Corporate Governance, Economic Reforms, and Development

Corporate Governance, Economic Reforms, and Development

The Indian Experience

Edited by

Darryl Reed

Sanjoy Mukherjee

OXFORD
UNIVERSITY PRESS

OXFORD
UNIVERSITY PRESS

YMCA Library Building, Jai Singh Road, New Delhi 110001

Oxford University Press is a department of the University of Oxford. It furthers the University's objective of excellence in research, scholarship, and education by publishing worldwide in

Oxford New York

Auckland Bangkok Buenos Aires Cape Town Chennai
Dar es Salaam Delhi Hong Kong Istanbul Karachi Kolkata
Kuala Lumpur Madrid Melbourne Mexico City Mumbai Nairobi
São Paulo Shanghai Taipei Tokyo Toronto

Published in India
By Oxford University Press, New Delhi

First published in India 2004

ISBN 019 566660 7

Typeset in Le Studio Graphique, Delhi 110 017
Printed at Pauls Press, New Delhi 110 020
Published by Manzar Khan, Oxford University Press
YMCA Library Building, Jai Singh Road, New Delhi 110 001

Contents

List of Tables and Figures

TABLES

FIGURES

Contributors

N. Balasubramanian is professor of corporate governance at the Indian Institute of Management Bangalore (IIMB), and chairman of the centre for corporate governance and citizenship, and, formerly, the chief editor of *IIMB Management Review*.

Jairus Banaji is an economic historian and activist. He has recently authored *Agrarian Change in Late Antiquity: Gold, Labour and Aristocratic Dominance* (Oxford) and co-authored a report on corporate governance while being a visiting fellow at Queen Elizabeth House, University of Oxford.

Asish K. Bhattacharyya is professor of finance and control at the Indian Institute of Management, Kolkata.

Sanjoy Mukherjee is coordinator at the Management Centre for Human Values (MCHV) at the Indian Institute of Management, Kolkata.

Ananya Mukherjee Reed is associate professor in the department of political science and director of the International Secretariat for Human Development and Democratic Governance at York University, Toronto.

Anant G. Nadkarni is general manager of Tata Group Corporate Social Responsibility.

Darryl Reed is associate professor in the division of social science and coordinator of the business and society programme at York University, Toronto.

Jayati Sarkar is associate professor at the Indira Gandhi Institute of Development Research, Mumbai.

Subrata Sarkar is associate professor at the Indira Gandhi Institute of Development Research, Mumbai.

ANUP SINHA is professor of economics at the Indian Institute of Management, Kolkata.

SHANKAR VENKATESWARAN, currently the executive director–India of the American Indian Foundation, is former chief executive of Partners in Change, a Delhi-based NGO that promotes the practice of corporate social responsibility.

Preface

The immediate background to this collection of essays was the awarding of a research grant by the Shastri Indo-Canadian Institute on the topic of 'Corporate Governance, Economic Reforms, and Development'. The three investigators of this project—Prof. S.K. Chakraborty, Prof. Ananya Mukherjee Reed, and I—had all been interested in the conjunction of these issues for some time. We had not been able to address it in a systematic fashion, however. Nor, given the breadth of this problematic issue and our own disciplinary limitations, had we been able to investigate the various facets of this nexus. The research grant enabled us to come together and take a more sustained look at this issue, as well as to engage others—academics, corporate leaders, activists—in discussion. This collection of essays is a result of these interactions. I along with other members of the research project, would like to thank the Shastri Indo-Canadian Institute for their support for this project.

The idea for the research project developed as a result of various discussions that I had in India in 1997–98. During that year I had the good fortune to be the Sir Ratan Tata visiting fellow at the Management Centre for Human Values at the Indian Institute of Management, Calcutta. I would like to thank the director of IIMC, Dr A.C. Bose, as well as numerous members of the faculty for their warm reception. I benefited greatly from the daily opportunities to engage in discussion and debate on the economic reforms and a range of related issues. I am particularly grateful to several IIMC faculty members who have contributed chapters to this collection. I would be remiss if I did not acknowledge a special debt of gratitude to Prof. Surendra Munshi, who has become a close friend over the past five years.

A special acknowledgement is due to the faculty and staff of the Management Centre for Human Values, who were incredibly hospitable during my stay as the Sir Ratan Tata visiting fellow and during subsequent visits. I want to thank my co-editor, Prof. Sanjoy Mukherjee, who has shown great dedication and attention to detail in bringing this project to fulfilment. I especially need to thank Prof. S.K. Chakraborty, the convenor of the Centre, without whom this project would never have got off the ground. An untiring spirit in the struggle for promoting greater corporate responsibility, Prof. Chakraborty has provided unwavering encouragement and support throughout the project, while maintaing his ability to engage in critical debate on the issues.

As is typically the case in projects like this, it is not possible to thank by name everyone who has contributed. This would include the numerous business leaders, government officials, academics, and activists who have taken time out of their schedules to talk to me and to respond to written requests for information. A couple of other contributions do need to be publicly recognized, however. Prof. N. Balasubramanian of IIMB, in addition to writing a chapter for this collection, hosted me during two visits that I made to Bangalore and was extremely helpful in setting up meetings with business leaders and academics in the area. Finally, and as always, my closest colleague, and most ardent critic, in this venture has been Ananya Mukherjee Reed.

March 2003 DARRYL REED
Toronto

Introduction

Around the globe, societies have been experiencing tremendous social, political, and economic change during the last quarter-century. Analysts of these processes of transformation invariably draw upon the notion of 'globalization', and more specifically 'economic globalization' as a conceptual anchor for developing causal accounts of the rapid change that has taken place. While different parties to the debate disagree about the extent to which globalization has been occurring and the nature of its effects, it is commonly acknowledged that the notion of (economic) globalization refers to changes in the ways that corporations produce goods and services (a transnationalization of production) and the associated changes to the national and international economies which facilitate this change at the firm level.

It is not only the extent of globalization and its effects that are disputed, however. Even more controversial is the evaluation of globalization and the various changes it has induced, as the existence of a global 'anti-globalization movement' makes clear. Of particular concern to many is the perception that in these processes of change the interests of large corporations are being promoted at the expense of ordinary people, especially the most vulnerable sections of society in the developing world. The purpose of this book is to examine this broad concern from a particular focus. This focus is the intersection of two particularly significant areas where change has been taking place over the past two decades—changes in the manner in which corporations are governed and changes in the efforts of developing countries to promote 'development'. As the title of this work implies, these two areas of change are linked through associated processes of 'economic reform'.

Historically it has not been common—for academics, business leaders, or the general public—to closely connect the notions of corporate governance and development. The former concept has most frequently been conceived rather narrowly in terms of the obligations of boards to shareholders, while the latter has primarily been understood to be the domain of the state, involving principally industrial and agricultural policy and rural development programmes. In actual practice, of course, there has always been some relationship between corporate governance and development as the manner and substance of corporate decision making has significantly affected development prospects. This impact, however, was to a great extent mediated by the state through its interventionist policy regime—a fact which largely enabled corporations to deflect criticism of their practices and shift it on to the bureaucracy and politicians.

Recently, though, processes of economic reform associated with the notion of globalization have been leading to a reduction in the role of the state in a variety of different areas. Under these circumstances, the links between corporate governance and development impact should become more direct (and more evident to most people). Indeed, the logic underlying the current reform process lays out in a very straightforward manner exactly how reforms to the governance system, broadly understood, should promote development. The removal of restrictions on corporate activities and the strengthening of market discipline is supposed to induce or force boards to monitor and work with management in creating more dynamic, efficient, and responsible business structures which will provide competitively priced and high-quality goods and services and produce profits for shareholders. In the process of doing this, firms will generate economic growth and employment through their activities in both domestic and foreign markets. According to this logic, those companies which are well governed will survive and possibly thrive, while those which are not will be taken over or perish. If, overall, there is a high level of (responsible) governance in the country, growth rates and employment generation will be high. The economic reform process in developing countries like India then is simultaneously changing the nature of corporate governance and introducing a new development strategy.

At the level of rhetoric, these connections between corporate governance and development are already being made, with corporations being publicly touted as the 'primary agents of development'. As just noted, this development impact is primarily understood to come from the firms' efforts to generate profits for their shareholders. There is also, however, an increasing emphasis being placed upon more direct involvement by corporations in the promotion of development under the rubric of corporate social responsibility. Again, it is the case that corporations in developing countries like India have long contributed to social causes. What is new is that a more specific 'development' focus is being advocated and implemented. Among other things, this has consisted of changes in the self-understanding of corporations in terms of their (stated) motives for engagement (a shift from philanthropy to corporate responsibility), in their manner of involvement (including cooperation with non-governmental bodies, the promotion of employee volunteers, etc.), and the activities in which they are getting involved (e.g. training and employment generation programmes, infrastructure programmes, etc.).

With the introduction of economic reforms in developing countries, and the shift in development strategy that they imply, there are some evident risks, especially for those sectors of the population most closely associated with the goals of development (the unemployed, women, children). Pressures to cut government spending (e.g. for food subsidies, education), to downsize the bureaucracy, to privatize public sector industries, etc., could be disastrous for large sectors of the population, especially if the promised growth from the private sector does not materialize. Given the stakes involved in more closely linking development prospects to private corporations, some obvious questions arise. The most basic of these are whether this new corporate governance model cum development strategy is likely to have the development impact that it promises or whether alternatives should be considered. An adequate answer to these questions, of course, depends upon the answers to a wide variety of other questions. These include: (1) positive (social science) questions about what the economic and corporate governance reforms actually entail, why they are occurring, and what their effects are; (2) normative questions about what development is, what our priorities should be, what responsibilities and rights different actors have; and (3) strategic questions about what the prospects for success of specific strategies and tactics are, and whether these prospects can change with alterations to larger economic and political structures.

Providing detailed answers to these questions is obviously a daunting task. This book is intended as a preliminary step in the investigation of these issues in the Indian context. While all the chapters in this work address all three questions noted above to some degree, they focus most primarily, on the positive analysis of the economic reforms—examining why the changes have occurred and investigating the nature of the changes and their effects so far. Most of the contributors also provide some strategic analysis, primarily in the form of recommendations intended to help boards (and markets) discipline management and ensure more responsible corporate governance. It is in the final chapter that the normative analysis of the relationship between corporate governance and development is most explicitly highlighted and problematized. The book unfolds in the following manner.

In the first chapter, I attempt to put economic reforms and the related changes to the system of corporate governance in India in a larger global and historical context. India has not been alone in implementing economic reforms and revamping its system of corporate governance over the last decade. Developing countries around the world have been engaged in similar projects. I start off the chapter by examining two traditional development strategies: import-substituting industrialization (which was employed in India) and export-led industrialization (employed in the newly industrializing countries of East Asia). While these two highly interventionist strategies shared some important commonalties, I argue that they had quite different outcomes, both in terms of economic growth and international competitiveness, which continue to impact on the development prospects of the countries that employed them. Next, I go on to provide a brief analysis of the causes and the nature of the governance reforms currently underway in developing countries. Here, I argue that structural changes in the international economy have combined with past problems of governance and development strategies to favour the adoption of an Anglo-American model of corporate governance (CG). This is not to say that the adoption of the Anglo-American model is necessarily the only logical choice for developing countries to make, but that these two structural factors have increased the ability of advocates of the model (both inside and outside of developing countries) to promote such a model (and introduced deterrents for adopting alternatives). In the next section, I offer a conceptual analysis of the development potential of the Anglo-American model of corporate governance and note several major concerns that have been raised about the model and its appropriateness for developing countries.

In Chapter Two, Ananya Mukherjee Reed and I investigate the changing nature of the historical links between corporate governance and development in India. The chapter starts out with an examination of the concepts of corporate governance and development. Here, a distinction between the formal mechanism of governance and the circumstances of governance is proposed as a basis for distinguishing different models of governance. Some preliminary reflections are offered, as well, on the possible ways in which corporate governance practices, policies, and institutions might contribute to development. The following sections examine in turn three historical models of corporate governance in India—a managing agency model (1850–1956), a business house model (1956–1991), and an Anglo-American model (1992–present)—each distinguished in terms of their formal mechanisms of governance and their circumstances of governance. As part of our analysis, the development impact of each historical model of governance is also investigated. The record indicates that in India, corporate governance practices and policies (for various reasons—but especially for the influence of Indian promoters), including those of the current governance model, have fallen well short of their promised development potential. We suggest that a major reason for this has been the inability of the state (and markets) to discipline corporations.

In Chapter Three, N. Balasubramanian takes up the issue of how economic reforms in India are changing board practices and, more specifically, promoting more responsible corporate governance. The chapter starts off with an argument for an expanded understanding of corporate governance that draws upon the notions of stewardship, trusteeship, and stakeholders. Balasubramanian argues that the best corporate boards are increasingly coming to realize that in order to be effective they must move beyond exclusive attention to the claims of shareholders and promote more collaborative solutions that seek to reconcile the different interests of shareholder and stakeholders. This trend, he argues, represents the emergence of an integrated model of corporate governance. Next, Balasubramanian goes on to examine how economic reforms are prompting Indian corporations to initiate reforms that move in this direction. Here, he first highlights the role of increased market pressure (in product, labour, and financial markets) as a disciplinary device. Next, he argues that with liberalization there has also been an increase in societal expectations of corporations, expectations which are forcing corporations to move beyond attention to profits alone and adopt a triple bottom line. The author next argues that in order for economic reforms to be effective, they need to be accompanied by corresponding civil service and administrative reforms. By way of conclusion, Balasubramanian delineates what he sees to be the key characteristics of the post-reform corporate board.

In Chapter Four, Anup Sinha examines the relationship between economic reforms and corporate philosophy and the development implications of this relationship. Sinha starts by explaining that market-friendly economic reforms have changed the business environment in three basic ways: allowing for greater freedom (to operate in markets), greater reach (in relating to other corporations across the world), and greater uncertainty (both about a firm's optimal structure, size, and strategy, and about the agenda for policy reforms). He argues that while such reforms do not alter the basic goals of the firm (to survive, earn profits for its stakeholders, and grow), they do inevitably force firms to rethink their corporate philosophy. More specifically, Sinha argues that each of the three changes in the business environment (greater freedom, reach, and uncertainty) induce changes to the underlying beliefs, claims to knowledge, and resultant strategies that firms employ to fulfil their core objectives. Here, Sinha points out that the resulting changes in corporate philosophy (as they relate, for example, to such issues as restructuring and mergers and acquisitions) are not always encouraging in terms of the development aspirations of countries like India. Sinha also points out, however, that such corporate policy options tend to cause a reaction among stakeholder groups, which needs to be taken into account by firms. More specifically, he argues, it calls for a corporate philosophy that manifests social responsibility as an outcome of strategy. Such a corporate philosophy not only involves responsibility to a wider range of stakeholders, but requires greater democracy and more responsible governance within the firm for its successful implementation. The need for such a corporate philosophy is especially great in developing countries like India, Sinha holds. Previously, he notes, public sector corporations in India were guided by such a philosophy of social responsibility, one which reflected the developmental concerns of the state. Over time, however, as these firms became caught between the 'rational' demands of planning efficiency and the 'irrational' intervention of political processes, the corporate philosophy of the public sector units degenerated from a deep social commitment to a position of 'anything goes' in meeting the political demands of special interest groups and lobbies. This indicated a failure to reconcile the core objective of being in business with the social commitment to harmonize development. Sinha believes that public sector units can regain this harmony and points to recent surveys that show them as among the most respected firms in the country. He argues, however, that the private sector in India also needs to develop corporate strategies based upon corporate responsibility due to changes in role expectations by the public. Such changing expectations derive from two sources—the sheer dimensions of social and economic deprivation in India and the decreased role of the state in delivering social services which has accompanied the market-friendly reforms. Sinha acknowledges that it may be difficult for Indian firms to live up to such expectations in a climate of increased (global) competition, but this is precisely the undertaking that corporate philosophy must take up. The task of philosophy, he argues, is to create spaces and guides to action that address the corporation's wider responsibilities, *without* compromising core objectives.

In Chapter Five, Asish Bhattacharyya takes up the issue of financial reporting. After a brief introduction to the field and a short account of the historical context, Bhattacharyya begins by examining the regulatory framework which guides corporate reporting practices. Until 1999, he notes, the Companies Act made no reference at all to 'accounting standards'. This omission implied that the government did not view compliance with the accounting standards set by the Institute of Chartered Accountants of India (ICAI) as necessary to provide a true and fair view of the performance and the financial position of the company. It was the changing information needs of a new generation of investors and providers of international finance that finally pressurized the government to incorporate the issue of accounting standards into the Companies Act. As a result, the Board's report must now include a *Directors' Responsibility Statement (DRS)*, wherein the directors attest that they have, among other things, chosen and consistently applied appropriate accounting standards, taken proper and sufficient care in the maintenance of adequate accounting records, etc. Next, Bhattacharyya discusses how in the early 1970s ICAI tried to promote mandatory accounting standards and how, when these efforts were not supported by government, ICAI's efforts to produce accounting standards and guidelines dropped off. Bhattacharyya then goes on to document how in the pre-reform era, compliance with ICAI standards remained low, a phenomenon that can be largely attributed to the fact that firms had little interest in improving the quality of financial reporting due to the relatively small percentage of public holdings in their companies. After a brief discussion of recent governance reforms, Bhattacharyya looks at current trends in financial reporting. Here, he argues that while there has been progress in financial reporting, this progress has not been across the board. One of the most obvious factors influencing reporting has been the desire of Indian firms to access foreign financing. Not surprisingly, Bhattacharyya reports, Indian companies, which either accessed or intend to access international finance, have raised the level of transparency and disclosure in their financial reports. Another factor contributing to increased disclosure, Bhattacharyya notes, has been the rise of the knowledge-based companies. As firms in these sectors, especially information technology, tend to have intangible assets (which are not recognized in the financial statements), they have an incentive to disclose such assets voluntarily as an additional information. On the negative side, Bhattacharyya notes that the ownership and control structure of Indian companies, still dominated as it is by promoters (who make extensive use of cross-holding to retain control), means that most companies still have little incentive to increase transparency and disclosure. As a result, there will continue to be a dichotomous situation in India with respect to financial reporting, with top-rung companies benchmarking their corporate financial reporting practices with international standards, while a second category of companies whose shares are not frequently traded attempt to circumvent the new regulations. As a result, Bhattacharyya argues, there is a need to increase regulatory activity so as to achieve an acceptable level of transparency and disclosure.

In Chapter Six, Jairus Banaji examines the role of institutional investors in India with an analysis based upon an extensive survey of senior business leaders, including CEOs, non-executive directors, fund managers, and accountants from audit firms. Banaji starts out by explaining how the Cadbury report led to a new model of governance—based upon market-based regulation, institutional investors, and codes of best practice—intended to produce greater transparency and accountability in business, boost investor confidence and increase the liquidity of the market. He then questions whether this model, developed in the context of developed economies, can be readily transposed into developing countries like India. Banaji argues that while the new Securities and Exchange Board of India (SEBI) code claims descent from the Cadbury report, it falls short of the Cadbury model in several important ways, including in its treatment of institutional investors. Before taking up these latter issues, Banaji first reports on opposing views of the nominee director system in India. He notes that while there have been problems with the system in the past, both the government and the corporations share in the blame for this. He argues that a more proactive role for nominee directors could be developed, but this would have to involve changes in the culture of the boardroom, less government control over financial institutions and, possibly, changes in how institutions appoint nominees. Next, Banaji looks at the treatment of nominee directors in the SEBI code, arguing that SEBI (reflecting the interests of the business houses) has largely muddied the waters by raising the issue primarily in relationship to concerns about insider trading. He argues that the issue of insider trading is logically independent of the question of board representation for institutional investors (and looks to full disclosure as the best antidote to the problem). Banaji then goes on to examine the role of foreign institutional investors (FIIs). Here, he contends that FIIs are very active in their relationships with management and have played a much larger role than is generally acknowledged in promoting professionally run, transparent, competitive businesses. He notes that FIIs are unlikely to seek board representation, but thinks that they can play an even greater role through actively voting their shares. This latter development will only come, however, as the market develops and larger long-term players enter the Indian market. This leads into a discussion on whether the new SEBI code (in combination with market pressure) is going to be adequate to promote greater boardroom responsibility. Here, Banaji points out that there is a real danger that the SEBI code might just serve as a façade to legitimize a system in which promoters are not held accountable. He argues that what is required is greater institutional monitoring and more regulatory intervention. With respect to the former, Banaji holds that greater institutional activism is required to supplement market pressures. Such activism, however, must be premised on the growing autonomy of the institutions from government control and interference, their increasing professionalization, and their responsiveness to their own shareholders and the public at large. With respect to the latter issue, Banaji argues that there is a need for regulatory measures which will help to ensure the independence of non-executive directors (e.g. requiring nomination committees, extending the definition of independence, etc.). To be effective, Banaji argues, these two governance agenda have to work together in a kind of symbiosis, with much greater input from institutional investors into the drafting of regulations and self-regulatory exercises and a publicly transparent articulation of institutional policy.

In his piece, Sanjoy Mukherjee reports on a survey on corporate governance and development in India. As part of the survey, senior executives of the top five hundred private sector corporations in India (Indian firms and MNCs) and selected senior executives from large public sector corporations were asked for information about their board structures and practices as well as their opinions on different issues relating to corporate governance and economic reforms. The findings of the survey can be summarized in three basic points. First, the CEOs and managing directors by and large supported the governance structures of the Anglo-American board pattern and, perhaps not surprisingly, downplayed the extent of agency problems. They almost uniformly thought that the most important factor in ensuring responsible governance was the moral leadership of the CEO or managing directors and generally expressed the belief that most senior executives lived up to this challenge (though they also suggested the need for more education around governance responsibilities). Second, with respect to economic reforms, the senior executives were largely supportive of the process, but downplayed the likely efficacy of many of the measures. They typically did not like measures that impinged on the autonomy of senior executives (e.g. the mandating of independent audit committees). Also, the importance of key aspects of the reform process normally emphasized in the literature (e.g. the role of financial markets, the legal system, shareholder rights, etc.), while not denied, was downplayed. Finally, and somewhat at variance with the faith expressed by CEOs, the survey indicated that while there had been some progress among firms in moving towards international best practices, there was still a long way to go. More specifically, it was found that the outside directors on most boards, especially those of family-controlled firms, could not credibly be classified as independent. This would indicate that the extent of the agency problem is far greater than most senior executives were willing to acknowledge.

In their Chapter, Jayati Sarkar and Subrata Sarkar investigate the effects of economic reforms on the development of the corporate sector in India. They start off with discussion of the corporate governance system and the quality of governance institutions in India in a comparative institutional perspective. Here, they argue that the Indian system, in relationship to the common distinction between banking and finance models of governance, is best portrayed as a hybrid model demonstrating characteristics of both. In terms of performance, however, they note that this traditional distinction has little explanatory value. Rather, categorizing governance on the basis of financial services and the legal system provides more fruitful results. The relative fecundity of this approach is demonstrated by comparing the ranking of the formal elements of India's governance system (which compare favourably with those of developed countries) with the implementation of its regulations (where it scores very low with respect to the rule of law, corruption, risk of expropriation, and weak accounting standards). Sarkar and Sarkar then go on to outline the important corporate governance reforms undertaken in India in the 1990s, including changes in the Companies Act, the regulation of capital markets and initiatives by banks and financial institutions as well as issuing of governance codes. They see these initiatives as generally being in line with the financial services and the law-based views, with policy makers and industry constituents attempting to create an enabling legal and regulatory framework to provide both banks and markets incentives to supply efficient financial services to the corporate sector. This review then provides the basis for their analysis of some major developments in the corporate sector over the past decade. Here the authors focus specifically on emerging corporate financing patterns, ownership and control structures, changing corporate strategies, the functioning of boards of directors, and the role of large shareholders in corporate governance. In their evaluation of the impact of the reform measures, while noting continuing agency problems rooted in the existing control structures, Sarkar and Sarkar are generally optimistic about current trends.

A less sanguine analysis of the current reform process is offered by Ananya Mukherjee Reed in Chapter Nine, where she investigates the role of profit strategies in promoting development. Starting with a theoretical approach to this issue, she first distinguishes different efforts to conceptualize the ability of corporations to foster economic growth and then discusses the applicability of these theories to the Indian case, with specific attention to the current context of economic reform. She argues against theoretic approaches—such as those underlying the current reforms—which claim that liberating private enterprise from both state control and inefficient state protection will unleash a new dynamism that will result in increased growth and employment. Instead, she favours positions that emphasize the importance of aggregate demand and contest the validity of Say's Law (the notion that supply creates its own demand), at least in the case of developing countries. On this basis, she argues that the crucial question for development becomes how to promote profit strategies that stimulate a virtuous cycle of aggregate demand, employment, and redistributive growth. In examining this question, Mukherjee Reed summarizes the major features of the profit strategies of Indian corporations, arguing that historically they have relied more on distorted market structures and a mediating role by the state to 'earn' high profits than they have innovation and increased productivity. While economic reforms were supposed to address the problematic business-state relations, the state has proved ineffective in imposing discipline on corporations (both through the legal system and through its function of encouraging the development of competitive markets), so as to force them to earn profits on the basis of innovation and increased productivity. As a result, the ostensible relationship between corporate profits, growth, and development is broken—and will remain broken until the issue of the influence of corporations over the state is seriously addressed—and millions of ordinary Indians pay the price.

In the next two chapters, the issue of corporate social responsibility (CSR) and the intentional efforts of corporations to promote development are examined. In Chapter Ten, Shankar Venkateswaran examines the role of non-governmental organizations (NGOs) in helping firms contribute more effectively to development. Starting off with the issue of CSR, Venkateswaran argues that in India the concept must reflect different priorities than have traditionally been advocated in the West. More specifically, the top priority must be engaging in activities that provide substantial benefits directly to local communities (followed by going beyond legal compliance in business activities and advocating public policy changes to benefit the disadvantaged). He next goes on to argue that firms and NGOs have capabilities and resources which tend to complement each other in the undertaking of development projects. Despite this potential for synergy, however, Venkateswaran notes that some 87 per cent of firms that undertake development activities do so without the cooperation of NGOs. There are a variety of reasons, on both sides, that account for this reluctance to cooperate. What is required to bridge the gap, Venkateswaran argues, is some sort of intermediary that can help allay the concerns and dispel the suspicions that both sides have and bring the potential partners together. Here, he provides an account of 'Partners in Change' as an example of such an intermediary. While seeing this organization as a success story, Venkateswaran recognizes that it has only just scratched the surface of the work that needs to be done.

In Chapter Eleven, Anant Nadkarni examines the changing understanding of CSR within one of India's leading business houses, the Tatas, long a leader in the field of corporate social involvement. Nadkarni explains that since the inception of economic reforms there has been a two-stage shift in the understanding of CSR in the Tata group. The first stage, which began with a series of consultations in the early 1990s, saw the emergence of a conviction that corporations should be involved in a conscious and dedicated effort to assist social reform as part of the larger ongoing societal project of building the nation. This new self-understanding was operationalized in part through the establishment of the Tata Council for Community Initiatives (TCCI), which was charged with the coordination of the CSR efforts of the various firms within the group. In line with its mandate, TCCI emphasized six themes: (1) developing long-term programmes with stakeholder groups; (2) promotion of a triple bottom line; (3) developing 'community champions' among its employees; (4) encouraging a corp of volunteers; (5) 'improving the quality of life' by focusing on activities involving important 'thrust areas'; and (6) developing environmental management and undertaking social audits. On the basis of action learning that occurred during the first stage, recently the Tata group has further deepened its self-understanding. As an 'enlightened business', it has now come to accept the need to align its CSR practices with the accepted tenets of development. Operationalizing this self-understanding poses tremendous challenges. The Tatas are focusing on four key areas: (1) institutions (to be based on the notion of community); (2) purpose (moving from a focus on the bottom line to the top line); (3) performance (developing new types of indicators); and (4) shifting from management to governance (to encourage more active involvement by stakeholders). While still early in the process, the House of Tatas believes that it is on the right road to becoming a 'development-driven business'.

Finally, in the last chapter, I investigate the normative analysis of governance and its relationship to development. I start by distinguishing two basic issues in the normative analysis of governance. There is the analysis of corporate governance responsibilities within the context of a given system or model of corporate governance, on the one hand, and the comparative evaluation of different models of corporate governance, on the other. In looking at the first of these two issues, I begin by distinguishing four basic roles of governance (accountability, monitoring, strategy formation, and policy development) and then investigate how stakeholder and non-stakeholder approaches differ in their treatment of these responsibilities with respect to the Anglo-American model. I then go on to ask whether and how different (Western and Indian) approaches to ethical theory might justify a specific responsibility on the part of corporations to promote development. Next, on the assumption of an obligation to promote development, I examine the implications of such a responsibility in terms of the four basic roles of governance noted above. Finally, turning to the broader question of the comparison of models of corporate governance, I raise the question of whether the Anglo-American model of governance is the most appropriate for developing countries. I do this by asking whether the Anglo-American model merely needs to be more effectively enforced, whether it needs to be supplemented with new measures or whether, for the sake of promoting development, we need to go beyond the Anglo-American model.

With programmes of economic reform, the relationship between corporate governance and development is going to come under ever-increasing scrutiny in the coming years, both in India as well as throughout the developing world. This is not just an academic issue, but one which will largely determine the life prospects of billions of people. In this volume we have investigated in the Indian context some of the factors that are likely to determine whether and how those responsible can be induced to govern the corporations in a manner that will significantly advance the development prospects of the larger population and the nature of the obligations that they have to act in this way. These are preliminary reflections on a very complicated issue that is evolving daily. It is hoped that they will stimulate others not only to think, but also to act and address the concerns that have been raised.

1

Corporate Governance Reforms in Developing Countries

Darryl Reed *

Corporate governance (CG) reforms are not unique to India, but are taking place in countries around the globe, potentially impacting the population of the entire planet. In developing countries, such reforms take place in a larger context that is primarily defined by previous attempts at promoting 'development' and recent processes of economic globalization. In this context, CG reforms (in combination with the liberalizing reforms associated with economic globalization) represent, in effect, a new development strategy for third world countries.

This chapter examines the larger context in which the corporate governance reforms in India are taking place, asking why such reforms are being undertaken around the globe, why they have been taking on the specific form that they have, and what the prospects are for such reforms contributing to development.

This chapter is organized into three sections. The first section offers a brief comparison of two interventionist development strategies, import-substituting industrialization and export-led industrialization. While these two strategies shared some important commonalties, they had quite different outcomes, both in terms of economic growth and international competitiveness, which continue to impact on the development prospects of the countries that employed them. The second section provides a short analysis of the causes and the nature of the governance reforms currently under way in developing countries. More specifically it argues that structural changes in

* This chapter is a revised and shorter version of a paper, 'Corporate Governance Reforms in Developing Countries', previously published in *Journal of Business Ethics*, 37 (3) May 2002, 223–47, and is reproduced with permission of Kluwer Academic Publishers.

the international economy have combined with past problems of governance models in developing countries to promote the move to an Anglo-American model of CG. The final section examines the development potential of the Anglo-American governance reforms and notes some of the concerns that have been raised.

The Background—Corporations and Development

Development is a broad concept with a variety of potential referents. Historically, as the notion of development emerged and became popular in the post-WWII era, it was closely, if not exclusively, identified with economic development and, more specifically, with industrialization. Through the link with industrialization, corporations have always been directly connected to the discourse on development. Over time, however, the discourse on development has greatly expanded. The concept of development, for example, is now commonly understood to include social, cultural, and political components in addition to the economic. The discourse has moved beyond a technical discussion of economic policy as well to raise normative issues about the justice of the international distribution of resources and opportunities, the priorities of development efforts, etc. (Mies and Bennholdt-Thomsen, 2000). As a result of the expansion of the discourse, development is being reconceptualized in different ways, e.g. as sustainable development (World Commission on Environment and Development, 1987), as human development (United Nations Development Programme, 1990: Haq, 1999), etc. Such reconceptualizations of development have significant implications for our understanding of the governance roles and responsibilities of corporations in development, a point that we take up below in looking at some of the concerns raised about recent reforms. Before moving on to discuss these implications, however, we must first briefly examine the nature of past efforts of developing nations at promoting (economic) development and the role of corporations in these efforts.

Import-Substitution Industrialization

In the post-colonial period, developing countries have typically associated development with industrialization and have adopted interventionist approaches to promote this goal. Two basic strategies have been followed. The first, import-substitution industrialization (ISI), was initially the preferred approach for most developing countries in the post-WWII era. The basic strategy of ISI was to develop an industrial base by protecting new or fledgling domestic firms from foreign competition and providing them with various forms of support. This strategy, which focused on production for the domestic market, often involved the use of strongly interventionist industrial policy to channel investment into the key sectors (e.g. the provision of cheap credit supplied by government development banks, licensing systems, etc.). Measures to protect the emerging industries included the use of high tariffs, overvalued exchange rates (to make imports more costly and domestic goods relatively cheaper), capital controls, and often a variety of subsidies (especially in the form of infrastructure). The ISI model meant different things in different contexts. In Latin America, for example, where the model was first employed in the inter-war period, the primary motivation for its adoption appears to have been a concern about vulnerability to foreign economic shocks and foreign political interests. In Asian countries like India, however, the adoption of the model in the post-colonial period seems to have been driven by the desire to rapidly increase industrial capacity (Banuri, 1991).

In the early stages the ISI strategy was relatively successful in many countries. Large and small industrial firms were supported and proved capable of supplying products to replace imports in a range of areas (especially consumer goods). Growth rates were also promising. By the 1960s, however, problems began to emerge. The basic indicator of development, growth, started to fall. Employment generation was insignificant with respect to demand. While the ISI model did allow some countries to develop a significant industrial base, large firms proved to be uncompetitive—providing expensive and poor quality goods for domestic markets and incapable of penetrating international markets. (In addition, these development efforts were also being associated with other problems, e.g. substantial environmental degradation, repressive political regimes, etc.). In the face of these problems, developing countries were forced to shift to an export promotion model (as Brazil and Colombia did in the 1970s) or to incur ever-increasing levels of debt (Pastor, 1995).

The reasons as to why the ISI strategy has not proven very successful are complex and differ from country to country. Many of the proximate causes of the problems of the ISI model seem relatively clear. First, firms were not subjected to competitive pressures. In product markets, not only did they enjoy captive markets, but they also received extensive subsidies in the form of credit and infrastructure. In the capital markets, especially in countries like India, there was virtually no opportunity for shareholders to exert any influence. Nor could effective redress to this situation be sought through the courts. Second, government subsidies (in the form of administered prices, infrastructure support, cheap credit) led not only to an inefficient allocation of resources, but also rising debts (which eventually forced liberalizing reforms). Third, inefficiencies were spawned through a variety of other channels related to the state such as poor administration of programmes (e.g. lack of accountability in loan repayments, etc.), corruption, the exercise of political influence and the lack of an effective legal system (Banuri, 1991).

While these basic mechanisms just delineated are generally undisputed, what is highly controversial is the nature (and relative importance) of the different underlying causes of the lack of development success. In particular, the debate revolves around two basic positions. On the one hand, it may be that there are inherent (and irremediable) problems involved in interventionist approaches to development strategy (e.g. rent-seeking behaviour, inability to gather and process information, etc.). On the other hand, the problems that emerged may have been more contingent in nature, e.g. poor planning and implementation, but also—and especially important with respect to governance—the ability of firms to influence government policy so that it operates in their interest rather than the interest of society as a whole.

This brings us to one final point about the model, the nature of the corporate structure that emerged from it. Most ISI states were dominated by large family-owned business groups. In India, as is well known, family-controlled business houses were able to build extensive empires ranging across numerous economic sectors. They were able to maintain control over their vast holding with a relatively small ownership stake through the use of interlocking directorates and intercorporate investments, etc. Their ability to maintain control (and ignore the interests of minority shareholders) was further enhanced by their reliance on debt finance, the weak state of the financial markets and an ineffective (and at times corrupt) legal system. Similar patterns of ownership and control were also evident in other developing countries such as Brazil (Rabelo and Vasconcelos, 2002), Mexico (Husted and Serrano, 2002), South Africa (Rossouw et al., 2002), etc.

Export-Led Industrialization

A second approach to industrialization and growth, which emerged in east Asia, is export-led industrialization (ELI). While the east Asian experience has often been looked at as a justification for a market-led approach to development, in point of fact the model was highly interventionist. (Indeed, in such areas as financial markets, Latin American countries typically had a much more liberal regime that did their east Asian counterparts.) Like the ISI model, the ELI approach was largely based upon the logic of the infant industry argument. It employed many of the same tactics to channel investment into key areas (e.g. development banks, licensing systems). It also used similar policies to protect domestic markets, e.g. import tariffs, undervaluing exchange rates, etc. Where ELI primarily differed from the ISI model was in its export orientation. But even here, the government took a very active role in encouraging firms to compete in foreign markets. In South Korea, for example, this first took place in the 1960s, with the military coup d'etat that brought Park Chung Hee to power in the spring of 1961. Park set Korea on the path of export-led development, first by focusing on light industries in the 1960s, then by undertaking a rather daring plan to promote heavy and chemical industries in the 1970s. Park adopted a carrot-and-stick approach to encourage Korean corporations to move into new areas, offering 'cooperation-contingent rents', while proving willing to throw business leaders into prison if they did not follow government policies (Amsden, 1989).

From the 1960s onward, the countries most closely associated with this model—the newly industrializing countries (NICs) of South Korea, Taiwan, Hong Kong and Singapore—achieved sustained high rates of growth and generated substantial employment. Perhaps most significantly, the NICs have created dynamic corporations capable of competing not only in the low end of international markets (light industries), but increasingly in leading sectors as well (heavy and chemical industries, knowledge-based industries). In comparison with the ISI model, the ELI states seem to have dramatically outperformed their rivals in other developing countries in terms of standard economic indicators. A more balanced evaluation of the 'development success' of the ELI model, of course, would also have to take into consideration the more negative aspects involved. These included the fact that the model largely operated in a repressive political environment in which worker rights were largely ignored (with women suffering a particularly heavy burden). Besides, there were rampant abuse of minority shareholders' rights, environmental degradation, etc. (Amsden, 1989; Haggard, 1990; Wade, 1990). Another controversial factor to take into account in evaluating the NICs and the ELI model is the recent Asian crisis. This is controversial in that, while many commentators see the model as the root of the crisis, others have argued the opposite, viz., that recent liberalizing changes in the early 1990s (induced by international pressures to open up domestic financial and product markets) were the source of the problem (Chang, Palma, and Whittaker, 1998).

With respect to issues of corporate governance, the basic corporate structure in the NICs was not unsimilar to that of the major ISI states. The South Korean structure, for example, closely parallels that of India with large family-controlled conglomerates (*chaebols*) dominating key industries.

Family groups, as in India, were able to maintain control over large empires through such means as interlocking directorates, intercorporate investment, etc. Other similar factors contributing to the ability of family groups to maintain control (and largely ignore the interests of minority shareholders, not to mention stakeholders) were debt financing (supplied through state-owned development banks), weak financial markets, and an ineffective legal system (Nam et al., 1999).

An intriguing question that arises in the comparison of the two state-led development models is why ELI seems to have been so much more successful (with appropriate caveats) than ISI in terms of traditional understandings of economic development, especially given the similarities between the two models (e.g. finance, corporate structure, industrial policy). There are several factors that possibly contribute to an answer. The first involves geopolitical factors in the form of the Cold War. Western, and in particular US, concerns about containing the Soviet Union provided countries like South Korea with several important advantages. These included not only relatively generous foreign aid packages, but also a benign trading relationship that allowed these countries to keep their domestic markets closed while enjoying access to foreign markets. Second, as noted above in the case of Korea, these countries had 'strong states' which were able and willing to force corporations to perform for the favours that they received from the state. Third, all these countries had a strong export orientation. Geography was in large part responsible for hoisting this orientation upon these countries (especially Hong Kong and Singapore which are, in effect, city states), but, as noted above, government also played a strong role in the promotion of exports. This export orientation served to subject firms to the discipline of the market, requiring them to meet international standards for quality and price. Scholars disagree about the relative importance of each of these three factors in the success of the NICs. They also disagree as to whether other countries might have successfully adopted this (or a similar) model (Cline, 1982). Where there is less disagreement is in the fact that it is increasingly difficult to employ the model in the new global economy (Bardhan, 1999).

The experience of the ISI and ELI models is important for understanding current governance reforms in several ways. First of all, it needs to be highlighted that while the relatively unsuccessful ISI model was interventionist, so was the relatively successful ELI model. While liberalization seems to be relatively easy to justify vis-à-vis the experience of the ISI model, the success of the ELI model gives one pause for thought. This is especially so when put in the larger historical context of industrialization. All previous industrializers, even the first- (e.g. UK, the US) and second-round industrializers (e.g.

Germany, France, Japan) all employed interventionist policies. In fact, there is no historic example of a country successfully industrializing (developing) in accordance with a market-led strategy. It is only after they become successful that countries tend to support more market-led approaches. What this means is that developing countries are now being asked (compelled) to develop according to a model that has no proven track record. Second, in many instances both models did succeed in terms of establishing large industrial corporations. At issue is the nature of these corporations, in terms of their governance practices, their relationship to the state and their ability to compete in international markets. In the case of the ELI model, corporations have proved themselves capable of competing in international markets, but their governance practices and their relationship to the state have been highly problematic. In the case of the ISI model, the corporations have generally been uncompetitive and have exhibited poor governance practices and questionable relationships to the state. Thus, in implementing governance reforms, developing countries are not starting in an institutional vacuum, but have to overcome ingrained corporate practices and interests, some of which are likely to oppose reforms and/or channel reforms in ways that undermine responsible governance. Moreover, they have to do so in a new global economy, the framework for which was largely developed by developed countries and, arguably, favours the interests of transnational corporations (TNCs).

Corporate Governance Reforms in Developing Countries

Over the last two decades, issues of corporate governance have gained increased prominence in countries around the globe. In the developed world, part of this increased attention to governance issues has been provoked by questionable business practices and scandals (e.g. in the UK, the bankruptcy of the Bank of Credit and Commerce International [BBCI] and Robert Maxwell's raiding of pension funds, the Savings and Loans scandal in the US, etc.). In some instances these events sparked a direct and specific response (e.g. the Cadbury Report) (Boyd, 1996). In developing countries too, there has been no shortage of scandals and questionable practices to incite interest in governance issues. The impetus for governance reforms, however, has deeper roots (both in developed and developing countries) that relate to the larger historical experience of the countries in question and structural changes in the global political economy. These deeper roots also affect the nature of governance reforms. In this section, the underlying causes of governance reforms are first examined. This is followed by a brief inquiry into the (Anglo-American) nature of the reforms.

The Underlying Causes of Governance Reforms

Two closely related factors contribute to an explanation of the recent processes of governance reforms. The first of these involves the past history of developing countries. As noted above, many countries employing an ISI model have seen the development impact of their policies wane over the last couple of decades. This downturn in development prospects has encouraged attention to governance issues for a couple of different reasons. On the one hand, it has given increased credibility to those who have always advocated liberalizing reforms (including governance reforms) and enabled them to have a more influential voice in the domestic political realm (Bhagwati, 1982; Krueger, 1990). On the other hand, poor economic performance has frequently resulted in debt crises in many developing countries (e.g. Brazil, Mexico, India). This situation has placed these countries under the direct influence of international financial bodies such as the International Monetary Fund (IMF) and the World Bank. As a condition of renegotiating loans, these international financial bodies have typically imposed a series of liberalizing measures, commonly referred to as structural adjustment programmes (Biersteker, 1990). Such programmes, as discussed below, require changes that bring increased attention to governance issues.

The structural adjustment programmes imposed by international financial institutions relate closely to the second factor influencing governance reforms, viz., major changes in the international political economy that are commonly discussed under the rubric of 'globalization'. Globalization, as a process of structural change, can perhaps best be understood in terms of a series of interrelated changes involving three basic structures, viz., methods of production, forms of state, and the international economy.

The first of these three areas of structural change can be conceptualized as a shift from a Fordist model to a post-Fordist model of accumulation (Lipietz, 1987). Cox (1994) explains this shift in accumulation strategy in terms of a distinction between core and peripheral aspects of the production process. Increasingly over the last couple of decades, large firms have been retaining only core aspects of the production process on a permanent basis (viz., research and development, finance, accounting, etc.), while contracting out other, more peripheral, aspects of the production process (e.g. production of component parts, maintenance, etc.). These changes in production relations are essentially designed to provide corporations with greater flexibility (which provide savings in terms of costs and advantages in capturing markets). While initially occurring within national boundaries (in Japan), the 'outsourcing' of peripheral aspects of production has rapidly spread across borders.

The second area of structural change, changes in the form of the state, has been conceptualized by Jessop (1994a) as a shift from a Keynesian Welfare State (KWS) to a Schumpeterian Workfare State (SWS). Jessop (1994b) argues that the KWS underwrote the social reproduction of Fordism through: (1) state management of aggregate demand; (2) competition policy, infrastructure development, transportation and housing policies; (3) the promotion of full employment and big business; and (4) the management of social problems and the promotion of mass consumption through welfare rights and social expenditures. The key traits of the SWS, by contrast, include: (1) economic policy focused on the promotion of innovation-driven structural competitiveness and (2) social policy designed to enhance business flexibility and competitiveness in a global economy (rather than promote redistribution with the nation state).

Third, there has been a shift in the international economic order from a 'liberal international' regime to a 'neo-liberal global' order. Of particular importance for our concerns are multilateral economic agreements. Over the last two decades, as individual countries have liberalized their economies, several new multilateral economic agreements and institutions (e.g. North American Free Trade Agreement [NAFTA], the Uruguay round of General Agreement on Tarisffs and Trade [GATT], the World Trade Organization [WTO], etc.) have come into existence. These agreements not only allow for increased flows of capital and goods across borders, but also put in place provisions that severely limit the ability of subsequent governments to (re)impose restrictions. These agreements have been essential in promoting the transnationalization of post-Fordist production. They (in concert with international financial bodies, e.g. the IMF, the World Bank) have also served as vehicles to encourage reluctant states in the developed world to introduce programmes of economic liberalization (Biersteker, 1995).

While evaluations of the (potential) development effects of globalization vary, one thing is clear. Processes of globalization (assisted by the end of the Cold War) have virtually eliminated the possibility for developing countries to continue with their previous development strategies, especially the unsuccessful ISI approach adopted by Brazil, Mexico, and India, but also the more successful ELI model employed by South Korea and other east Asian countries. Shifts in the form of state (induced in large part by structural adjustment programmes), have resulted in the opening up of domestic markets to foreign investment and foreign goods as well as a shift to a market-oriented industrial policy. Changes in the international economy (e.g. trade liberalization) have also contributed to countries opening up their domestic markets and altering their interventionist industrial policies (e.g. reducing and eliminating subsidies). Finally, changes to production relations (and in the form of state) have resulted in increased capital mobility, which in turn requires liberalization of financial markets to induce (foreign) investment. The net effect of these structural changes is that firms in developing countries are being weaned off state support (e.g. subsidies) and protection (e.g. high tariff barriers), and forced to compete in a global economy, while states are under pressure to liberalize in order to attract foreign capital.

It is in this context that governance reforms must be understood. For developing countries to compete in a global economy, governance reforms are important for several reasons. First, they help to provide legitimacy for governments undertaking unpopular liberalizing reforms by indicating to the public that the government is not merely cutting back on spending, but it is also developing a more effective corporate structure that will generate the conditions for growth and development. Second, they are important in promoting greater efficiency among domestic firms and enabling them to compete against the TNCs that are entering into their previously protected markets. Third, they are essential for increasing investor confidence, which is particularly important as governments are eliminating traditional sources of cheap credit offered through development banks.

The Anglo-American Nature of the Reforms

Governments in developing countries are not just introducing corporate governance reforms, however. They are introducing corporate governance reforms that are largely in line with a particular model of corporate governance, viz., an Anglo-American model. Typically, Anglo-American models of corporate governance are defined as insider (vs outsider) or finance (vs banking) models. Historically, Anglo-American models have been characterized by: (1) a single-tiered board structure which gives almost exclusive primacy to shareholder interests (e.g. the board is elected exclusively by shareholders, shareholders have strong rights grounded in company law); (2) a dominant role for financial markets (both as the major source for investment funds and as a disciplinary mechanism to address the agency problem); (3) a correspondingly weak role for banks (which typically provide a small proportion of investment funds, cannot hold shares, do not have nominee directors, etc.): and (4) little or no industrial policy involving firms cooperating with government agencies (and labour bodies).

Why are developing countries favouring an Anglo-American model? There are several possible contributing factors. One has to do with the past experience of the countries themselves. For some countries (e.g. India, Nigeria) there are strong historical ties with the Anglo-American model (e.g. their company law is firmly rooted in British company law) that make further movement in this direction appear natural to some. Another possible factor is that the lack of success of their previous interventionist models has served to discredit elements commonly associated with other models (e.g. a major role for bank finance, the use of industrial policy). It is also the case that, insofar as the previous interventionist system bred uncompetitive firms, strong financial markets present themselves as an important tool for promoting more competitive domestic firms.[1] As we noted above, whether in point of fact past failures were directly attributable to the ISI model is disputed (Taylor, 1991). What is undisputable, however, is that key domestic (business and political) actors have presented past failures as a justification for liberalization and for moving towards an Anglo-American model. Business interests generally tend to favour the Anglo-American model and have been outspoken in opposing the adoption of any other models of governance, especially models that provide a role for stakeholder involvement (e.g. employees), like the German model (Confederation of Indian Industry, 1998).

Another reason for the move to an Anglo-American model has to do with debt and the influence of international financial institutions. As noted above, as a condition of renegotiating loans, international financial bodies imposed structural adjustment programmes on developing countries. These programmes included a variety of features that induced a move to an Anglo-American model of governance. For one, fiscal cutbacks pressurized governments to reduce credit supplies, diminishing the role of bank finance and direct bank influence in governance (e.g. a decreased emphasis on nominee directors) and leading to a much greater role for equity financing. An emphasis on equity financing (and shareholder interests) was also encouraged through requirements that states deregulate financial markets and relax controls on foreign portfolio investment (FPI). States were also forced to abandon strong interventionist industrial policy (e.g. licensing regimes, labour market interventions, etc.) and dramatically reduce direct participation in production (e.g. privatization of national industries). Again, the wisdom of the structural adjustment programmes can be questioned (Stallings and Perez, 2000), especially as they were applied in the aftermath of the east Asian crisis (Stiglitz, 2000). There is no doubt, however, that they have encouraged developing countries to move in the direction of the Anglo-American model.

Structural adjustment programmes reflect a general approach by business and political elites to economic reforms. Dubbed by Williamson (1990) as 'the Washington Consensus', this approach advocates liberalizing reforms in a range of areas (viz. fiscal discipline, public expenditure priorities, taxation, financial markets, trade, privatization policy, deregulation, property rights, foreign direct investment, exchange rates). It is this 'consensus' that has shaped not only IMF and World Bank policy, but also the neo-liberal form that processes of globalization have taken. This neo-liberal character of globalization serves to promote an Anglo-American model of corporate governance. In the neo-liberal environment, where domestic firms have to increasingly raise funds in equity markets (due to declines in bank capital) and states are seeking to induce foreign investment—FPI to finance domestic firms and foreign direct investment (FDI) to generate employment and stimulate key sectors of the economy—shareholder interests have to be given priority. This necessitates a liberalization of capital markets, changes to company law, etc. Similarly, other aspects of the neo-liberal global economy (e.g. trade agreements) undermine the use of interventionist industrial policy associated with non-Anglo-American governance models. In effect, the Anglo-American model of corporate governance is a logical micro-level complement of the macro neo-liberal global economy.

One final point about the 'consensus' needs to be highlighted with respect to governance concerns. This so-called consensus was largely induced by lobbying efforts and negotiations involving large TNCs in developed countries and the dominant economic powers. TNCs have exercised their influence at the level of the nation state (e.g. in supporting the Thatcher and Reagan revolutions, in lobbying for trade liberalization) through the creation of strong business lobbies (e.g. the Business Roundtable in the US, the Business Council on National Issues in Canada) as well as through the establishment of and participation in unofficial multilateral bodies (e.g. the Trilateral Commission, the Bilderberg Conferences, the Mont Pelerin Society, etc.). For their part, the dominant economic powers (e.g. the US, Japan, the EU) have asserted their influence through multilateral organizations whose participation is (largely) restricted to developed countries (e.g. the G-7, the Organization for Economic Cooperation and Development [OECD], etc.). Through these organizations, the dominant economic powers have laid the basis for key changes in the international economy, inviting 'participation' from developing countries only after they have reached basic agreement among themselves (Cox, 1987; 1994). These practices have contributed to the widely held perception, as expressed in 'Seattle', that processes of globalization tend to largely reflect the interests of TNCs in developed countries.

Corporate Governance and Development in a Global Economy

As noted above, changes in the systems of corporate governance in the developing world are taking place in the wake of processes of structural change in the international economy and (in the case of many countries) less than fully successful interventionist development projects. But while developing countries may be giving up on interventionist development models, they have not given up on their development aspirations. The major justification offered for economic liberalism and deregulation is that it will have a greater 'development impact' than previous interventionist programmes. The main source of this development impact is expected to be private corporations, which are increasingly being portrayed as the 'primary agents of development'. The adoption of an Anglo-American model of corporate governance is understood as a key element in unleashing the 'development potential' of corporations. In this section, we offer a brief account of the logic of the development potential of the Anglo-American model of corporate governance and examine some of the concerns raised about the model.

The Development Potential of the Anglo-American Model

Changes in corporate governance in developing countries occur in the context of broader policies of economic liberalization and cannot readily be separated from the latter. Together, these liberalizing reforms are intended to induce changes that will generate high levels of sustained growth. Within the dominant understanding of economic liberalism, development is typically understood to come about as a result of economic growth (e.g. growth increases employment which enables people to more adequately provide for their own needs with respect to health, education, etc.). There are three basic channels through which these reforms are intended to work.

First, the reforms are intended to increase available investment funds. One aspect of this is increasing the pool of potential investors by increasing investment opportunities, especially for foreign investors. This involves changing limits on foreign direct investment (e.g. allowing foreign firms to hold majority interests in companies), encouraging cooperative agreements between foreign and domestic firms (e.g. joint ventures), allowing for foreign portfolio investment, achieving current account convertibility (so as to allow for the repatriation of profits), and encouraging investments by domestic institutional investors (e.g. allowing pension funds to invest in the stock market). A second element involves increasing investor confidence, both among foreign and domestic investors. This goal is achieved through a variety of means including reforms to company law (e.g. to strengthen shareholder rights and increase transparency), reforms to capital markets (e.g. allowing prices to be established by the market, making listing requirements more stringent), and reforms to the banking sector (e.g. the elimination of soft loans based upon industrial policy rather than market evaluations). These reforms should not only increase the pool of available investment funds, but also improve the efficiency of the allocation of such funds, including increasing the prospects for funding ventures in the new, more dynamic sectors of the economy.

Second, the reforms are designed to increase the competitiveness of domestic firms. The basic measures here involve exposing domestic firms to increased market pressure, both in the financial markets and product markets. Increased pressure in financial markets involves, as noted above, opening up domestic markets to foreign investors as well as the elimination of soft financing through domestic (often nationalized) banks as well as capital account convertibility (which enables domestic investors to invest their funds abroad). Increased pressure in product markets is achieved through trade liberalization, liberalization of FDI, the reduction and elimination of subsidies (including the privatization of heavily subsidized public sector firms), the elimination of industrial policies that restrict entry into particular industries, etc. These measures should have the effect of forcing domestic firms, among other things, to professionalize management, to rationalize their holdings (e.g. concentrating on core competencies, hiving off unrelated businesses), to be more innovative in product design and marketing, to improve their use of technology (e.g. through licensing agreements, joint ventures, etc.), to focus more on export markets, and even to transnationalize themselves.

Third, the reforms are also commonly understood to serve another important function, viz., decrease the ability of the bureaucracy and politicians to engage in 'rent-seeking' behaviour which undermines economic efficiency. The basic argument here is that economic liberalization, by decreasing the size of the state and the number of interactions that business has to have with government (viz., for licences, loans, etc.), will decrease the ability of government to extract rents and limit the inefficiencies involved in this behaviour (Bhagwati, 1982; Krueger, 1974).

The net effect of governance reforms, then, is intended to be the generation of growth through the combination of attracting foreign direct investment and increasing the competitiveness of domestic firms. As part of the virtuous circle of generating profits for their shareholders, competitive firms not only provide goods and services desired in the marketplace but also create jobs which enable local people to meet their basic needs (and help to reduce or eliminate the need for government programmes).

Concerns About the Model

A variety of concerns have been raised about the development potential of the Anglo-American model. Some of these problems may best be described as transitional in nature, (i.e. establishing the conditions for the model to function effectively), but others are more inherent and serve to call into question the efficacy of the model. In what follows, we examine some of the major concerns that have been raised.

Responsible Ownership

One of the major concerns of the model has to do with the prospects for generating responsible ownership. This situation is typically understood in terms of the agency problem. As La Porta et al., (1999) have suggested, in developing countries the primary agency problem has historically been between majority and minority owners (and not between owners and managers). There are two versions of this problem, however. The one most frequently commented upon involves domestic firms, where the problem is primarily one of families with controlling interests vis-à-vis small domestic shareholders. While the reforms mentioned above are supposed to address this problem, given the prevalence of agency problems in the developed world, there would seem to be relatively little reason for optimism with respect to the prospect for success in developing countries.

A second agency problem involves domestic stakeholders and foreign firms, typically large TNCs that were previously forced to set up less than wholly owned subsidiaries in developing countries due to restrictions on ownership placed by national governments. Historically, there has been a lot of concern about whether the management of TNCs look out for the interests of domestic shareholders as much as they do for the shareholders of the parent company (e.g. by repatriating profits to the parent company, and foreign shareholders, in questionable ways) (Krasner, 1985). This concern has not abated during liberalization as foreign TNCs have taken to setting up wholly owned subsidiaries to compete with their own partially owned firms. In doing so, they have been accused of hiving off the more profitable parts of their operations for their wholly owned subsidiaries (and foreign shareholders) (Varma 1997).

The Nature of Investment

A second concern about the potential development impact of the new model of corporate governance involves the nature of the investment that is being induced. Here, both FPI and FDI are important. With liberalization of international financial markets over the last decade or more, there has been a substantial increase in both the amount and the mobility of FPI. The short-term focus of portfolio managers has had a tremendous impact not only on individual companies but also on national economies. The most striking example of this was the recent 'Asian crisis'. This behaviour, best explained in terms of Blair's (1995) concept of 'market myopia', is significant not only because it can contribute to national and regional economic crises (Chang, Park, and Yoo, 1998), but also because it results in a general tendency for firms to under-invest, a phenomenon which has an obvious negative development impact (Porter, 1990; Prahalad, 1997).

Turning our attention to FDI, there are several points of concern that relate to development. One area involves the nature of the investments, in particular whether they entail greenfield operations or mergers and acquisitions. If new investment primarily takes the forms of mergers and acquisitions, it is likely to have only a limited development impact at best, as it is not creating new jobs (and indeed may result in a net loss of jobs in so far as mergers and acquisitions tend to be accompanied by retrenchment). There is clear evidence in countries like India that mergers and acquisitions are being favoured over greenfield projects (Khanna, 1999). A closely related issue is how foreign firms finance new projects. If the financing is being done within the host country, then again the development impact is compromised as it brings in no new investment funds into the country, but merely drives out competing projects. A final issue is the question of costs associated with inducing FDI. More and more developing countries find that they have to provide corporations with a range of incentives to invest (tax holidays, regulatory concessions, infrastructure improvements, etc.). These costs not only devalue the benefit of new investment, but undermine the abilities of governments to raise funds and allocate them to social and educational programmes (which may be equally or more important in promoting development).

Another area of concern relating to FDI involves the fact that significant amounts of FDI are invested in private (non-listed) companies (often wholly owned subsidiaries of TNCs). While such investment might generate some significant development impact (again depending upon its form, the sector in which it occurs, how it is financed, etc.), it does little to contribute to the development of a vibrant and liquid stock market. The development impact of such investment might as well be limited by the fact that such firms have fewer ties to a country (e.g. through domestic shareholders) and therefore might have a weaker commitment to remaining in the country.

Maintaining Competition

A third area of concern has to do with competition, especially as it relates to the ability of domestic firms to compete with TNCs. The development potential of the Anglo-American model rests upon the premise of the benefits of competitive markets. To the extent that markets are not competitive, the development impact is weakened. While the liberalization of markets has generally had salutary effects on domestic firms (e.g. forcing them to be more innovative, more efficient in their production techniques, etc.) it is not clear that domestic firms will be able to compete with TNCs (Rabelo and Vasconcelos, 2002), nor that competitive markets can be maintained otherwise. The fear is that as TNCs move into markets in developing countries, they can over time use their established competitive advantages in combination with other advantages (e.g. size, access to cheaper financing, etc.) to buy up competitors or force them out of the market. Possible results of such moves could include oligopolistic domination of global markets and increased susceptibility of individual countries (especially smaller countries) to macro-economic shock (e.g. if TNCs decide to consolidate production in another country, find a better investment climate, etc.). Such a threat of oligopolistic control is given credibility by the preference, noted above, of foreign firms to engage in mergers and acquisitions rather than greenfield operations, as well as by the recent wave of mergers and takeovers among TNCs. Such oligopolisitc control, as Joan Robinson (1932) pointed out years ago, obviously has a negative development impact as it not only limits the amount of goods and services produced, but also reduces consumption and employment generation.

Even if a tendency among TNCs towards oligopololistic control could be effectively curbed, most developing countries would still want to ensure, for economic and not merely political reasons, that domestic firms could compete with their foreign rivals. While under the assumption of perfect competition, it should not make any difference where corporations are headquartered and owners reside, in practice it is probably rational for governments to prefer domestic firms because they may be less likely to relocate, it may be easier to extract tax revenue from them (e.g. they cannot use transfer prices to manipulate profit levels), etc.

Political and Legal Development

As noted above, in many interventionist economies in the developing world the relationship between corporations and government was characterized by a combination of inappropriate political influence by corporations and 'rent-seeking behaviour' by government. This relationship amounted to a distorted symbiosis in which politicians and bureaucrats sought to extract 'rents' from corporations in return for consideration of the corporation's economic concerns, e.g. obtaining licences, loans, etc. (Bagchi, 1993). One of the arguments for economic liberalization is that it is supposed to decrease the ability of government to extract rents by decreasing the number of interactions that business has to have with government (viz., for licences, loans, etc.) (Krueger, 1974). However, while under liberalization the ability of government to extract rents may decrease, this does not necessarily imply that the ability of corporations to influence government also decreases. On the contrary, as we noted above, with the processes of globalization there has been a significant shift in power between states and firms that has undermined the public policy of autonomy of states. This shift in power often allows corporations to negotiate virtually as equals with the governments of developing countries (Strange, 1994). While states do retain significant power, which they could in principle exercise, they are generally reluctant to do so because of the perceived need to 'induce' foreign investment. A more general concern here is that the emphasis on corporate governance is being used as a justification on the part of governments (in both developed and developing countries) to avoid any discussion about the possible need for more effective (binding) international regulation (e.g. in such areas as climate control, biodiversity, international labour standards, anti-trust law, etc.).

The political influence of corporations relates to another concern. A key condition for the effective functioning of an Anglo-American model is a legal system that can uphold contracts in a fair and timely fashion. Indeed, in recent literature on corporate governance a strong case has been made that an effective legal system is more important than the choice between banking and finance models in determining the success of a corporate governance system (Levine, 2000). Initiating reforms in the legal system presents a major challenge for developing countries, as entrenched interests have to be overcome. Even if such reforms can be initiated, however, there is a tremendous risk that large corporations will dominate the agenda, as they are more capable of 'representing' their interests (e.g. reforms to bankruptcy law, company law, etc.). The concerns of other stakeholders (e.g. consumers, labour, local communities, etc.) by contrast, are less likely to be effectively addressed (Sheikh and Rees, 1995).

Social Development

Traditional growth (and development) theory has typically given priority of place to economic over social development. The standard understanding was that if economic development takes place, it will create employment and people will generally be able to take care of their own social development needs (i.e. education, health, etc.). Recent empirical work in the field of development, however, has challenged this contention (Haq and Streeten, 1982; Dreze and Sen, 1995). As a result, development economists like Nobel-prize winner Amartya Sen are increasingly arguing that economic development does not so much induce social development as it depends upon it. Based on the most successful examples of recent economic development (viz., the NICs), Sen (1998a) argues that it was the early investment by these countries in education (especially primary education), health and other social programmes that allowed for their subsequent economic success. Similarly, Sen argues, it is the previous investment made by China in social programmes that have provided the basis for the rapid economic growth which that country is currently undergoing. By contrast, Sen claims, the failure of countries like India to invest in primary education and basic health care continues to undermine their potential for economic growth and development.

Development economists such as Sen (1998b) argue that proponents of economic liberalization, who generally advocate Anglo-American corporate governance reforms as well, make a fundamental mistake by assuming that the freeing up of economic opportunities for business necessarily involves funding cuts and a reduced presence by government in other activities, viz., the provision of social welfare programmes. On the contrary, governments in developing economies have a key role to play. Because of the relatively low cost of health and education programmes in these countries, a tremendous impact can be made without affecting the efforts to stimulate economic recovery. Indeed, such efforts provide the necessary basis for long-term growth and development. Even low-cost programmes, however, do require funding which must eventually come from tax revenues. Corporations, however, undermine the tax base of developing economies and induce a 'race to the bottom' by engaging in what has been termed 'regulatory competition' (i.e. playing one country off against another for such benefits as low tax rates, tax holidays, subsidies, less stringent regulatory standards for labour and the environment, etc.).

Conclusion

Through its programme of economic reform, India has been changing not only its model of CG (to bring it more in line with the textbook Anglo-American model) over the past decade, but also its development strategy. While the past history of the Indian corporate sector and the Indian state's efforts to promote development helps to account for these recent changes, they are only a partial explanation at best. Driving the reforms are processes of economic globalization involving interrelated changes at the level of the firm (a transnationalization of production), nation states (especially the leading post-industrial economies), and multilateral bodies. These larger processes, which have induced a significant change in the rules of the game of the international economy, account for why not only India but virtually all developing countries are introducing programmes of economic reforms, reforms that are promoting the spread of an Anglo-American model of governance.

Adapting to the new rules of the game (including subjecting their domestic firms to increased competition) should have some salutary effects for developing countries, especially in addressing problems of governance which have previously plagued their domestic corporate sectors—if policies are well designed and successfully implemented. One major concern in this regard is that liberalizing reforms may only be selectively pursued and implemented in developing countries in line with the interests of key corporate sectors and bodies. Another key concern is that effective implementation of governance reforms implies associated reforms in other sectors, most notably in the realm of the judiciary. Again, many developing countries, like India, face major challenges in developing and implementing such complementary reforms.

Even if India and other developing countries are able to effectively implement a full package of reforms, other questions remain. The fact that changes have been made to the rules of the game in the international economy does not imply that everyone is now competing on a level playing field. One potential concern for developing countries is that, while governance reforms might help to make their domestic corporations more competitive, it is not clear that they will be adequately competitive to remain in the market in the medium to long term. There is a real risk of an emergence of oligopolistic control over global markets in key economic sectors, with domestic firms in developing countries slowly being swallowed up by their larger transnational rivals. Moreover, even if domestic firms are able to become and remain globally competitive, it is not clear that the success of the corporate sector will necessarily be a sufficient engine to integrate the masses currently on the margins into the economic mainstream. Nor is it clear that government will be able to play an active and effective role in addressing the plight of the marginalized under the new models of corporate governance and development.

Thus, while there are some reasons to be hopeful that economic reform programmes (which have been largely forced upon developing countries) can induce important changes in the way corporations are governed in developing countries like India, the long-term efficacy of these changes and their likely development impact remain an object of deep concern.

Notes

1. Both of these points are obviously less true of the NICs. First, interventionist models have not been discredited to the same extent, e.g. many commentators still see a strong role of the state in channelling investments funds, etc. Second, the model has produced internationally competitive firms. Many commentators see the recent problems as resulting from, rather than requiring, rapid liberalization and deregulation (especially of financial markets) (Chang, Palma, Whittaker, 1998).

References

Amsden, A. (1989). *Asia's Next Giant: South Korea and Late Industrialization*, New York: Oxford University Press.

Bagchi, A.K. (1993). 'Rent Seeking, New Political Economy and the Negation of Politics', *Economic and Political Weekly*, 21 August, pp. 1729–36.

Banuri, T. (1991). 'Introduction', In *Economic Liberalization: No Panacea*, (ed.) T. Banuri, Oxford: Clarendon Press, pp. 1–27.

Bardhan, P. (1997). *The Role of Governance in Economic Development: A Political Economy Approach*, Paris: OECD.

Bardhan, P. (2001). 'Development Thinking Today in an Asian Perspective', Global Finance and Development Symposium sponsored by the World Bank, Tokyo, Japan, 1–2 March, Accessed at: http://www.worldbank.org/japan/sympo/bardhan.htm.

Bhagwati, J.N. (1982). 'Directly-unproductive (DUP) activities', *Journal of Political Economy*, 9 October, pp. 988–1002.

Biersteker, T. (1990). 'Reducing the Role of the State in the Economy: A Conceptual Exploration of the IMF and World Bank Policy', *International Studies Quarterly*, Vol. 34, No. 4 (Dec 1990), pp. 477–92.

——— (1995). 'The "triumph" of liberal economies in the developing world', In *Global Change, Regional Response: The New International Context of Development*, (ed.) B. Stallings, Cambridge: Cambridge University Press, pp. 174–96.

Blair, M. (1995). *Ownership and Control: Rethinking Corporate Governance for the Twenty-first Century*, Washington: Brookings Institute.

Boyd, C. (1996). 'Ethics and corporate governance: The issues raised by the Cadbury Report in the United Kingdom', *Journal of Business Ethics*, 15 (2), pp. 167–83.

Chang H.J., G. Palma, and D.H. Whittaker (1998). 'The Asian Crisis: Introduction', *Cambridge Journal of Economics*, 22, pp. 649–52.

Chang H.J., H.J. Park, and C.G. Yoo (1998). 'Interpreting the Korean crisis: Financial liberalisation, industrial policy and corporate governance', *Cambridge Journal of Economics*, 22, pp. 735–46.

Confederation of Indian Industry (1998). *Desirable Corporate Governance—A Code*, Delhi: CII.

Cox, R. (1987). *Production, Power, and World Order*, New York: Columbia University Press.

_____ (1994). 'Global Restructuring: Making Sense of the Changing International Political Economy', In *Political Economy and the Changing Global Order* (eds.) R. Stubbs and G.R.D. Underhills, Toronto: McClelland & Steward, pp. 45–59.

Dreze, J. and A. Sen (1995). *Economic Development and Social Opportunity*, New Delhi: OUP.

Haggard, S. (1990). *Pathway from the Periphery: The Politics of Growth in the Newly Industrializing Countries* Ithaca, NY: Cornel University Press.

Haq, M. and P. Streeten (eds) (1982). *First Things First: Meeting Basic Needs in Developing Countries*, Washington: World Bank.

Haq, M. (1999). *Reflections on Human Development*, Delhi: OUP.

Husted, B., and C. Serrano (2002). 'Corporate Governance in Mexico', *Journal of Business Ethics*, 37 (3), pp. 337–48.

Jessop, B. (1994a). 'The transition to post-Fordism and the Schumpeterian workfare state', In *Towards a post-Fordist Welfare State*, London: Routledge, pp. 13–37.

_____ (1994b). 'Post-Fordism and the State', In *Post-Fordism: A Reader*, (ed.) A. Amin, Oxford: Blackwell, pp. 251–79.

Khanna, S. (1999). 'Financial Reforms and Industrial Sector in India', *Economic and Political Weekly*, XXXIV (45), 6 November.

Krasner, S.D. (1985). *Structural Conflict: The Third World Against Global Liberalism*, Berkeley: University of California Press.

Krueger, A. (1974). 'The Political Economy of the Rent-Seeking Society', *American Economic Review*, 64, pp. 291–303.

_____ (1990). 'Government Failures in Development', *The Journal of Economic Perspectives*, 4 (3), pp. 9–23.

La Porta, R., F. Lopez de Silanes, and A. Shleifer (1999). 'Corporate Ownership Around the World', *The Journal of Finance*, 54 (2), pp. 471–517.

Levine, R. (2000). *Bank-Based or Market-Based Financial Systems: Which is Better?* Minnesota: Institute of Financial Studies, Carlson School of Management, The University of Minnesota, Working paper *0005.

Lipietz, A. (1987). *Mirages and Miracles: The Crisis in Global Fordism*, London: Verso.

Mies, M. and V. Bennholdt-Thomsen (2000). *The Subsistence Perspective: Beyond the Globalized Economy*, New York: Zed Books.

Nam, I.C., J.K. Kim, Y. Kang, S.W. Joh, and J.I. Kim (1999). 'Corporate Governance in Korea', Proceedings of the OECD Conference on Coporate Governance in Asia: A Comparative Perspective (Korean Development Institute, Seoul). Accessed at: http://www.oecd.org/daf/corporate-affairs/governance/roundtables/in-Asia/1999/.

Pastor, M. Jr (1995). 'Latin America, the Debt Crisis and the IMF', In *International Political Economy: Perspectives on Global Power and Wealth*, (eds) J. Frieden and D. Lake, 3rd edition, New York: St. Martin's Press, pp. 320–34.

Porter, M.E. (1990). *The Competitive Advantage of Nations*, New York: Macmillan, The Free Press.

Prahalad, C.K. (1997). 'Corporate Governance or Corporate Value Added: Rethinking the Primacy of Shareholder Value', In *Studies in International Corporate Finance and Governance System*, (ed.) D.H. Chew, New York: OUP, pp. 46–56.

Rabelo F. and F. Vasconcelos (2002). 'Corporate Governance in Brazil', *Journal of Business Ethics*, 37 (3), pp. 321–35.

Robinson, J. (1932). 'Imperfect Competition and Falling Supply Price', *The Economic Journal*, 42 (168), pp. 544–54.

Rossouw, G.J., A. van der Watt, and D.P. Malan (2002). 'Corporate Governance in South Africa', *Journal of Business Ethics*, 37 (3), pp. 289–302.

Sen, A. (1998a). *Development as Freedom*, New Delhi: OUP.

Sen, A. (1998b). 'Theory and Practice of Development,' In *India's Economic Reforms and Development: Essays for Manmohan Singh* (eds) I.J. Ahluwalia and I.M.D. Little, Oxford: OUP.

Sheikh, S. and W. Rees (1995). *Corporate Governance & Corporate Control*, London: Cavendish Publishing.

Stallings, B. and W. Perez (2000). *Growth, Employment, and Equity: The Impact of the Economic Reforms in Latin America and the Caribbean*, Washington: Brookings Institution Press.

Stiglitz, J. (2000). 'What I Learned At The World Economic Crisis', *The New Republic On-Line*, http://www.tnr.com/041700/stiglitz041700.html.

Strange, S. (1994). 'Rethinking Structural Change in the International Political Economy: States, Firms and Diplomacy', In *Political Economy and the Changing Global Order*, (eds) R. Stubbs and G.R.D. Underhill, Toronto: McClelland & Steward, pp. 103–15.

Taylor, L. (1991). 'Economic Openness: Problems to the Century's End', In *Economic Liberalization: No Panacea*, T. Banuri, Oxford: Clarendon Press, pp. 100–47.

United Nations Development Programme (1990). *Human Development Report 1990*, New York: OUP.

Varma, J.R. (1997). 'Corporate Governance in India: Disciplining the Dominant Shareholder', *Management Review*, 9 (4), pp. 5–18.

Wade, R. (1990). *Governing the Market: Economic Theory and the Role of Government in East Asian Industrialization*, Princeton NJ: Princeton University Press.

Williamson, J. (1990). *Latin American Adjustment: How Much Has Happened?* Washington: Institute for International Economics.

World Commission on Environment and Development (1987). *Our Common Future*, Oxford: OUP.

2

Corporate Governance in India

Three Historical Models and Their Development Impact

Ananya Mukherjee Reed and Darryl Reed

Linking issues of corporate governance and development would not necessarily strike most people as an obvious thing to do. In India and many other countries of the developing world, however, these two sets of issues have long been connected, first through the economic policies of colonial powers and later through the interventionist development policies established by national governments. Most recently, the connections between corporate governance and development have been expressed in the notion that in the new era of economic reforms, corporations are becoming the primary agents of development.

The purpose of this chapter is to examine the changing nature of the historical links between corporate governance and development in India. It does so by distinguishing three different historical models of corporate governance in India—a managing agency model (1850–1956), a business house model (1956–1991), and an Anglo-American model (1992 to date).

The chapter comprises four sections. First, a short account is provided of the basic concepts of corporate governance and development, and the possible relationship(s) between the two. The next three sections investigate, in turn, the three historical models of corporate governance in India. In each instance, the origins of the model, the formal mechanisms of control, the circumstances of governance, and the development impact of the model are investigated.

A Relationship between Corporate Governance and Development

As noted above, the relationship between corporate governance (CG) and development may not be immediately clear to most people. In order to make the connections more readily apparent, this section examines the question of what the concepts of CG and development entail and then goes on to take an initial look at some possible ways in which CG practices, policies, and institutions might contribute to development.

What is Corporate Governance?

Three Approaches to the Analysis of Corporate Governance

Before attempting to offer any definition of corporate governance, it is first important to recognize that the study of CG can be undertaken for different purposes and from different perspectives. More specifically, CG can be undertaken from three distinct analytical approaches, viz., the positive, the normative, and the strategic (Donaldson and Preston, 1995; Reed, 2002), each of which makes different claims, problematizes different questions and tends to employ different academic disciplines. Positive analysis makes claims of truth. It problematizes how we can know existing states of affairs and their causes. Normative analysis makes claims of goodness and correctness. It problematizes the criteria by which we (ethically or morally) evaluate people, policies, effects, etc. Strategic analysis makes claims of effectiveness. It problematizes how we can most effectively achieve given ends. Different academic disciplines problematize these different forms of analysis. Social science disciplines and history problematize positive analysis. Ethics and political philosophy problematize normative analysis. Business and related professional disciplines along with public policy problematize strategic analysis. This distinction between the three forms of analysis is important because it can help us to separate different issues involving the relationship between corporate governance and development (e.g. how corporate governance has affected development, whether there are any responsibilities of governance to promote development, how governance practices might contribute to development in a more effective fashion). The various chapters in this collection emphasize these different forms of analysis to different degrees. In this chapter, we first take up the positive analysis of corporate governance by examining different historical models of governance in India and their development effects. We then go on to employ more strategic analysis in raising questions about how emerging corporate governance practices and models in India might (not) contribute to development. In a later chapter, Reed takes up more of the normative analysis of CG by asking whether there are any governance obligations to promote development.

Narrow vs Broad Definitions of Governance

In line with the distinction made above, it is possible to offer three formal definitions of CG. From the perspective of positive analysis, a formal definition of CG might simply refer to (actual) CG as the manner in which corporations are governed. From the perspective of normative analysis, (responsible) CG governance is the manner in which corporations should be governed. From the perspective of strategic analysis, (efficacious) CG is the manner is which corporations can most efficiently achieve their given ends. Such formal definitions are by nature uncontroversial. What is at issue is the content of more substantive (positive, normative, and strategic) conceptions of CG. Such substantial conceptions of CG presuppose more specific understandings of what counts as a corporation, what counts as governance, and what types of effects (and people affected) are relevant. As a result of different views on these issues, substantive conceptions of CG range from the very narrow to the very broad (Tricker, 1994).

The narrowest conceptions of CG offer very restricted answers to all three of these questions. First, they limit their understanding of corporations, restricting it not only to large, for-profit firms, but to such firms operating under specific regulatory environments (e.g. US corporations, Anglo-American corporations). Second, they restrict their understanding of governance to the activity of the board of directors (and, as just noted, to a particular form of board structure). Third, they limit their analysis of governance issues to the fiduciary obligations that directors owe to shareholders. Effects on other stakeholders (e.g. employees) are either ignored, shunted to the realm of some other field of study (e.g. industrial relations, personnel management), or considered only to the extent that they have some possible impact on shareholders.

Broader understandings can extend this narrowest conception of CG in any or all of three basic directions: (1) they can examine the effects of corporate decision making on other (stakeholder) groups (e.g. employees, suppliers, etc.); (2) they can extend their analysis to alternative forms of corporations (e.g. employee-owned firms, co-operatives, etc.); and (3) they can examine different national and regional models of CG (e.g. the Japanese model, the German model, the Scandinavian model), as well as changes in governance models within individual countries over time.

Different Models of Governance

If one adopts a narrow understanding of CG, comparison of different empirical models of governance is largely restricted to the analysis of board practices and mechanisms. This approach may be adequate for trying to understand differences across firms, sectors, or countries with a common system of governance (e.g. within a given country like the US or across countries like Canada, the US, and the UK). To the extent that factors other than board practices come into play in determining corporate performance (e.g. industrial policy, the banking and financial systems, etc.), this approach is not generally very helpful in analysing differences across governance systems. Such comparative analysis requires a broader understanding of governance, one that incorporates the analysis of other factors (besides board practices and mechanisms) that can influence how corporations are governed. One approach to providing such an account is to distinguish between the 'formal mechanisms of governance' and the broader 'circumstances of governance' (Reed, 1998; Mukherjee Reed, 2001).

The formal mechanisms of governance can be understood as those legally sanctioned practices and policies that formally enable certain types of actors to affect how the corporation is governed. These formal mechanisms would include such things as board structures, management agreements, shareholder rights, etc. In the case of most major English-speaking countries, for example, the formal mechanisms would include a single-tiered board structure, election of directors by the shareholders, as well as various shareholder rights including the right to introduce resolutions. It also includes various restrictions on who can be a shareholder in a company and a representative on the board of directors (e.g. restrictions on banks and financial institutions). In Germany, by contrast, the formal mechanisms are quite different. There is a two-tiered board system consisting of a supervisory board and a management board. In the supervisory board workers in large firms are allocated 50 per cent of the seats. Moreover, financial institutions can also be represented on the supervisory board (with major banks usually having representation on the boards of all large firms) (Clarke and Bostock, 1997).

The circumstances of governance can be understood as factors that influence how the formal decision makers (viz. board members, shareholders) make their decisions regarding the governance of the corporation. A range of factors is potentially involved here, but the most significant of these tends to be the nature of the capital market. In the case of the Anglo-American countries, for example, capital markets tend to be relatively strong and readily allow for mergers and acquisitions, including hostile takeovers. In Germany and Japan, however, capital markets have tended to be relatively weak and hostile takeovers are virtually unheard of. Other significant areas of difference that can have an effect on the governance of firms include the banking/credit system, tax policy, macro-stabilization policy, and industrial planning.

In the following sections, we shall use this distinction between the formal mechanisms of governance and the circumstances of governance to identify different historical models of governance in India.

What is Development?

Development is a contested notion which admits of a variety of different definitions and dimensions. Historically, as the concept of development emerged and became popular in the post-WWII era, it was closely, if not exclusively, identified with economic development and the field of development economics. While (mainstream) development economists differ on some questions, they have tended to share the same basic assumptions. Most characteristic has been a focus on national economic output (viz., growth), with an underlying assumption that this was dependent upon or related to levels of industrialization. The key project, therefore, has been the development of an industrial economy. While other aspects of development (viz., socio-cultural, political) were not entirely ignored, they were seen as secondary in the sense that economic development was understood to provide the necessary basis for sustained development in these areas (i.e. a developed, industrial capitalist economy was understood to provide a necessary basis for stable political democracy and the meeting of basic needs and other social development goals). Similarly, while efforts have been made to incorporate some measure of distribution into this economic understanding of development, economic growth (measured in terms of per capita GNP) remains the dominant criterion (David, 1997; Martinussen, 1997).

While the basic approach of mainstream development economics has long been contested, oppositional voices over the last couple of decades have become much louder and more effective in challenging the dominant paradigm and reconceptualizing the notion of development. One key advance has been the incorporation of other dimensions (viz., the socio-cultural and the political) and related concerns (e.g. the gendered nature of economic development, impact on the environment and future generations, etc.) into the study of development. The success of these efforts is perhaps most visibly reflected in the emergence of new conceptions of development, e.g. as sustainable development (World Commission on Environment and Development, 1987), as human development (United Nations Development Programme, 1990; Haq, 1999), as freedom (Sen, 1998), etc.

These new conceptions of development have moved the discourse beyond a technical discussion of economic policy to raise normative issues about the justice of the international distribution of resources and opportunities and the priorities of development efforts. In terms of priorities, for example, a much greater emphasis has been placed upon meeting basic needs. Such conceptions also have implications in terms of economic policy, specifically inferring the need to allocate more emphasis to local (rural) development efforts and less to large industrialization projects and commercial activities (Mies and Bennholdt-Thomsen, 2000). Another key achievement has been to alter how we officially measure development. In line with the evolving understanding of development, a new index was proposed and eventually adopted by the UNDP, viz., the Human Development Index (HDI). The HDI consists not only of an economic measure (in which per capita GDP is calculated in terms of purchasing power rather than exchange rates), but also social measures such as literacy and life expectancy (UNDP, 1990; 2000). More recently, a Gender Empowerment Measure (GEM) has been added, but political indicators remain more controversial and have not yet been incorporated into the index.[1]

The Relationship Between Governance and Development

Corporations (through their governance practices and policies) can have a positive (or adverse) development impact in any of the three dimensions of development noted above—economic, socio-cultural, and political. Such impact can occur in three basic ways (Reed, 2001). First, CG practices can promote (impede) development through their efforts to maximize shareholder value. As this will be discussed in more detail later, it is sufficient to state here that this typically involves firms contributing to economic growth and employment generation through the pursuit of profits in a competitive market environment. To the extent that markets are less than perfectly competitive, the direct economic (and subsequent social) development impact of corporate activity is adversely affected as growth and employment generation suffer (while corporate profitability remains high). Second, corporations can consciously decide to take the development impact of their business activities into consideration while developing strategies and tactics. In terms of economic development impact, this would include such considerations as plant location (e.g. in underdeveloped regions and rural areas), choice of appropriate technology (so as to generate more employment in labour-surplus situations), product selection (e.g. developing products that optimize the use of local resources by improving the productivity of small producers, but which might not be the most profitable for the firm), etc. In terms of political development, it would involve such considerations of business-government regulations as lobbying practices, campaign donations, etc. Third, corporations can contribute to development through their non-business activities, such as philanthropy and corporate social responsibility programmes. Such programmes are typically directed at economic (small business) development or social development (e.g. the provision of social services).

Both the three-dimensional conception of development (i.e. economic, political, and socio-cultural) and the aforementioned threefold understanding of how business can contribute to development can be played out in terms of the three different forms of analysis noted above (i.e. the positive, normative, and strategic). From the perspective of positive analysis, the basic questions that arise are: (1) how do CG policies, practices, and decisions involving the business and corporate responsibility practices of the firm affect (promote/inhibit) economic, social, and political development and (2) are there differences in results among different models of CG. From the perspective of normative analysis, the basic questions are: (1) what responsibilities do those actors governing the corporation have (in terms of their business and social responsibility agenda) to promote economic, social, and political development and (2) are the results that tend to be generated by some models of governance better than other models. From the perspective of strategic analysis, the questions become: (1) how can corporations within a given governance framework most effectively live up to their responsibilities to promote economic, social, and political development and (2) how can we develop models of governance that are more likely to promote our desired development results.

In the remaining part of this chapter, we shall focus on the positive analysis of the relationship between governance and development, focusing specifically on how different historical models of CG have emerged in India and what impact they have had on development.

The Managing Agency Model (1850–1956)

While it is undoubtedly true that there has been increased interest in and discussion of issues of CG in recent years, concern about how corporations are governed is not new. Indeed, it goes back virtually to the founding of the first joint stock companies. What has changed in recent years is that more attention has been paid to the academic analysis of CG and the term has received greater currency in public policy debates. Thus, when looking back at the past, much of the public concern about and academic analysis of corporations was not expressed in terms of 'governance'. The same also holds with respect to issues of 'development'. While concerns were raised about what today are considered development issues—and the impact of corporations on development—it was often done in terms of a different vocabulary. By drawing upon the distinction made above between formal structures of governance and the circumstances of governance, it is possible to examine more explicitly the nature of governance structures in the past and, most important with regard to our concerns, how they have affected development. In this section we begin this process with an analysis of the managing agency model of CG.

Origins of the Model

Managing agents were individuals or business firms (partnerships or private joint stock companies) which contracted with joint stock companies to manage the affairs of the latter. The managing agency, if not an institution entirely unique to India, is certainly most closely identified with India and took its most elaborately developed form there. While it has been argued that the emergence of the first managing agency can be dated as far back as 1809 (Rungta, 1970), the institution only began to have significant impact with the passing of the first Indian Companies Act of 1850 and subsequent emendations in 1857. By paving a firm foundation for the establishment of joint stock companies (e.g. through the provision of limited liability), these developments allowed for the spread of the managing agency system (Sharma and Chauhan, 1965: 29; Rungta, 1970).

Underlying the spread of managing agencies were the particular political-economic conditions of the day. British merchants were the first managing agents. What confronted them in India in the middle of the nineteenth century was a potentially rich resource base, a large labour supply and a consuming public (Lokanathan, 1935: 15–16). The development and exploitation of this resource base had not been undertaken due to, among other reasons, a lack of financial and managerial resources. This meant that for the initial entrepreneurs who could bring the necessary financial and managerial resources together, there was tremendous potential for making very high profits. British merchants with experience in the region proved up to the task and realized this potential through the institution of the managing agency. The initial area of operation for British managing agents was in and around Bengal, the seat of imperial power in India. In line with British colonial policy, British managing agencies developed the rich resource base (e.g. jute, coal, tea) for export rather than for industrial production in India (Sharma and Chauhan, 1965: 149ff.; Rungta, 1970).

Not long after the establishment of British managing agencies in and around Bengal, Indian managing agencies began to emerge on the west coast of India, especially in and around Bombay, but also in Ahmedabad. These initial agencies, which were predominately established by merchant families, focused on the cotton and textile industries. Such families were not only aware of the potential of industrial production and the role of joint stock companies in its promotion, but had the capital to invest. However, as the marginal productivity of capital in their hands was high, they did not want to tie up their capital for long periods and were not willing to take up industrial production if it did not provide high rates of return. The managing agency contract provided them with an appropriate vehicle to address these concerns. By promoting firms and then controlling them through managing agency contracts, such merchant families were able to reap high profits without tying up their own capital. For some, the managing agency contract would also later prove an effective vehicle for extending their business interests into many new fields and eventually to building vast industrial empires (Rungta, 1970: 229–30).

As business enterprises, such managing agencies served three basic functions. First, they started or 'promoted' new companies. Typically what would happen is that the managing agency would start a company with its own capital. After it became successful, they would then sell off most or all of its shareholdings, but still retain control of the company on the basis of a managing agency contract. Second, managing agencies might be asked to manage existing companies. In such instances, managing agencies were sought because of their managerial expertise, as demonstrated by their track records. Thirdly, managing agencies provided important financial functions. Here, their ability to attract new investors, to secure bank loans, etc., made managing agencies attractive to investors in joint stock companies especially at a time when the credit system was not yet fully developed and capital markets were still in their infancy.

Formal Mechanisms of Control

The defining characteristic of the formal mechanism of control in this model is the managing agency contract. Through this device the managing agents (generally as partnerships or private joint stock companies) were able to exercise control over other firms. Managing agents typically established the managing agency contract (and their control over the firm) before promoting a firm or before selling off control of an established firm. A variety of provisions within the contract (e.g. long or unlimited terms of office, penalties for dismissal of the agency, etc.) would help to ensure that the managing agents could not be readily removed by shareholders. As the managing agents had a wide range of powers (viz., investment decisions, appointing directors, etc.) they were not merely managers, but exercised the functions of CG as well. In many cases, the companies that the managing agents managed did not even have boards, or if they did, the boards were entirely composed of the managing agents (Sengupta, 1983: 16). Due to its 'advantages', the managing agency became the dominant form of control among industrial firms in India, with 95 per cent of firms under managing agencies in 1955, the year before measures were taken to gradually eliminate the institution (Baig, 1971: 80).

Circumstances of Governance

The second factor defining the managing agency model consists of a range of macro-economic circumstances under which the managing agencies operated. The first such circumstance was undeveloped capital markets. The undeveloped nature of the capital markets (indeed, the very absence of stock markets when the first managing agencies were founded) had a twofold significance. On the one hand, it meant that there was an important financial role to be fulfilled and opportunities for whoever could fulfil it. It was managing agents who proved to have the ability to step in to fill this void, an ability that meant they were attractive to firms not only (or even primarily) for their management skills. On the other hand, the undeveloped capital market meant that there was virtually no market discipline to be imposed upon managing agents. A second important circumstance of control was a weak credit system. This enabled the managing agents to play a key role in securing working capital for managed companies, fulfilling, in effect, the same role as British discount houses (Chaudhuri, 1975: 44). Again, this was another non-management role that made managing agents attractive to companies. Third, the system was characterized by lax government regulation. In the absence of legislation against the abuses of power by managing agents, including the methods used to attain and maintain control over firms, the contracts they established were legally binding and their legality was upheld by the courts over the objections of shareholders (Rungta, 1970: 234). Moreover, the British government was not in a mood to regulate the system more effectively as it 'considered it more important to keep Indian law in line with British law so that British investors would know where they stood' (Rungta, 1970: 259). Finally, it needs to be noted that government policy systematically favoured European over Indian entrepreneurs (Bagchi, 1972;

Ray, 1979). While this discrimination slowly eroded over the decades as India moved towards independence, it was only on the eve of independence that Indian managing agencies were able to sufficiently offset this bias to overtake European managing agencies in terms of size.

Development Impact

Assessing the developmental impact of the managing agency model is complicated by its historical association with a colonial regime, which was not intended to promote development but, on the contrary, largely worked to undermine local development aspirations. In one sense, however, there were some positive economic developmental effects, which primarily came in the form of facilitating investment and introducing better management techniques. These developments, however, represented, at best, an ad hoc approach to structural problems, which turned out to be quite dysfunctional. The structural problems were a lack of well-developed financial markets and a dearth of professional management. These responses must be considered dysfunctional insofar as the managing agencies were able to maintain control with small (or even no) shareholdings, had little incentive to take into account the concerns of small shareholders, and ultimately did little to encourage the development of a wider shareholding public (Rungta, 1970). Another development that might be considered positive, but which also turned out to be dysfunctional in many ways, was the emergence of large business houses. While the rise of such business entities might be considered necessary for the emergence of a dynamic modern economy, in practice they did little in this regard. Investment funds did not get effectively allocated to key sectors. While this was due in part to colonial policies, it is also the case that managing agency system contributed to economic concentration. This allowed the large business houses to reap huge profits in traditional sectors and did not push them into new areas. At the same time, economic concentration (and the practices of many of the business houses) inhibited their potential contribution to economic growth and employment (Chaudhuri, 1975).

While it is hard to argue that the managing agency effectively promoted development through standard market incentives, it could be argued that this was not the entire story as individual firms and business houses did intentionally try to take their development impact into account. A commonly cited example of this, of course, is the Tata Iron and Steel Company (TISCO) in Jamshedpur, established by J.R.D. Tata (Keenan, 1943). There were two significant developmental impacts of this venture. On the one hand it could be argued that TISCO represented an effort by nationalist industrialists (at the expense of their own profit margins) to contribute to laying the basis for the economic development of a new, independent Indian state. An alternative—less flattering, but not insidious—interpretation is that this represented good, long-run business strategy by the Tatas, ensuring that they would be the dominant player in the field in the future. Which of these two interpretations is correct is hard to determine, especially insofar as the Tatas themselves have tended to uphold the compatibility of sound business investments and corporate responsibility. The other intentional developmental impact of Jamshedpur comes in the form of a series of very progressive labour measures (which were only adopted much later as Central government schemes).[2]

The Tatas were not alone, of course, in their concern about the future of India and the responsibilities of corporations more generally. The founders of a number of other Indian business houses, such as Ghanshyam Birla (Jaju, 1985), and Ardeshir and Pirojsha Godrej (Karanjia, 1997) were not only associated with Gandhi in the nationalist struggle, but also adopted the latter's concept of 'trusteeship' in understanding their corporate responsibilities. It is hard to find examples, however, of how this understanding may have directly motivated them to incorporate development concerns into their business decisions (in the same way as the Jamshedpur example is often cited). Rather, their commitment tended to be expressed more through charitable donations and philanthropic activities.

Another potential area of development impact relates to political development. As noted above, Indian business leaders played a key role in the nationalist struggle. As such, it could be argued that they contributed to political development in a significant way. Yet, while the ousting of the British and the establishment of a democratic state was undoubtedly a very positive development, the story is more complicated than that. At issue are the ways in which they contributed, their motivations, and the nature of the political system that would emerge in the new, independent India. In particular, the question is whether business leaders used their power to unfairly determine the nature of the political institutions and the basic economic development strategy of the new state. As the authorship of the *Bombay Plan* indicates, the fact that business leaders largely determined the post-independence economic strategy can hardly be doubted (Thakurdas, Tata, and Birla, 1944). Whether they unduly used their influence in this venture and in the determination of the form of India's political institutions, however, is open to question.

The Business House Model (1956–1991)

Origins of the Model

With independence, major changes in the Indian economy were inevitable. The basis for these changes had been prepared beforehand through the complex network of interests and activities that were loosely woven together in the form of the Indian National Congress. The Congress was to a large extent a microcosm of Indian society. In it were represented a broad spectrum of conflicting interests divided along geographic, ethnic, religious, caste, class, and ideological lines, but united in their common desire to throw out British rule. Despite the wide range of interests represented, there was a surprising degree of agreement on many key issues such as the need for uplifting the masses by dramatically increasing per capita income, support for small- and medium-sized business, the goal of a self-reliant economy not dependent upon foreign technology, and a strong role for government planning, including a large role for the state in direct economic production. There were, of course, significant differences also. These involved, to use the language of the *Bombay Plan*, the degree to which 'individual liberty and freedom of enterprise' were to 'suffer a temporary eclipse' (Thakurdas, Tata, and Birla, 1944).

The basic form of the post-independence economy was characterized by the combination of an 'Import-Substituting Industrialization' (ISI) strategy for promoting economic development and limited welfare state schemes.[3] The ISI approach developed by India involved strict restrictions on the import of consumer and capital goods as well as foreign exchange, a mixed economy which restricted the activities of large companies and promoted small- and medium-sized firms as well as state-owned enterprises, economic planning, and a wide range of government support programmes, especially in the area of industrial financing. In addition, the government would also pass a new Companies Act, which was designed to gradually eliminate the institution of the managing agency, better safeguard the rights of shareholders, and protect the interests of the general public. These various factors would shape the nature of the new form of CG that was to emerge in independent India (Government of India, 1955; 1956).

While there was a strong role for the public sector in the Indian economy, this role, as elaborated in early planning documents, was often much stronger on paper than in actual practice. The private sector retained a key role in the economy, even in the 'commanding heights'. As private sector involvement was largely dominated by family-controlled business houses (although there was still significant foreign investment, this was regulated to a great extent and generally involved partnerships with the Indian business houses), this model can be referred to as the 'business house model' (Mukherjee Reed, 2001).

Formal Mechanisms of Control

The defining characteristic of the formal mechanism of control in this model was the superseding of the managing agency contract by an elected board of directors. The basis for this switch was laid down in the Companies Act of 1956. While the Act did not abolish the managing agency as a form of organization, it did strongly discourage it. As a result, the vast majority of new firms after 1956 chose to register as 'board-managed firms' (or selected the closely related option of having a managing director). The intention of the act was to bring the management, whatever its form, squarely under the control of a board of directors. In this sense, the act closely paralleled the formal understanding of the Anglo-American model in which, to use contemporary language, the role of the board was understood to be governance, while management was responsible for the day-to-day operations of the firm. The Act also contained provisions concerning a number of other areas (e.g. disclosure norms, rules for AGMs, maintenance of records, limits on the number of directorships an individual could hold, removal of directors, etc.) which, in principle, served to protect shareholder interests and bring the system more in line with the spirit of the traditional Anglo-American model (Government of India, 1956).

While similar to the Anglo-American models in some of its characteristics, the business house model also distinguished itself in several ways. One area of difference was that the Company Act subjected many more corporate decisions to government approval. Companies, for example, required Central government approval for such matters as the appointment of whole-time directors and managing directors, their salary levels, tenure, etc. Such intervention, which involved wide powers of discretion, was ostensibly intended to help promote, among other things, greater income equality and prevent economic concentration. This level of intervention was unparalleled in any Anglo-American system (Gupta, C.B., 1984; Sharma and Chauhan, 1965; Sengupta, 1983).

A second major contrast with the Anglo-American model involved the institution of the 'nominee director', which enabled banks and other financial institutions to demand of companies the right to 'nominate' a director to represent their interests on the board. Such nominee directors could be either employees of the nominating institution or outsiders. The source, the role, and the functioning of such nominee directors tended to differ both depending upon whether the firm was in the public or private sectors and whether the firm was deemed to be 'sick'.[4] The main impetus for the practice of having nominee directors in the private sector was the Report of the Industrial Licensing Policy Inquiry Committee (ILPIC)—more commonly known as the Dutt Committee—which imputed a twofold importance to such directors, viz., helping to prevent economic concentration and ensuring that public interest and not merely private profit guided corporations. On the basis of the Dutt Committee Report, the Central government issued guidelines in 1971 to public financial institutions for the appointment of nominee directors and the convertibility of debt to equity (Sengupta, 1983: 218–21). While nominee directors sat on boards of the entire range of corporate ventures, the incidence of their presence, however, was highly correlated with the size of the firm, with some 87 per cent of the largest firms having nominee directors (Gupta, 1989).

Circumstances of Governance

Two factors in particular defined the circumstances of governance in the business house model. The first of these was the nature of the capital market. Up until the 1950s the contribution of capital markets in India remained relatively unimportant (as the number of shareholders remained but a very small fraction of the population) while at the same time commercial banks tended to shy away from financing industry. This changed somewhat in the 1950s as commercial banks, especially the State Bank of India (SBI) and its subsidiaries, began to play a greater role in the field of industrial finance. In addition, the government fostered other financial institutions with the special intention of financing and developing industry. These included public financial institutions (PFIs) sponsored by both the Central government and the states.[5] The former included the Industrial Finance Corporation of India (IFCI) founded in 1948, the Industrial Credit and Investment Corporation of India (ICICI) established in 1951, and the Industrial Development Bank of India (IDBI), which came into being in 1964. The basic guidelines governing the operation of these institutions, as laid out in the Third Five-Year Plan were to ensure 'that their support to new entrants into industry and to medium and small enterprises as well as to cooperative undertakings is both speedy and adequate. They should also devise suitable criteria for assessing progress in this direction' (cited in Chaudhuri, 1975: 250). In addition to banking and term-lending institutions, the government also sponsored investment institutions such as the Life Insurance Corporation of India (LIC), the Unit Trust of India (UTI), and the General Insurance Corporation (GIC). Another key factor that affected the operation of the capital markets was the institution of the Controller of Capital Issues (CCI). Established in 1947, the government granted the CCI, as part of its efforts to channel investment funds to priority areas, the power to establish share prices (rather than allowing them to be set in the market).

A second major factor defining the circumstances of control consisted of government restrictions on and intervention in market competition. These were designed to achieve two broad goals. The first goal was to promote economic development. To this end the government: (1) imposed import restrictions (on consumer and capital goods); (2) regulated foreign exchange; (3) promoted exports (by linking import licences and resource allocation to export targets); (4) financed infrastructure projects and research and development; (5) channelled investment into key priority sectors; (6) restricted the areas in which large private sector firms could operate through an industrial licensing programme; and (7) nationalized some industries. The second major goal, which existed in some tension with the first, was to control economic concentration and monopolistic practices. The key measures that were taken towards this end were: (1) the development of a large public sector; (2) the promotion of small- and medium-sized firms (incentive programmes, cheap credit, etc.); (3) restrictions on the areas in which large corporations could operate (viz., through the industrial licensing system); and (4) the passing of the Monopolies and Restrictive Trade Practices Act (MRTPA). These latter restrictions on and interventions into the market, then, were actually intended to strengthen market competition.[6]

Development Impact

It is commonly acknowledged that India's economic development efforts during the interventionist period and under the business house model were less than fully successful. While upto the mid-1960s, growth rates were relatively high, growth became very sluggish after that. Not only this, but even unemployment remained high, real wages stagnated, and the corporate sector proved incapable of producing high-quality, internationally competitive products. What is less widely recognized is that, despite this less than stellar performance, the profits of large corporations in India remained very high—far outstripping, for example, profit rates in those countries commonly recognized as the development success stories, such as Korea and the other newly industrializing countries of east Asia. From the perspective of standard economic theory this is a bit of a paradox, as firms should only be earning such profits on the basis of innovative practices and products, which should involve dynamic growth and increases in employment. How is this to be accounted for?

Business leaders in India have long criticized the licence-permit raj as an inefficient system, which imposed unnecessary and costly restrictions upon business, including the need to make payments at various level of the bureaucracy and to political parties. Yet, while there were inconveniences for business (in terms of having to make pay-offs, having plans delayed and operations slowed down, etc.), what is less commonly acknowledged by business is that there were also important advantages insofar as the government provided subsidies (especially cheap credit) and protected markets. What is most significant, however, is not just that business received favours, but that they were not held accountable. The industrial system meant that there was little competition in product markets. Cheap credit meant that there was little pressure from shareholders through financial markets. An inefficient legal system made the courts an inefficient mechanism for imposing discipline. Nor did the government prove willing or able to link the benefits it offered to economic performance—again, in contrast to the example of Korea, where similar policy arrangements were in place, but the government forced business to perform to reap any benefits (Mukherjee Reed, 2001). Chapter Nine will discuss in greater detail the impact of this credit policy, which resulted in a massive default of the corporate sector and led to a complete collapse of the public banking system. Some authors have appropriately labelled this as the 'Great Indian Bank Robbery' involving a drainage of the public capital to the amount of Rs 110,000 crores. As they have argued, 'This is the money that India Inc. owes and won't pay back. Here's what it could pay for: all our defence bills for 2 yrs. Or an expressway in every state. Or a school in every village.'[7]

With respect to the issue of corporate responsibility, most leading Indian business continued to follow the example of their founders in acknowledging the notion that they had social obligations. Again, the House of Tatas and its flagship TISCO continued to lead the way with a wide range of initiatives including a Rural Development Society (providing integrated rural development programmes including education, medical and sanitation services, family planning, drinking water, adult literacy, afforestation, vocational training, and the encouragement of rural industry, entrepreneurship and handicrafts), a Tribal and Harijan Welfare Cell (whose main goal is raising the socio-economic status of tribals and Harijans by providing education, health care, drinking water, and vocational training), a Community Development and Social Welfare Department (which provides medical and health programmes, the promotion of sports and cultural education and activities, and vocational training), and a Centre for Family Initiatives (focusing on family planning activities, women's health issues, childcare and health campaigns). Other business houses followed in a similar, if not as extensive, fashion. Arvind Mafatlal, the former chairman of the Mafatlal group, for example, advocated such measures as businesses 'adopting villages' to help eradicate poverty (Mafatlal, 1973), while the chairman of Hindustan Lever, T. Thomas (1991), advocated and initiated some involvement in 'integrated rural development'.

While major corporate houses were involved in corporate philanthropy and community development projects during this period, it has been difficult to assess how 'socially responsible' they actually were, either in terms of the resources that they made available or in terms of the manner in which they have used them. Part of the problem is that firms have generally been rather tight-lipped about these matters, just as they have been of other aspects of their operations (Kasbekar, 1983). Despite calls for corporations to be more forthcoming with such information since at least the 1960s, the first social audit by an Indian company during this period was only conducted in 1980 by TISCO (Cherumilam, 1982). Until recently, few have followed TISCO's lead. There are reasons to suspect the development efficacy of corporate programmes, however, for a number of reasons. First, much of the money that was allocated did not go to high-priority development areas, but was directed to more highly visible activities (e.g. the arts, religion, sport). Second, the general approach to assistance programmes tended to be based more on a charity model rather than a development model (see Nadkarni's Chapter Eleven in this volume). Third, the commitment of the business houses was often dubious. Some business leaders either played down the notion by stressing the need to pursue profits over all else or have denied that such an obligation to 'charity' exists at all (Krishna, 1992). Concerns about the lack of corporate social responsibility, however, were expressed by various government agencies and commissions. The High Powered Expert Committee on Companies and the MRTP Act (better known as the Sachar Committee), for example, saw fit to declare that 'in the development of corporate ethics, we have reached a stage where the question of social responsibility of business to the community can no longer be scoffed at or taken lightly' (Government of India, 1978). Even business leaders themselves, most notably perhaps J.R.D. Tata, criticized business for not living up to its basic obligations of fair business practice, not to mention the failure to address social responsibilities.[8]

In terms of political development, as was noted earlier, business has often portrayed itself as a victim of the rent-seeking behaviour of bureaucrats and politicians. While there can be no doubt that successive Indian governments extracted a price from business (and punished any who were not willing to pay), it is also the case that the business houses were not entirely innocent victims and that they were in large part beneficiaries of the system (which, among other things, provided them with extensive protection from competition and a variety of subsidies). Rather than one-sided predatory activity, the business-government nexus of the time is better characterized as a combination of inappropriate political influence by corporations and 'rent-seeking behaviour' by government. This relationship amounted to a distorted symbiosis in which politicians and bureaucrats sought to extract 'rents' from corporations in return for consideration of the corporation's economic concerns, e.g. obtaining licences, loans, etc. (Bagchi, 1993).[9]

The Anglo-American Model of Governance (1991 to date)

Origins of the Model

In the 1980s the United States under Reagan and the United Kingdom under Thatcher led the way in what would become a global trend by introducing programmes of radical economic liberalization. These programmes involved both marketization (i.e. giving greater play to the market in solving economic problems) and deregulation (i.e. a substantial withdrawal of the state not only from direct economic activity, but also from the regulation of the economy and the provision of a variety of social services). These liberalizing policies (including the liberalization of trade, foreign investment, and international financial markets) have been strongly implicated in the increased transnational economic activity that has occurred over the last two decades, commonly referred to as globalization.

In India, the fiscal crisis of 1991 and the resulting need to approach the IMF led the government to move in the same 'reform' direction. Initially, the reform process induced by this crisis only had the appearance of an economic stabilization programme. Soon, however, it became clear that the key players in the reform process had a more ambitious plan that they hoped to enact. Although they had adopted a much more gradualist approach than most of their eastern European counterparts, the finance minister at the time, Dr Manmohan Singh, and his successor, P. Chidambaram, were clearly moving along the lines of the new consensus of liberalization and deregulation. Concerns arose, however, that with the election of a BJP-led government the reform process would slow down and be very selectively implemented. It was thought that key sectors of the business community, reputed to have the ear of the BJP leadership, were more concerned about insulating themselves from competitive pressures (e.g. through continued tariffs on consumer goods) than with becoming competitive. As it has turned out, while the concerns of Indian business have not gone unheeded by BJP-led governments (as evidenced by such policies as 'buy-back' provisions in the new company law), the liberalization process has continued.

These policies of economic reforms undertaken have implied a change in the model of corporate governance. The form most closely associated with these reform policies, of course, is the Anglo-American model, characterized by a single-tiered board structure, in which representation is limited to directors elected by shareholders, and strong reliance on capital markets as a disciplinary tool.

Formal Mechanism of Control

As part of the larger liberalization process, in 1999 the Government of India amended the Companies Act, 1956. Before examining these changes, it is important to note that the 1956 Act was already largely in line with the basic understanding of the Anglo-American mechanism of control. While the 1956 Act formally allowed for a range of management/corporate governance options (including, for example, direct management by the board of directors), in practice most companies adopted the standard Anglo-American option of a single-tiered board composed of a mix of inside and outside directors including a managing director/CEO (who tended to occupy the position of chairperson). The current reforms are largely intended to make this formal mechanism function as it was intended to, by addressing the agency problem (which has long afflicted virtually all countries with the Anglo-American model). To this end, a variety of measures have been adopted, including the strengthening of certain shareholder rights (e.g. postal balloting on key issues), the empowering of SEBI (e.g. to prosecute defaulting companies), increased sanctions for directors who do not fulfil their responsibilities, limits on the number of directorships, changes in reporting, and the requirement that a 'small shareholders nominee' be appointed to the board of companies with a paid-up capital of Rs 5 crore or more. Overall, changes in the area of corporate responsibility during this period were relatively minor and did not constitute significant changes to the model of corporate governance.

There is one area concerning the formal mechanism of control in which significant change has, however, been taking place. This involves the role of nominee directors. Under the business house system, public financial institutions were instructed to appoint nominee directors both on the basis of lending and equity holding (and to convert debt into equity). Because of the extent of their lending and equity holdings, such institutions had the potential to attain levels of board representation that would have given them a significant voice, if not outright control, in most large publicly held companies. In the newly liberalized economy, however, there has been a strong tendency to play down the role of nominee directors (see Chapter Six by Banaji). Rather, the key institutional players are placing the primary emphasis on the role of the capital market in disciplining firms. This is true both of regulatory bodies such as SEBI and public financial institutions such as UTI.[10] In a well-functioning market system, it is argued, financial institutions do not need to have board representation. For its part, the finance ministry abolished the convertibility clause in loan agreements as part of its budget proposals for 1992–1993, further weakening the ability of public financial institutions to promote nominee directors (*Economic Times*, 15 October 1996).

Circumstances of Governance

The second defining characteristic of the model of corporate governance comprises the circumstances of governance. Here, significant changes have taken place in a number of different areas. Four areas of change in particular might be noted. First, with respect to capital markets, a number of key changes have taken place: 1. the repeal of the Capital Issues Control Act and the establishment of SEBI has meant that stock prices are now determined on the basis of market forces with no intervention by the government; 2. market pressures and SEBI guidelines have led to greater disclosure; 3. investors enjoy greater protection (through stricter controls over brokers and promoters); and 4. there are greater prospects for (hostile) takeovers. Second, there has been a liberalization of the banking sector through a twofold strategy involving macro-policy reforms intended to remove the external constraints on the system and micro-policy reforms designed to resolve the internal constraints that have plagued the system. The former policies included reducing the pre-emption of bank resources (viz., through reducing the cash reserve ratio), simplifying the maze of interest rates, and reducing the directed credit programmes and greater latitude for private banks. Among the latter polices were the introduction of prudential norms to ensure greater transparency, the establishment of debt recovery tribunals, the recapitalization of banks and the introduction of Memoranda of Understanding (MOUs) between banks and the RBI to 'tone up' management (Velayudham, 1997). Third, with respect to industrial policy, liberalization brought an effective end to the licence-permit raj and opened up capital and consumer markets alike to competition. This move was complemented by the removal of similar restrictions on investment and expansion that were part of the MRTPA. Finally, in the area of foreign trade, significant changes include: (1) the virtual abolishment of restrictions on the import of raw materials and capital goods;

(2) liberalization of the consumer market (including reductions in tariffs and a reduction in the list of goods that can be imported against special import licences); and (3) liberalization of the foreign exchange policy with replacement of the Foreign Exchange Regulation Act (FERA) by the new Foreign Exchange Management Act (FEMA).

The Development Impact

While the Anglo-American model is still relatively new, we now have a ten-year span over which to assess its impact. One approach to evaluating the development impact of this new model of governance is to look at how advocates justify it (and the economic reforms that have accompanied it). Here, we can note three basic claims with respect to the model's economic impact.[11] First, it is argued that the model, by liberalizing business, will result in increased corporate growth (and profits) which will provide the basis for sustained macro-economic growth. Second, as a result of the latter, the overall level of opportunities and benefits for society will increase. For the greatest mass of the population, employment generation will represent the most significant opportunity. Third, in addition to increased growth and employment, advocates argue that the reforms will provide benefits to (minority) shareholders in terms of greater transparency in corporate dealings and increased opportunities for shareholder participation.

While such claims provide a potential justification for adopting an Anglo-American model, they only constitute an actual justification to the degree that they can be supplemented by arguments based upon evidence that the model will live up to its claims. In what follows, some indication (though by no means a systematic analysis) is given of how well the new model is functioning with respect to these three economic criteria.

Corporate Profitability and Growth

Under the new Anglo-American model, it should not be at all surprising if corporate profitability were to increase. Reformers would argue this is what should occur and, if it does, it will be salutary for the economy as a whole. The actual results, however, have not been as unequivocally 'positive' as the reformers have predicted. Let us begin with some simple measures of corporate growth, viz., sales and fixed asset formation, as well as total output. As Figure 2.1 illustrates, there has been substantial growth in corporate sales, although the trajectory of growth is markedly volatile. A similar volatility characterizes growth of profits, especially when we consider the profit before interest, depreciation, and tax (PBDIT) (See Figure 2.2).

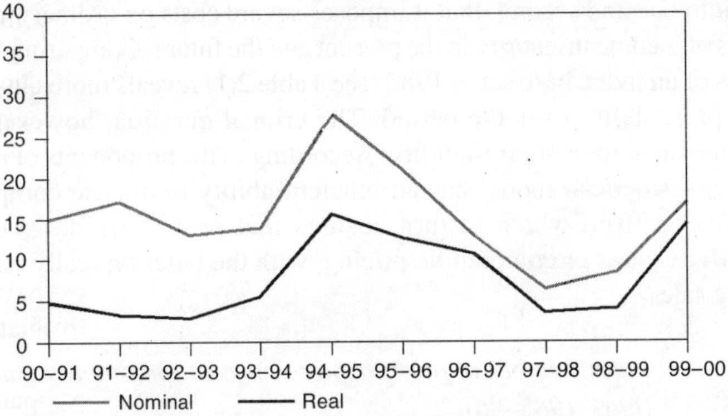

Fig. 2.1 *Growth in sales (%), 1990–91 to 1999–2000*

Source: Centre for Monitoring the Indian Economy (CMIE) Corporate Sector Database accessed online at www.cmie.com on 15 February 2003.

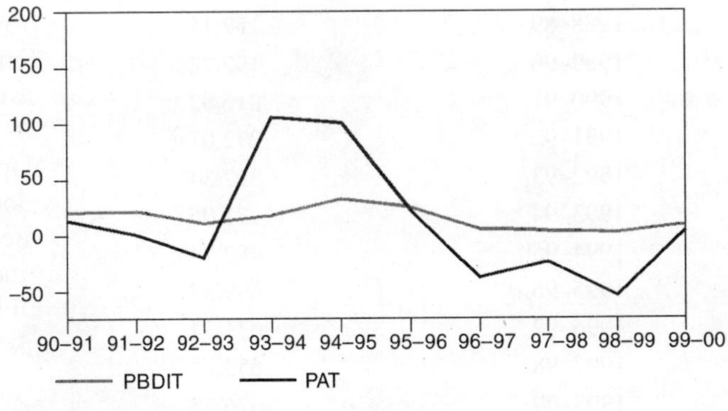

Fig. 2.2 *Growth in profit before interest, depreciation, and tax (PBDIT) and profit after tax (PAT), 1990–91 to 1999–2000*

Source: Centre for Monitoring the Indian Economy (CMIE) Corporate Sector Database accessed online at www.cmie.com on 15 February 2003.

Many observers take this volatility simply as an indication of the increasing marketization of the economy, and ascribe to it a positive value. While there is some validity in this view, it merits further analysis in the light of two issues that seems to have emerged: first, that it has become increasingly difficult to get the economy out of a recession every time it enters into one and second, that it imposes severe costs on ordinary citizens in terms of income insecurity in the present and the future. Comparing PBDIT in terms of an index base set in 1985 (see Table 2.1) reveals more clearly the rise in profitability over the period. The critical question, however, is to determine the source of profitability. According to the proponents of reform, the Anglo-American model has an inherent ability to impose competitive pressures on firm, which in turn ensures that profits are derived from productivity gains or competitive pricing, with the latter typically reflected in rising sales.

TABLE 2.1 *Index number of profit before depreciation, interest, and tax (base 1985–86)*

Year	*Index*
1985–86	100
1986–87	110.9
1987–88	123.76
1988–89	152.11
1989–90	192.72
1990–91	216.62
1991–92	272.07
1992–93	312.34
1993–94	371.06
1994–95	482.74
1995–96	599.57
1996–97	631.34
1997–98	659.75
1998–99	676.25
1999–00	471.47
2000–01	814.54

Source: Calculated from the *Indian Corporate Sector* (CMIE), May 2002.

In the Indian case, it is now commonly acknowledged that corporate incomes in the pre-liberalization era were mostly in the form of 'rents' rather than profits. The development of an Anglo-American model was expected to alter this. Did it? It is now a well-documented fact that the growth in corporate incomes immediately following liberalization was due, to a significant extent, to a spurt in *other incomes*, i.e. incomes derived from sources other than a company's primary line of business. The main sources of these incomes have been investments in the financial sector, in real estate, commodities, and other stocks, (which also had a very significant inflationary impact on these sectors). In 1993–94 and 1994–95, for example, the proportion of corporate funds invested in the financial sector were as high as 21 per cent and 13 per cent respectively by some estimates, in contrast to about 5 per cent during 1985–1993.[12]

Unfortunately, the standard measures of corporate performance do not reflect these structural properties of corporate incomes and profits. Most importantly, they cannot provide much indication as to whether any genuine economic value addition has occurred. This inadequacy of accounting profits has for some time now plagued institutional shareholders especially with regard to their investments in the developing world. The recent focus on *shareholder value* by management theorists, consultants, and institutional investors largely reflect this concern and has led to the adoption of indices of *economic* profits rather than *accounting* profits.

One key initiative in this area has been the development of the notion of Economic Value Added (EVA™). EVA attempts to reflect the difference between a company's accounting profit and the cost of capital to indicate to shareholders whether their invested capital has been efficiently utilized, i.e. if there has been an addition to the market value of their capital. Developed by an American management consultant Stern Stewart, EVA has been popularized in countries like India, Brazil, and Mexico, primarily to protect the interest of foreign investors. Since 1995, a large number of Indian companies have been using EVA and indeed, some startling results emerge when one compares companies on the basis of economic value rather than accounting value. A study undertaken in India in 1997 revealed the following:

- Of the top 100 companies that were studied, as many as thirty-six companies reported *negative economic profits* (i.e. they have a rate of return lower than the cost of capital invested);
- Three out of the top five value creators—Oil and Natural Gas Corporation (ONGC), Videsh Sanchar Nigam Limited (VSNL) and Bharat Petroleum Corporation Limited (BPCL)—operate under monopolistic conditions;[13]
- For most companies, there exist huge discrepancies between ranking in terms of their economic profits and their after-tax profits; and
- The discrepancies between economic and accounting profits are equally significant for public sector corporations and private sector corporations.

Table 2.2 presents the rank discrepancies revealed by the study.

TABLE 2.2 *Economic profits, market profits, and market-value added of selected companies*

Company	*Management*	*Rank by Profit After Tax (PAT)*	*Rank by Economic Profits (EP)*[a]	*Rank by Market Value Added (MVA)*[b]
ONGC	Govt. Executives	1	1	1
IOCL	Govt. Executives	2	89	2
Reliance Industries	Ambanis	3	9	4
TELCO	Tatas	4	6	7
HPCL	Govt. Executives	5	16	9
VSNL	Govt. Executives	6	4	6
IPCL	Govt. Executives	7	43	29
SAIL	Govt. Executives	8	98	8
BHEL	Govt. Executives	9	90	11
NALCO	Govt. Executives	10	67	16
TISCO	Tatas	11	97	18
Bajaj Auto	Bajaj	12	3	14
BPCL	Govt. Executives	13	5	12
Hind Lever	Professional	14	2	3
Larsen & Toubro	Professional	15	96	17
Hindalco	Govt. Executives	16	30	10
ITC	Professional	17	10	5
Grasim	Birlas	18	85	37
Tata Chemicals	Tatas	19	71	25
Indian Rayon	Birlas	20	31	66

Source: KPMG (1998).

[a] EP = [PAT – weighted average cost of capital] ÷ total capital;

[b] MVA = total capital employed – [current value of company's shares and debt]

These findings are indeed significant from the point of view of capital efficiency, and in particular, from the point of view of the shareholder. Those who champion the EVA approach argue that a company should be rewarded (punished) *only* according to whether it creates/destroys shareholder value. They go even further to argue that remuneration of managers should be tied to their performance measured in terms of value creation. While these may be important arguments—and they are certainly beginning to convince a number of leading Indian firms—a switch to a focus on capital efficiency or shareholder value is not likely to redress the problems of macro-level growth. In fact, it might even worsen the possibilities of growth. For, as the list of top performers indicates, high EVA-MVA rankings are associated with monopolistic firms that do not function on principles that are necessarily growth generating. Further, the implications of maximization of shareholder value on the economy are ambiguous at best, since value can be easily maximized through a number of growth-impeding corporate strategies including retrenchment, sell-offs, and mergers. Of course, indices like EVA are not intended to reflect systematic differences between monopoly profits and competitive profits or between profits that arise from reducing the size of the workforce. As such, the shift to EVA-based strategizing by companies cannot in itself provide much cause for optimism.

Transparency and Increased Control by Shareholders

A prime manifestation of the absence of control or influence by shareholders is the existence of financial irregularities. While it is generally difficult to prove financial abuse, one area in which dominant shareholders clearly took advantage of the deregulated capital market and abused the rights of minority shareholders is preferential share options. Between 1992 and 1994, dominant groups, both in Indian and foreign firms, took advantage of this device to 'earn' hundreds of millions, all in a perfectly legal manner. Thirty top foreign firms, for example, amassed more than Rs 300 crore through this device while ten major Indian firms received Rs 1500 crore (*Economic Times*, 8 August 1994).

While this particular abuse was largely curtailed in 1994 (when SEBI ruled that the price of preferential offerings could not be below the average share price of the previous six months), the issue of transparency in the stock market continues to plague India in a manner that reveals some underlying contradictions in the Anglo-American model. A couple of issues can be noted in this regard. The first is the recurrence of stock market scams, which have continued to afflict India since 1992, the year capital market regulations were substantially liberalized. In 2001, for example, Indian small investors were caught in a scam involving even greater sums of money and a larger number of actors than the one mentioned above. SEBI's preliminary investigation of this scam in May 2002 revealed that Rs 2900 crore were transferred out of the country through five Overseas Corporate Bodies (OCBs) between March 1999 and March 2001. These OCBs had together invested just Rs 777 crore in the Indian market but remitted a whopping Rs 3677 crore out of the country. This direct flight of capital occurred through a number of companies such as European Investments, Far East Investments, Wakefield Holding, Brentfield Holdings, and Kensington Investment. Three of these companies have a paid-up capital of just US $10.[14] The Joint Parliamentary Committee which investigated the scam blamed the two critical financial institutions—SEBI and the Reserve Bank of India (RBI).[15]

Integrally connected with the stock market crisis is the serious crisis of India's public financial institutions like the Unit Trust of India (UTI). In 2001, UTI was the largest single investor in Indian markets, and controlled assets worth Rs 60,000 crore, a quarter of which was invested through its flagship fund, the US-64. It is estimated that some twenty million investors had investments in US-64. Many of these were small investors who bought US-64 with their voluntary retirement funds and were dependent on it for income security. In July 2001, UTI suspended sales and repurchases of US-64, as it did not have enough reserves to finance such transactions. As of June 2002, a year after the suspension, UTI's financial situation was, according to T. Bandyopadhyay ('Saving a Leviathan', *Business Standard*, 29 June 2002), as follows:

- The Trust's assets under management have shrunk to a five-year low. Its market share, which once hovered at around 85 per cent, has come down to around 50 per cent. The total investible fund has fallen to Rs 48,706 crore in May 2002 from Rs 55,202 crore in June 2001. During this time, the US-64 corpus has shrunk from Rs 16,432 crore to Rs 12,330 crore.
- Gross non-performing assets in corporate debt is around Rs 6800 crore or 33 per cent of its total debt portfolio. There is also a pile of illiquid stocks in its equity schemes.
- The US-64 scheme alone has borrowed Rs 3185 crore from the banks to meet redemption pressures. Then, there is another Rs 5000 crore borrowed from various other in-house schemes. This apart, the government is supporting the fund to bridge the gap between the net asset value and the promised return on the limited redemptions of the US-64 units. So far, about Rs 300 crore has been reimbursed by the government on this account.
- The Development Reserve Fund (DRF) of the Trust, which is the cash reserve to meet shortfalls in its assured return schemes, is shrinking fast. The DRF corpus is now pegged at around Rs 950 crore after UTI drew Rs 617 crore to meet the shortfall in one of its monthly income plans—MIP-97—on 30 April.

- MIP-97 is one of the many assured return schemes that will continue to mature until March 2006. These schemes could bleed UTI to death if the government distances itself from the organization and the stock markets remain subdued. On 30 June 2002, three more assured return schemes were to mature, creating an additional deficit of Rs 1000 crore in the UTI balance sheet.
- Between October 2002 and 30 June 2003, when the UTI's financial year ends, four more income plans will mature and the shortfall could be at least Rs 700 crore.

As many readers would recall, UTI's first crisis occurred in 1999, induced by a highly problematic private placement deal involving shares of Reliance Industries Limited (RIL). The response to that crisis was a bail-out package of Rs 3300 crore to UTI. The second crisis cost the taxpayers about five times as much—a package to the tune of Rs 14,500 crore which was finalized in August 2002.[16] As of 31 December 2002, UTI recorded cumulative negative reserves of Rs 7359 crore.

The investigations into the 2001 crisis revealed that its source also lay in exactly the same set of causes—doubtful investments, bail-out of chronic industrial defaulters (such as the Essar group), and investment in a variety of volatile software scrips and stocks pushed by stockbroker Ketan Parekh (the chief player in the stock market scam of 2001).[17] In 1999, the RIL investments revealed the extreme danger inherent in UTI's shift towards equity and away from debt. The Deepak Parekh Committee, which investigated the 1999 crisis, recommended that its equity exposure, which then stood at 70 per cent, should be brought down to 40 per cent. Following that recommendation, however, not only did such a shift not occur, but the equity investments of UTI became increasingly problematic. Investments were frequently made, for example, in companies that UTI's own internal research team had ruled against (e.g. Cyberspace Infosys where Rs 24 crore was invested). In other cases, investments in companies were increased after the erosion in share prices.

The 'development impact' of the UTI crisis is enormous, especially if calculated in terms of health care, education, and poverty alleviation programmes. Yet, as Dalal has observed, 'the government will, in all probability, get away with the massive bailout without so much as a protest. That is because social activists in India and NGOs have yet to understand the enormity of the leakage of scarce resources to privileged investors and industrialists through organisations such as the UTI and development financial institutions'.[18]

Employment

With the introduction of the Anglo-American model, the expectation was that employment would increase as labour market conditions gradually came to simulate those in the more liberalized Anglo-American markets. The 2002–03 Economic Survey indicates that the exact opposite has occurred. There is a decline in growth rate of employment during the 1990s despite a comparatively higher growth rate in GDP, indicating a decline in the labour intensity of production. The absolute number of unemployed has grown during this period due to a near stagnation of employment in agriculture. Employment in the organized sector, which was hardly 8.34 per cent (with only 2.58 per cent in the private sector), shows a further decrease of 0.6 per cent over 2000. In this period, employment in the private sector rose by a mere 0.1 per cent (Government of India, 2003).

As Table 2.3 and Table 2.4 show, the share of wages in the value of production has declined uniformly across all types of corporate firms—from 10.43 per cent in 1985–86 to 6.75 per cent in 1994–95. It has also been uniform across both large corporations (especially Multinational Corporations, MNCs), as well as smaller, private firms—where the share of wages has declined from 12 per cent to 5 per cent (CMIE, 1996: 50). The declining trend continues between 1995 and 2001.

If forces acting to increase employment are not readily evident, forces acting to increase unemployment certainly are. One of the key vehicles through which this occurs involves voluntary retirement schemes (VRSs). In the private sector, the largest firms administered VRSs worth Rs 100 crore each year between 1993 and 1997.[19] Particularly affected have been sectors where high growth is envisaged in the coming years, and the permanent exclusion of a section of Indian workers from these sectors merits some concern. VRS might seem to be an attractive option for corporations trying to 'right size', especially insofar as the law only requires companies to pay up to fifteen days' salary for every completed year of service. From some perspectives, they might also provide a rational solution to facilitating structural change in labour markets. In practice, however, their attractiveness is limited by the way the industrial relations system in India functions, which, somewhat ironically, contributes to even greater unemployment. Part of the problem lies in the fact that, while by law companies only have to offer a relatively small amount for VRS, typically, state governments will not ratify the schemes unless they have support from the trade unions. This obviously increases the costs of such schemes and, in conjunction with other costs and problems associated with state intervention, often makes it more feasible for companies to shut down entire operations rather than lay-off a section of the workforce.

TABLE 2.3 *Share of wages in the total value of production (per cent): 1985–86 to 1994–95*

	1985–86	*1989–90*	*1990–91*	*1991–92*	*1992–93*	*1993–94*	*1994–95*
Public Sector	9.79	9.83	9.61	9.54	9.44	9.32	6.53
Private Sector	11.16	9.04	8.68	8.16	8.0	7.42	6.85
Indian Private Sector	11.46	9.18	8.84	8.28	8.03	7.36	6.77
Large Houses	11.28	9.27	9.03	8.52	8.34	7.87	7.31
Other Private Cos.	12.28	8.82	8.13	7.47	7.11	6.05	5.32
Foreign Companies	11.83	9.81	9.01	8.51	8.47	8.34	7.73
All Companies	10.43	9.44	9.13	8.81	8.65	8.22	6.75

Source: CMIE, *The Indian Corporate Sector*, 1996, p. 50.

TABLE 2.4 *Share of wages in the total value of production (per cent): 1994–95 to 2000–01*

	1994–95	*1995–96*	*1996–97*	*1997–98*	*1998–99*	*1999–00*	*2000–01*
Government	4.8	5.4	4.7	5.1	4.9	4.3	3.9
Central Government	4.7	5.4	4.6	4.9	4.8	4.2	3.8
Central Government Taken over	33.3	35.1	34.7	46.7	51.4	55.4	61.4
Central Government Others	4.4	5.1	4.3	4.6	4.4	4	3.7
Private Sector	5.1	4.9	5	5.3	5.5	5.4	5.1
Indian Private Sector	4.9	4.7	4.9	5.1	5.4	5.3	5
Indian Business houses	5.2	5	5.1	5.4	5.6	5.4	4.9
Top 50 Business houses	5.8	5.6	5.6	5.7	6	5.7	4.8
Other Business houses	4.2	4.1	4.4	4.7	5	4.9	5.1
Other Private Indian	4.1	3.9	4.1	4.3	4.6	4.9	5.1
Foreign Private Sector	5.7	5.5	5.5	5.9	5.9	5.7	5.8

Source: CMIE, *The Indian Corporate Sector*, May 2002, p. 171.

In the public sector, a total of 129,049 workers had availed of the VRS by April 1999. The amount released for this purpose was Rs 23 billion between 1992–93 and 1998–99. During 1998–99 a budgetary provision of another Rs 2900 crore has been made for VRS with the expectation that a similar amount would have to be set aside every year for the next five years. Of the total number of workers retrenched, about 11,367 (approximately 10 per cent) have been redeployed over the past six years, approximately at the rate of 2000 workers per year as against a retrenchment rate of 21,000 per year (Government of India, 1998–99).

The retrenchment of workers through various voluntary retirement schemes, in a market where unemployment is already high, has resulted in the reversal of some of the material and political gains secured by the Indian workforce. One obvious reason for this has been the recessions that have plagued the Indian economy in the past decade. Another major reason, however, has been the increasing presence of MNCs. While MNCs, as we noted above, have induced a tremendous increase in salaries in select labour markets, they have also introduced various practices which tend to increase unemployment and make it more precarious, e.g. flexible employment, less job security, subcontracting, etc. The situation is likely to get worse in the near future as domestic firms, which currently do not have a viable exit strategy, have been lobbying for bankruptcy laws based on the US example.[20]

Conclusion

As a country, India has long expressed its aspirations in terms of 'development'. From the perspective of potential development impact, there is a lot at stake in recent debates in India over corporate governance reform. In this chapter, we have tried to examine the relationship between corporate governance and development in a larger historical context. We have done this by distinguishing three different historical models of corporate governance (based upon formal mechanisms of control and circumstances of governance) and examining their development impact. What we have not yet done is to compare the different models and account for similarities and differences.

While there is not enough room here to go into a detailed discussion on the various aspects of (economic, social, and political) development, it is important to point out one key similarity between the models in terms of their economic development impact. This is the fact that the corporate sector (and the industrial sector more generally) has not been able to affect the rate of poverty in the country. As Datt, Kozel, and Ravallion (2003) have argued, there is virtually zero correlation between growth rates and the (share-weighted) growth elasticities of poverty across states in India in the 1990s. This is not unique to the 1990s, however. Trend growth rates in India's non-farm economy from 1960 to 1993–94 were also uncorrelated with the weighted growth elasticities of poverty. The differences across states in the non-farm growth elasticities of poverty are largely explicable in terms of differences in initial rural development and initial human development

This phenomenon, which runs counter to the logic of mainstream economics, raises an obvious question. How are we to account for this historic lack of connection between industrialization and development? Datt, Kozel, and Ravallion provide a partial answer to this question by pointing out that initial deficits in human development prevent the poor from participating in industrial growth. This answer is partial in that it only explains the supply side of the problem. There is also a demand side that needs to be considered in tandem.

In order to understand the demand side of the equation, one has to look at profit strategies. Here, one finds that the most critical factor that has been consistent across the different models of CG has been the inability of government and market pressure to link corporate profits to innovation and productivity gains. This was true not only during the interventionist period, but, as Mukherjee Reed argues in greater detail in Chapter Nine, continues to be the case in the post-interventionist state. Surpluses generated by corporations in India have typically not been 'economic profits' based upon innovation, but 'rents' which have emanated from market imperfections, market manoeuvres, and state policy. It is this approach to generating profits that breaks the link between corporate performance (profits) on the one hand, and growth and development on the other. The task of governance reforms is to establish this link in a systematic fashion.

If corporate strategies help to account for the low development impact of the corporate sector across models of corporate governance, corporate influence provides us with the key for understanding why large firms have been able to effectively pursue such strategies. What such influence means is that economic reforms, of whatever nature (and at whatever level), are not likely to be successful unless they are accompanied by political and legal reforms that can effectively limit the influence of corporations outside of the economic realm. Ultimately, responsible corporate governance must be predicated upon responsible political governance.

Notes

1. Proponents of this approach, while acknowledging the importance of freedom (political democracy) as another important area of development, have chosen not to incorporate such concerns into their own measure, preferring that such issues be evaluated by a different political freedom index (Haq, 1999).

2. TISCO introduced, for example, an eight-hour working day (1912), free medical aid (1915), a welfare department (1917), school facilities for children of employees (1917), work committees (1919), leave with pay (1920), workers' accident compensation (1920), a technical institute for training (1921), maternity benefits (1928), a profit-sharing bonus (1934), retiring gratuity (1937), and compensation for injuries on the job (1979).

3. State-aided and/or state-led accumulation was not only an important strategy in India (Bardhan, 1984; Bagchi, 1972; 1982), but was the reality of many, if not most, Third World countries from the 1950s to quite recently. The most notable and successful example of this are the east Asian states, but Latin American countries, most notably Brazil and Peru, have also had high degrees of state aid in accumulation (Evans, 1979; Stepan, 1978).

4. 'Sick' industrial firms are defined as firms which (a) have earned cash losses (b) have high current liabilities relative to their current assets, and (c) have had their net worth eroded by 50 per cent or have suffered an erosion of their paid-up capital. (Government of India, 1984: 70).

5. In addition to their ability to exert control over firms through equity holdings, PFIs also held considerable powers as lenders. These included: (1) the right to appoint one or two nominees to the board (generally a total of only two nominees are appointed by all institutions combined); (2) the right to require the borrowing company to broaden its board of directors; (3) the right to approve the (re)appointment of the managing director; (4) the right to approve certain other key appointments (e.g. finance director, technical director); (5) the right to specify what matters may be submitted for the board's approval; (6) the right to restructure the top management set-up; (7) the right to approve selling/purchasing arrangements; (8) the right to appoint management/technical consultants and auditors who will report directly to the shareholders; and (9) in the case of the IFC, the right to take over management in some circumstances (Gupta, 1989: 129–32).

6. There was an apparent tension between the two goals of promoting economic development and controlling concentration. Whether this tension was the result of an ineluctable trade-off (between the promotion of growth and equity) or was due to a lack of political will is a question of some debate. In any case, one key aspect of the practical resolution of this tension over the years tended to take the form of the government imposing and then relaxing (or ignoring) restrictions on large companies.

7. Dalal, S. et al, 'The Great Indian Bank Robbery', *Indian Express*, Sunday, 1 December 2002.

8. J.R.D. Tata, *Industrial Times*, 17–30 December 1979.

9. It has been suggested that some corporations, most notably the Tatas, tried to avoid participating in such 'rent-seeking behaviour' (at least at the highest levels)

and that they frequently paid a price for this (e.g. through delays or denials in granting licences. See, for example, Verma (1987).

10. This was confirmed by one of the authors in interviews with top executives of both these institutions.

11. It is, of course, also important to analyse the model with respect to its political and social impact. While we are not able to offer a systematic analysis of social development here, in Chapter Ten, Venkateswaran gives some indication of the intentional efforts of corporations to contribute to social development. Similarly, while short of a systematic account, in Chapter Nine Mukherjee Reed makes clear the impact of a lack of corresponding political reform to go along with current economic reforms.

12. Indira Gandhi Institute for Development Research (1998: 128).

13. This seems to be the case worldwide: in the US the top three are Microsoft, Coca Cola, and Intel; in the UK, Shell, Glaxo, and Lloyd; in Brazil, Telebras, Telesp, and Brahma.

14. Dalal, S. 'KP scam: Bigger than 1992', www.rediff.com, 19 July 2001.

15. 'Stock scam: JPC slams RBI over poor governance', Press Trust of India, 26 October 2002.

16. *Business Standard*, 2 September 2002.

17. Dalal, S. 'UTI gets another dole without stricter accountability?', www.rediff.com, 24 December 2001.

18. Dalal, S. 'UTI gets another dole without stricter accountability?', www.rediff.com, 24 December 2001.

19. The figures are estimated from CMIE's data on some major restructuring efforts in the private sector, and VRS schemes of the public sector discussed in the media (1996: 50, Table 52).

20. Existing policies seek to protect employment by inducing 'sick companies' to seek help from the public financial institutions and the Board For Industrial & Financial Reconstruction (BIFR). Once signs of 'industrial sickness' begin to appear, boards and managements of companies are expected to approach the financial institutions and the BIFR to put together a revival strategy that involves fresh financing and concessions. While the intentions behind these measures are commendable (protection of employment and investments made out of public money), there is ample evidence that the possibility of receiving these concessions have induced firms to use them for financing corporate restructuring (as in the case of Dunlop India Ltd). Also, there is evidence that the roles played by the government and its various agencies, including the BIFR, are rather ambiguous. Broadly speaking, they have tended to respond much better to revival plans proposed by managements/promoters rather than workers. In one particularly illustrative example, workers had put up equity amounting to Rs 9 crore out of their wages to finance the revival of an ailing jute mill. The proposed scheme got no attention from the various authorities for about three years, a delay that compromised the viability of the scheme and the earnings of the workers in a very significant way (Narayanan, 1994).

References

Bagchi, A.K. (1972). *Private Investment in India: 1900–39*, Cambridge: Cambridge University Press.

_____ (1982). *The Political Economy of Underdevelopment*, Cambridge: Cambridge University Press.

_____ (1993). 'Rent Seeking, New Political Economy and the Negation of Politics', *Economic and Political Weekly*, 21 August, 1729–36.

Bardhan, P. (1984). *The Political Economy of Indian Development*, Oxford: Basil Blackwell.

Baig, N. (1971). *Pattern of Company Management in India*, Aligarh: Navman Prakashan.

Centre for Monitoring the Indian Economy (CMIE) (1996). *The Indian Corporate Sector*, Delhi: CMIE.

_____ (1998). *The Indian Corporate Sector*, Delhi: CMIE.

_____ (1999). 'An Analytical Overview–May 1999', http://www.cmie.com/products/eis/index.htm (accessed 28 February 2003).

Chaudhuri, A. (1975). *Private Economic Power in India: A Study in Genesis and Concentration*, New Delhi: People's Publishing House.

Cherumilam, F. (1982). *Business and Government*, Bombay: Himalaya Publishing House.

Clarke, T. and R. Bostock (1997). 'Corporate Governance in Germany: The Foundations of Corporate Stucture', In *Corporate Governance: Economic and Financial Issues*, (eds) K. Keasey et al., Oxford: Oxford University Press, 233–51.

Datt, G., V. Kozel, and M. Ravallion (2003). 'A Model-Based Assessment of India's Progress in Reducing Poverty in the 1990s', *Economic and Political Weekly*, 25 January.

David, W.L. (1997). *The Conversation of Economic Development: Historical Voices, Interpretations and Reality*, New York: M.E. Sharpe.

Donaldson, T., and L.E. Preston (1995). 'The Stakeholder Theory of the Corporation: Concepts, Evidence, and Implications', *Academy of Management Review*, 20 (1), pp. 65–91.

Evans, P.B. (1979). *Dependent Development*, Princeton: Princeton University Press.

Government of India (1955). *The Second Five Year Plan, 1956–61*, New Delhi: Planning Commission.

_____ (1956). *The Companies Act*, New Delhi: Ministry of Law, Department of Justice and Company Affairs.

_____ (1978). *Report of the High Powered Expert Committee on Companies and the MRTP Act*, New Delhi: Controller of Publications.

_____ (1984). *Report of the Committee to Examine the Legal and Other Difficulties faced by Banks and Financial Institutions in Rehabilitation of Sick Industrial Undertakings*, New Delhi: Controller of Publications.

_____ (1998–99). *Annual Report*, New Delhi: Department of Industrial Development.

_____ (2003). *Economic Survey, 2002–2003*, New Delhi: Ministry of Finance.

Gupta, C.B. (1984). *Managerial and Executive Remuneration in India*, New Delhi: Allied Publishers.

Gupta, L.C. (1989). *Corporate Boards and Nominee Directors*, New Delhi: Oxford University Press.

Haq, M. (1999). *Reflections on Human Development*, New Delhi: Oxford University Press.

Indira Gandhi Institute for Development Research (1998). *India Development Report*, Mumbai: Indira Gandhi Institute for Development Research.

Jaju, R.N. (1985). *G.D. Birla: A Biography*, New Delhi: Vikas Jaju.

Karanjia, B.K. (1997). *Life's Flag is Never Furled: Godrej—A Hundred Years, 1897–1997*, New Delhi: Viking.

Kasbekar, K. (1983). 'The Secretive Sector: Should Companies Reveal More?' *Business World*, 31 January–18 February, pp. 66–75.

Keenan, J.L. (1943). *A Steel Man in India*, New York: Duell, Sloan and Pearce.

KPMG. (1998). 'Business Standard Value Survey', *The Strategist Quarterly*, January–March.

Krishna, C.G. (1992). *Corporate Social Responsibility in India: A Study of Management Attitudes*, New Delhi: Mittal Publications.

Lokanathan, P.S. (1935). *Industrial Organisation in India*, London: George Allenard Unwin.

A. Mafatlal, (1973). 'Social Responsibilities of Business and Industry', In *Industrial Development of India: Policy and Problems*, (ed.) C.N. Vakil, New Delhi: Orient Longman.

Martinussen, J. (1997). *Society, State and Market*, London: Zed Books.

Mies, M., and V. Bennholdt-Thomsen (2000). *The Subsistence Perspective: Beyond the Globalized Economy*, NY: Zed Books.

Mukherjee Reed, A. (2001). *Perspectives on the Indian Corporate Economy: Exploring the Paradox of Profits*, London: Palgrave.

Narayanan, M.S. (1994). 'Industrial Sickness: Review of BIFR's Role', *Economic and Political Weekly*, 12 February.

Ray, R. (1979). *Industrialization in India, Growth and Conflict in the Private Corporate Sector, 1914–47*, New Delhi: Oxford University Press.

Reed, D. (1998). *Three Historical Models of Corporate Governance: An Examination of Corporate Economic Responsibility in India*, Calcutta: Indian Institute of Management.

_____ (2001). 'Will Freeing up Corporate Activity Lead to Development? (and Why Should Corporations Care?)', *General Business Review*, April–June, pp. 8–20.

_____ (2002). 'Management Education in an Age of Globalization: Some Insights from Critical Theory', In *Rethinking Management Education*, (eds) C. Wankel and R. DeFillippi, Greenwich CT: Information Age Publishing.

Reserve Bank of India (1999). 'Performance of Private Corporate Business Sector, 1998–99', *RBI Bulletin*, October.

Rungta, R.S. (1970). *The Rise of Business Corporations in India: 1851–1900*, Cambridge: Cambridge University Press.

Sen, A. (1998). *Development as Freedom*, New Delhi: Oxford University Press.

Sengupta, N.K. (1983). *Changing Patterns of Corporate Management*, 2nd revised edition, New Delhi: Vikas Publishing House.

Sharma, T.R. and S.D.S Chauhan, (1965). *Indian Industries*, Agra: Shiva Lal Agarwala & Co.

Stepan, A. (1978). *State and Society: Peru in Comparative Perspective*, Princeton: Princeton University Press.

Thakurdas, P., J.R.D. Tata, G.D. Birla, A. Dalal, and J. Mathai (1944). *The Bombay Plan for India's Economic Development, a Brief Memorandum Outlining a Plan of Economic Development for India*, London: Penguin.

Thomas, T. (1991). *To Challenge and to Change*, New Delhi: Viking.

Tricker, R. (1994). *International Corporate Governance: Text, Readings and Cases*, NY: Prentice Hall.

United Nations Development Programme (1990). *Human Development Report 1990*, New York: Oxford University Press.

—— (2000). *Human Development Report 2000*, New York: Oxford University Press.

Velayudham, T.K. (1997). 'Prologue', In *Banking Reform in India: Managing Change*, (eds) R Subramanian and T.K. Velayudham, New Delhi: Tata McGraw-Hill.

Verma, H.S. (1987). *Industrial Families in India*, New Delhi: Concept Publishing Company.

World Commission on Environment and Development (1987). *Our Common Future*, Oxford: Oxford University Press.

3

Economic Reforms, Corporate Boards, and Governance

N. Balasubramanian

In India, the notion that corporations can and should contribute to development is not new. Gandhiji clearly conceptualized such obligations in terms of the notion of 'trusteeship'. However, till now, corporations and their boards have not fully lived up to the ideals of trusteeship and have not had as significant a development impact as they might have had. This paper discusses the potential impact of economic reforms on corporate boards of directors with an eye on understanding whether, by encouraging more responsible and effective corporate governance, they will contribute more efficaciously to development.

In this chapter I first discuss briefly the origins of the corporate form of business organization, together with the concept of the board of directors and the roles and responsibilities that it is charged with. This is followed by an examination of the thrust of economic reforms, with special reference to the corporate form of business organization. The paper concludes with an assessment of the initial impact of the reforms on corporate boards and some speculation on the nature of the challenges that the reforms will pose for corporations and their boards as the reform process continues to unfold in the first years of the new millennium.

Origins of the Modern Corporation

The corporate form of activity appears to have begun in early Middle Ages, with towns, universities, religious orders, guilds of trades, people, and so on being treated as distinct entities quite separate from those comprising them. Such corporate entities could and did own considerable assets in their own name. None of these assets, however, were held in the form of *shares*, as we understand that term today. The origins of the notion of limited liability also seems to go back to this period, with the English courts by the fifteenth century upholding the principles that if something was owed to a group, it was not owed to the individuals and that individuals did not owe what a group owed. These principles would later evolve into the full-blown concept of limited liability as it pertains to the shareholders of joint stock companies.[1]

The origins of the modern business corporation can be traced to growth in the size and complexity of businesses, in financial, technological, and geographical terms. In financial and geographic terms, the origins of the corporation have clear links to the seafaring entrepreneurs from Europe who set out in search of the riches of the Orient. Their efforts to procure commodities like silk from China and spices from India not only sowed the seeds of international trade (and perhaps coincidentally, colonization and empire building!), but changed the nature of business. Such ventures were very risky and required significant financing. Few individuals or partnerships were able or willing to marshal the requisite capital by themselves. As a result, the substantial funds required to finance such expeditions had to be raised from a 'public' that went beyond kith and kin and a close circle of friends. Subsequently, technological innovations associated with the industrial revolution (e.g. the steam engine) led to dramatic increases in the size, complexity, and costs of projects (e.g. railroads) and further spurred the need for finance. It also induced the rise of a class of professional managers.

Gradually then, over the course of several centuries, the traditional practice of business in which 'owners managed and managers owned' changed dramatically. First, the ownership of business was dispersed, with ever larger number of people holding shares, most of whom had nothing to do with the management of the actual business. Later, as dispersal of ownership proceeded, professional management came to play an increasingly large role in running the corporation, often effectively wresting control from owners altogether.

As corporations have grown in size and complexity—some of them are larger than the total GDP of several sovereign countries—so too has their impact on people's lives. While part of the impact has been positive, a range of concerns has also been expressed about how these corporations operate. Their sheer size has almost inevitably led to financial and political clout, which in turn has caused an adverse reaction among citizens around the world, who wonder how the positive and negative impact of such mammoth entities can be balanced.[2] As a product of economic freedom and entrepreneurial aggression, the modern corporation promises to be a continuing challenge to society's ability to harness its potential benefits while simultaneously attempting to contain its ill effects.

The Corporate Board and Governance

The initial joint stock companies, especially those involved with long-distance international trade, were inevitably very risky ventures. Part of the risk—in the form of acts of God, piracy, etc.,—was largely unavoidable. Other aspects, however, in the form of fraud and incompetence, were not. Concerns over these risks eventually led not only to the development of joint stock company with limited liability, but also to the first rudiments of a system of disclosure and transparency aimed at those who were invited to contribute to the funds pool of the company. Clearly, while most of the investors did not expect to have anything to do with the management of the affairs of the company, which was left to the promoters, they needed to be reassured about their investments. The institution of the corporate board was founded on the basis that some group of respectable and trustworthy people, maybe many of them part of the dominant shareholding group, should look after the interests of the 'sleeping' shareholders of the company. That many corporate boards did not, and regrettably even now do not, discharge this trusteeship role is partly the justification for the ongoing efforts in legislation and regulation to demand compliance.

The notion that there are risks associated with a divorce between ownership and management is not new. Indeed, concern about the potentially adverse effects of such separation goes at least as far back as to the days of Adam Smith.[3] As Smith noted, directors, 'being the managers rather of other people's money than their own', cannot be expected to watch over it 'with the same vigilance with which the partners in a private copartnery frequently watch over their own'.[4] In Smith's time, however, the corporation was still a new innovation and there was relatively little separation between ownership and control. While this situation changed over the course of the nineteenth century, it was only in the 1930s that the research of Adolph Berle and Gardiner Means[5] first rigorously demonstrated a secular trend towards a separation of ownership and control. This discovery, of course, laid open the path for the formulation of the principal-agent problem. In recent decades, this conceptual framework has come to dominate calls for reform, in particular the imperative of strengthening corporate boards so that they can exercise their supervisory domain over executive management and ensure that all the created wealth in the business is reserved for and distributed to its rightful owners, the shareholders.

Recently, however, cross-national research conducted by Professor La Porta and others[6] has called into question the universality of the trend discovered by Berle and Means towards separation of ownership and control. The extent of separation of ownership from management control appears to be a function of the development of the economy in general and its capital markets in particular in the respective countries. In many cases, the predominant situation is still controlled by a dominant group of shareholders, not management (though it should be noted that in such situations, owner control does little to protect the interests of those minority or external shareholders who are not part of the dominant group). Another interesting dynamic involves the experience of developing countries like India, which in the post-WWII decades were to some extent influenced by socialism and adopted forms of central planning. In these cases, the state turned out to be the dominant owner in control of management, and the perils of ownership-control divorce continued to apply (with equal if not even greater force as far as the residual shareholders and large blocks of stakeholders were concerned).[7]

It is in this context that much greater emphasis is now being placed on the need to populate corporate boards with *independent* directors who have no material pecuniary relationships that may impair their judgment on matters relating to the company and its shareholders.[8] Together with moves to ensure *independence* of the companies' auditors,[9] these initiatives recognize and address the imperatives of accountability and fair play in protecting the interests of the vast majority of shareholders who do not have the benefits associated with operational control of their corporations.

The Stewardship Role of the Board

It has become common to understand the responsibility of the board to shareholders, especially in the Anglo-Saxon world, in terms of *stewardship* and *trusteeship*. Nowhere is the corporate board's stewardship role better articulated than in the Canadian guidelines.[10] Stewardship, the guidelines state, refers to 'the responsibility of the board to oversee the conduct of the business and to supervise management which is responsible for the day-to-day conduct of the business. In addition, as stewards of the business, the directors function as the catchall (*sic*) to ensure no issue affecting the business and affairs of the company falls between cracks'. Similar views, even if differently couched, predominate in many other countries around the world.

These concepts of stewardship and trusteeship, of course, are not new to India. Indeed, they go back to ancient times and have long been understood to hold in relationships between people and the maliks. The *Isa Upanishad*, for example, admonishes people not to covet another's property[11] (as does the Tenth Commandment in the Old Testament). In more recent times, Gandhiji elaborated the concept of trusteeship to help Indian landlords and industrialists better understand their roles and responsibilities.[12] A leading adherent of the trusteeship concept was L.S. Vaidyanathan, the first managing director of the state-owned Life Insurance Corporation of India, and earlier of Oriental, the leading insurers, who reportedly reminded his officers constantly that they were dealing with *widows' monies* and hence must observe the highest levels of prudence in spending insurance funds. Later-day materialism and cross-border influences may have eroded to a degree the belief in, and adherence to these fundamental values ingrained in the population. One can, therefore, do with some restatement and reinforcement of these values from time to time—perhaps, by persuasion, failing which by legislation!

The Stakeholder Debate

In this discussion so far, the board's accountability to shareholders has been the central theme. The principal ground for this shareholder primacy in terms of board accountability is the fact that they are what Easterbrook and Fischel[13] call *residual claimants*. Claimants other than shareholders, such as creditors and employees, have contractual relations with the firm, which subject them to minimal risk. Shareholders, however, do bear significant risk in their investments, with their claims coming into play only after those of other claimants. It is for this reason that they are generally understood to have the right to the profit of the firm's activities and to make decisions.

While this appears to be an accepted position in most countries—particularly those of Anglo-Saxon origin, control, or influence—increasingly the residual claimants theory is being subjected to critique, as it is argued that the corporation should be accountable to a wider spectrum of stakeholders. One particularly strong line of argument that has been advanced, most notably by Margaret Blair, challenges the notion that only shareholders make investments and take on risks.[14] While this approach does not dismiss the notion of shareholders as residual claimants out of hand, it argues that in many firms, especially those involving knowledge-workers, the theory is not applicable because employees too (in addition to shareholders) invest (viz., in specialized skills) that contribute to the wealth-creating efforts of the firm and that these investments involve some costs. In addition to this position which focuses on a particular type of employee, a wide array of other arguments have been advanced by environmental and other social activists to bolster their stand that the corporation should be held accountable to other societal actors as well.

As the debates proceed with escalating intensity, there is an emerging trend that has been clearly discernible in corporate governance frameworks across the world, particularly since the late 1990s. There is increasing recognition that the dictum of shareholder primacy and its wealth maximization goals cannot and should not be pursued to the exclusion of the claims and interests of other stakeholders. Thus, for example, the OECD guidelines on corporate governance,[15] while accepting the creation of long-term economic gain to enhance shareholder value as the central mission of corporations, postulate that 'corporations must function in the larger society' and state that individual national governments may temper their economic objective to address non-economic objectives as well. More recently, in India, the Securities and Exchange Board's code of corporate governance[16] has reiterated the fundamental objective of corporate governance as being the *enhancement of shareholder value, keeping in view the interests of other stakeholders.*

Who is a Stakeholder?

It is important then to identify who actually qualifies as a *stakeholder*. The expression, 'stakeholder', is itself of fairly recent origin. It first appeared reportedly in 1963, in an internal memorandum at the Stanford Research Institute in the context, curiously, of upholding the notion that shareholders are the only group to whom managements need to be responsive. According to the influential definition offered by Edward Freeman,[17] the term stakeholder refers to any individual or group who can affect, or who is affected by the achievement of the organization's objective. Ada Demb and Fred Neubauer[18] identify six groups of commonly distinguishable stakeholders: providers of funds (shareholders, banks, etc.), employees, general public, government, customers, and suppliers, with claims not necessarily in that order. These categories, of course, admit of a range of actors (e.g. employees will cover both the top management group including executive directors as well as the other groups of gold-, white-, and blue-collared workers) and can vary over time (e.g. increasingly, suppliers will include not just traditional relationships with firms providing goods and infrastructural facilities, but also include a variety of outsource vendors and contractors, besides other providers of technology, knowledge, and service).

While there is a range of stakeholders, interestingly if not surprisingly, in the debates on corporate governance most of the attention has been focused first on shareholders and then on employees. Customers have also been the object of some attention, but not so much for their stake in the company as for the company's stake in ensuring they are satisfied with (and continue to buy) the company's products and services. Other stakeholders, especially in developing countries, seem to receive less attention. The general public, for example, is often given short shrift as a stakeholder group, though this may change as societal activism continues to rise. Governments, too, seem to have been forced into a more defensive posture with programmes of economic liberalization, and appear to be less willing or able to defend their interests through regulatory and punitive measures. Suppliers too appear to be a group ill provided for in terms of corporate accountability, a situation that needs attention particularly in these days of outsourcing and subcontracting. A vendor or subcontractor putting up a business unit that is virtually for the captive consumption of a larger organization should surely qualify for the status of stakeholder by any definition. How many outsourcing businesses, however, consider the vendors' interests when deciding on their own action plans?

Towards an Integrated Corporate Governance Model

Kautilya, the great Indian political strategist (circa AD 100–150), postulated in his discourse on the duties of the king: 'In the happiness of his subjects lies his [the king's] happiness; in their welfare, his welfare.'[19] Much of this ancient wisdom applies to the present-day corporation as well. The *real* stakeholders, including the shareholders, certainly constitute the population of the corporate kingdom. The associated issue is also one of clearly differentiating between the real stakeholders (who have a *stake* in the company) and others who are at best, *constituencies*, as Adrian Cadbury terms them.[20]

There is near unanimity among academics, regulators, and corporate managers on the imperatives of coexistent and collaborative solutions to the shareholder-stakeholder problems. Many authorities see some cogency in the notion of a mutually complementary governance model that looks after the interests of shareholders and real stakeholders, one where there is no irreconcilable conflict with the more traditional principal-agent finance model. In an award-winning 1987 essay, Cornell and Shapiro[21] distinguished between the *explicit* and *implicit claims* of non-investor stakeholders and concluded that the latter (for example, tacit promises of continuing supply, timely delivery, product enhancements, job security, etc.) have significant implications for corporate financial policy, which is itself founded on the principal-agent theory of shareholder supremacy. Similarly, Hill and Jones[22] in 1992 developed a stakeholder-agency theory. If ethical behaviour is the strategy that maximizes long-term profits, they argued, shareholders (principals) should encourage their managers (agents) to practise such initiatives. The recent emphasis on organizational reputation and acceptability in competitive markets for financial and human resources (among others) is a further manifestation of the harmony between stakeholder and shareholder interests.[23]

On the larger issue of societal interests, OECD guidelines admit that at times there may be a trade-off between short-term social costs and long-term benefits to society in having a healthy, competitive private sector. They recommend that societal needs that transcend the responsive ability of the private sector should be met by specific public policy measures rather than by impeding improvements in corporate governance and capital allocation. Companies should recognize and respond to the needs of their employees (and not just stop at periodical announcements that '*employees are our most important assets*'), since it would help in wealth maximization for shareholders. Where the competitive capability of the corporation is at stake while trying to meet other stakeholders' claims, the government should handle the issues through appropriate *public policy* initiatives.

Could this be the beginning of an integrated corporate governance model that seeks to straddle the competing claims of shareholder primacy and stakeholder stridency? Certainly, it would appear to be the most balanced approach to corporate governance in recent decades. There is indeed striking evidence that successful corporations have almost always practised these precepts, though, perhaps, without labelling them with such clarity. General Electric Company, currently the world leader in terms of market capitalization, provides an impressive example. Its former, long-time CEO, Ralph Cordiner, called its top management a *trustee* responsible for managing the enterprise 'in the best balanced interest of shareholders, customers, employees, suppliers, and plant community cities'.[24] Decades later, Jack Welch, its celebrated CEO until recently, presided over the corporation rated the 'Most Admired Company' in the world in a 2000 Fortune survey, with the criteria for this evaluation including key stakeholder measurements.[25]

India is not without its own examples. The Wipro Corporation,[26] which is among the top companies in the country in terms of market capitalization, states in its five-year vision that it puts 'its people first', a claim that is confirmed by the fact that a whopping 78 per cent of its employees perceive the company to be the best organization for them to be in. Its compatriot, Infosys Technologies, thrives on its objective of making thousands of its employees millionaires through the company's stock-sharing programmes, while retaining a top slot in the capital market and attracting international investors.

The corporate board's role thus appears to be to steer a middle course, one that protects and enhances shareholders' wealth while satisfactorily 'managing' the real stakeholders' aspirations in a manner not prejudicial to shareholders' interests.

Economic Reforms

How, if at all, do economic reforms in a country impact upon standards of corporate governance and boards of joint stock corporations? International experience in recent decades suggests that their beneficial influence can be significant, even if at times, especially in the shorter term, their human consequences may tend to be less than humane. This latter fallout, more often than not, has been the result of ruthlessly weeding out non-value-adding inefficiencies that globally competitive business activity could ill afford to carry. Translated into action initiatives, a large proportion of such 'improvements' had to come from *downsizing* uneconomic businesses and operations. The resulting loss of jobs further exacerbated the common predicament of countries with insulated economic environments, a situation characterized by abysmal poverty, raging unemployment and an absence or inadequacy of social security cover for the most vulnerable sectors of society. In theory at least, these 'passing' problems would be addressed in *due* course, the duration usually being determined by the magnitude of the problems themselves.

Even though the reform process in India commenced in the 1980s, its deliberate articulation and implementation was heralded only in the 1990s by the then Congress government and pursued thereafter by its successors. The basic goal of the reforms eventually was to bring about a competitive, free market economy. This meant gradually dismantling the complex maze of licences controls, and other hurdles that had been assiduously built up over the previous four decades and more, by no means an easy task. In retrospect—now more than a decade into this process—progress achieved in this direction has indeed been impressive, especially in the last two to three years. The accomplishments are all the more impressive considering the fact that the country is firmly wedded to democracy, with full adult franchise free from any gender or other bias.

The principal impact of these reforms on business has been felt in the market place. At long last, the *customer* regains his pride of place as king. As Gandhiji wrote decades ago, everyone in the business value chain must recognize that they owe their existence to the customer, without whom there would indeed be no need for business. The customer consequently has not only the choice of goods and services from alternative vendors but also the right to seek value for money. With various manufacturers and service providers vying for custom, the inexorable forces of competition will drive down the margins to a barely adequate level, leaving no room for cost inefficiencies in the manufacturing and service delivery processes.

With the opening up of the economy to both domestic and global competition, companies will have to upgrade their performance levels, eliminating all non-value-adding activities in their entire operations. It is more than likely that some international players with the advantage of economies of scale and technological superiority will provide stiff competition for domestic industry, not only through legitimate, but also illegitimate means such as dumping. Industry must gear itself up as quickly as it can, seeking and obtaining breathing time from the government to enable it to compete effectively. In a liberalized environment, though, there can be no room for permanent and secure protective tariffs against such incursions. Being a signatory to the ongoing WTO agreements on trade and tariffs, the country will have to brace itself to meet such competitive situations with sustained confidence in its own competitive competence and entrepreneurial aggression.

On other fronts as well, businesses will feel the impact of economic liberalization. With employers seeking to tap the limited pool of skilled workers, expectations of wages and rewards will naturally escalate. The information technology and software businesses based on knowledge workers have been striking examples in recent times. It is not unnatural for a given contributing factor to claim an especially large share of the added value (and consider this fair), even if it be at the expense of some other factor in the chain. Free and competitive markets will determine the price at which such resources and skills can be hired and retained. The solution, in such situations, lies not in bemoaning the *expense* but in containing the *cost* through improved productivity and management.

The other important implication flowing from economic liberalization concerns the use of money. Similar to the costs of inefficiency in operations and elsewhere, the costs of inefficient use of money could also be passed on to the hapless customer in an insulated and protected economy, but not in the post-liberalization world since the customer will not pay for cost inefficiencies. Businesses will have to get used to operating with hand-to-mouth inventories and the shortest possible cycle times in all processes. As George Stalk Jr. and Thomas Hout postulated several years ago, competing against time is as important, if not more important, than competing with other business competitors.[27] Businesses tying up less money in their activities will thus have an inherent advantage over others. Firms will also have to be conscious of the cost of equity or owners' risk-bearing funds that they employ. With businesses becoming riskier post-liberalization—partly on account of the market, but even more so because of the lack of possible bail-out options in the event of failure[28]—rewards expected by providers of equity funds will increase, and thus add to the cost of capital used in business. Reducing the pool of funds employed in business thus affords an opportunity to reduce equity funds required and consequently their costs as well.

A significant component of an economic reforms process is the reduction of state involvement in activities other than the business of government. Privatization of state-owned enterprises in non-strategic fields brings with it both opportunities for better utilization of national investments and challenges in terms of democratic and collaborative transition from public to private control. The track record of the country during the last decade of the twentieth century (when the reforms agenda was put in place) is more than satisfactory, with several state-owned enterprises now being traded in the secondary capital markets following partial divestment of shareholding by the government. Within the constraints of political democracy and the imperatives of coalition politics, further initiatives on divesting in major sectors like aviation, telecommunication, oil exploration, refining and distribution, and power generation and transmission are at different stages of implementation.[29] With these moves and others to follow, such privatized corporations will have to undertake major programmes for upgrading governance in their organizations. These will include restructuring and reorienting their corporate boards and revamping their board processes. Competencies, independence, fair play, accountability, and transparency will have to be the watchwords for the directors and executives of these corporations in transition.

A principal feature of economic reforms in India, as in similar situations in most other countries, is the opening up of opportunities to overseas investors, either in terms of direct foreign investment in domestic corporations or through trading in local company stocks on the domestic secondary capital markets. These transnational players bring with them demands for good governance based on international best practices. Equally, as Indian corporations begin (as indeed many of them already have done) accessing international markets for their financial requirements, they will be required to comply with such governance practices as are applicable in those countries.[30] Domestic corporations will thus be under increasing pressure to step up their adherence to internationally acceptable governance standards in such areas as board composition and independence, accounting standards, transparency in financial and other reporting, corporate citizenship, social responsibility, and so on.

The overarching fallout, then, of economic liberalization is, on the one hand, to squeeze out the unreasonable rents or margins that were earlier possible and, on the other, to drive businesses towards elimination of inefficiencies in producing and delivering goods and services to the customer.

Eliminating the excess fat in the system, like in human beings, is good overall, but the process is not entirely painless. Simultaneously, companies in both private and public sectors will also have to eschew unscrupulous control-related perquisites that they could get away with in a closed and monopolistic business environment.[31] Those who cannot meet these challenges will find themselves lagging behind, and even falling by the wayside. A well-managed corporate will heed these warnings well in time and prepare itself to convert these challenges into opportunities. These are probably the toughest tasks with which economic reforms confront corporations and their boards.

Corporate Citizenship and the Triple Effect on Society

A corollary of economic reforms is the societal expectation that corporations behave as good corporate citizens.[32] As mind-boggling advances in information and communications technologies propel people across the world to the status of citizens of a global village, a diminishing asymmetry in the knowledge base is the order of the day. Good (and bad) practices in one part of the world are picked up with astonishing speed. As standards of living and expectations of quantity of life go up in the developed world, less fortunate citizens elsewhere in the world begin first to dream of, and next to demand that concerns for safety, the environment, and other perceived social ills be addressed by their own businesses and the government.

In this ambience, corporations need to reconfirm and reiterate to themselves that they operate within a larger society. This society provides them with a sanction to operate—but a sanction oriented towards a common good which includes not only themselves and their shareholders, employees, and managers. Without a contribution to a larger purpose, there will be no social cohesion between and among government, business, and society. With such an understanding and appreciation of these imperatives, however, the country and business can thrive.

As the OECD governance document proffers, it is indeed advisable that corporations be allowed to concentrate on their task of achieving their economic objectives, but the varying stages of development in different countries may dictate a diversity of approaches towards achieving objectives that may not strictly be economic. This is where corporations with their managerial, financial, and other resources and strengths will be expected to step in and help in the process of achieving growth in desired directions.

Authorities have identified four stages in what is inherently a continuum between the two extremes of responses to societal demands. At one end is the total denial of any responsibility towards society, a position Nobel-laureate Milton Friedman advocates. Recognition of some responsibility comes next, mainly through the medium of discretionary philanthropy. More advanced corporations, in the third stage, reactively discharge social responsibilities mandated by legislation or regulation, or even societal protests and activism. The ultimate is proactive engagement, where corporations strive to achieve leadership in conceptualizing, assessing, and addressing societal obligations on their own initiative and without legal or activist prodding. This is like a state of *corporate nirvana*—a state that is particularly difficult to achieve (especially in societies that are governed in a less than ideal manner) but once reached, bestows on the corporation the shine and status of the North Star.

Several corporations internationally have made significant progress towards this exalted state, among them Motorola, Levi Straus, the Body Shop, to name just a few. They have taken the lead in following high-principled policies relating to business ethics, child labour, environmental protection, and so on. In India too, there are a few worthy of emulation, both internationally and domestically, including: the Tatas in Jamshedpur for running a township that puts to shame many municipal corporations; Infosys for its massive efforts at comprehensiveness and transparency in financial reporting; the Indian Space Research Organisation for implementing its Vikram A. Sarabhai Trust that provides succour to their employees not otherwise covered by insurance or other similar protection; and Wipro through its Azim Premji Foundation for upgrading the quality of elementary education and minimizing school dropouts.

Businesses impact on society in three basic ways: environmentally, socially, and economically. Under the first category fall such items as emission and waste control, energy usage, product life cycle/ recycling, and sustainable development. Social impact would cover areas such as equal opportunities, community regeneration, human rights, education and culture, and so on. Wealth generation, (productive) job creation, ethical business practices, corruption and bribery, and product value would constitute the elements of economic impact. In each of these areas, the way a corporation chooses to act will determine its claim to good corporate citizenship or otherwise. There is a move to encourage such triple-bottom-line focus and reporting among Indian corporations on a much wider scale than is presently evident.[33]

Government and Governance

An oft-overlooked aspect in discussions on economic reforms and corporate governance is the role of government at the political and bureaucratic levels (both as a role model and as an arbiter). In broad terms, politicians—especially in the case of the Cabinet in a ministerial form of government—have the dual role of policy making and implementation. It is not unusual to have prime ministers of countries and chief ministers of states referred to as chief executives of their respective domain. In a presidential form of government such as obtains in the United States, the president is of course the chief executive assisted by his chosen team of politically appointed advisors. The civil service or bureaucracy is of course the substantive and in many ways *the* executive influencing, advising, and implementing policy. Economic reforms and their impact on corporate governance can hardly be separated from the imperatives of governance reforms in the government itself, represented by the politicians and the bureaucrats, who continue to influence and determine the way business is carried on in the country. Elsewhere in the world, civil service reforms are also a topic of concern, especially because their enlightened society demands value for money from their rulers and their representatives.[34] A major initiative that needs to be mounted by countries like India embarking upon economic liberalization measures is to ensure that as part of the process, appropriate civil service and administrative reforms are also tackled to improve service quality and delivery. The cost of government impacts business and society not only in terms of its own expenditure but also the indirect costs of delayed or denied opportunities that have to be borne by businesses and the civic society flowing from unintended bureaucratic interference and operating inefficiencies.

The Post-Reforms Corporate Board

With all resource providers seeking money for value in a fiercely competitive environment, corporations will have to generate enough cash and profits to bid for and obtain their required share of monetary, human, and other resources. The investors providing funds to the companies and ensuring liquidity of their securities in capital markets are more than likely to expect that their claims are looked after by corporate boards because in the final analysis they also have to create wealth for *their own* share owners. With the opening up of the financial sector and the entry of international players in the marketplace, requirements of more stringent governance will be the order of the day. Similarly, with Indian corporations tapping international financial markets for funds, the more developed and stringent governance requirements of those countries will also need to be complied with. In addition, the mandatory requirements of the SEBI (Kumar Mangalam Birla) report became applicable in March 2002 to companies that account for approximately 80–85 per cent of the total market capitalization on the Indian stock exchanges. (Companies adding up to more than 50 per cent of such capitalization were already covered by March 2001.) All in all, corporate boards in the post-reforms era will have to operate in a much more efficient, professional, and transparent manner than they may have been used to before in an insulated economy.

The emerging demands on corporate boards are already discernible. In 1998, the Confederation of Indian Industry published its guidelines heralding probably the first formal recognition by Indian industry of the need to respond to changing circumstances on this front.[35] Admittedly, the document fell short of ideal practices in many respects,[36] but it was a bold and visionary step in the right direction. In 2000, the Securities and Exchange Board of India (SEBI) published its report on corporate governance, following which several requirements have been mandated on companies by stock exchanges through their listing agreements.[37] The government has already brought in and is continuously contemplating legislation[38] to amend the Companies Act that would usher in several improvements in the governance of corporations. The country's Central bank, the Reserve Bank of India, has already issued its recommendations as applicable to banks.[39] The most recent government initiative is the Naresh Chandra Committee Report, many of whose recommendations are widely expected to be implemented.[40] The message for listed corporations and their boards is clear: improved governance is no longer just a preferred objective of the limited few, but the harsh reality of the marketplace.

What would be the profile of the post-reforms corporate board?

- Clearly, it will be professional. This does not mean that the days of family-controlled corporations are over but only that the demarcation between ownership and control, on the one hand, and management, on the other, will be much more evident.[41] Nothing precludes a family member also being a successful director, if by training and inclination he or she is suited for the position. Others may have to be satisfied with the fruits of ownership.
- Its members will be people with managerial and technical expertise, who can guide and oversee operating management in the discharge of their functions. Most importantly, it will have a large proportion of *independent external* directors who can without fear or favour advise, admonish, and control operating management on issues of policy and performance.[42] (To make this transition a little less uncomfortable, SEBI has provided for a category of directors who will be non-executive but may not be independent.)
- Board chairs are likely to be separate from CEOs; even when this is not so, senior lead directors may be required to chair board meetings.[43]

- Board processes will be more exacting and call for adequate time commitments from members. Rubber-stamp boards will be a relic of the past. There will be greater clarity of the board's role and the matters that should receive their attention and consideration. Following the SEBI report, stock exchanges have, for example, enumerated many of these items in their listing agreements.
- Board committees will be commonplace, with the audit committee taking the pride of place as the first among equals. Its duties are indeed onerous and its members will have to commit extra time and effort.
- Transparency in reporting will be a prime responsibility of the board. It will have to ensure that appropriate accounting practices have been applied in the preparation of the company's financials and that any material changes during the reporting period are fully debated and justified.
- Independent audit is a key component of corporate governance and the future boards will have to ensure that such auditors are appointed with due care and attention to their independence and professional competence.[44] The board or its audit committee will have to discuss with such auditors any concerns they may have about the credibility of the financials, not only on the acceptability but also the appropriateness of the accounting and reporting practices.
- The board must be conscious of the continuing stability and security of the company and ensure that their assessment is predicated on a going-concern basis.
- Internal control will be a focus area of concern for the board. It will have to ensure that appropriate systems are in place and are complied with on a regular basis.
- In return for their extended scope of services and responsibilities, the board is likely to compensate its members more appropriately than was possible before. Stock options, profit-based commissions, and the like will be more readily available to attract and retain board-level talent.
- As a corollary, boards and their members will be under continuing pressure to perform, with negligence and delinquency leading to likely litigation. (An incidental beneficiary will be the insurance business, which can market appropriate products to cover these risks!)
- Accountability to shareholders will be the cornerstone of board and management philosophy. Enhancing corporate performance and

enriching shareholders through legitimate and transparent policies and practices will be their highest priority. This is not to say that there will be no accountability to other stakeholders like customers and employees. These objectives are not mutually exclusive, and in fact, depending upon their respective importance in the value-adding process, their satisfaction will often be a precondition to achieving shareholder satisfaction.

- Increasingly, boards will have to address themselves to issues of corporate social responsibility and good citizenry. Unless they strive to make their companies more admired and better places to work in, their chances of recruiting and retaining the kind of resources that they need will be slim indeed. They will also have to realize that corporations function under the authority and with the sanction of the societies and communities they operate in and that they would do well to provide demonstrable evidence of their concern for the issues that confront those constituencies.
- With the increasing levels of transparency, corporations will have to spruce up their image in terms of corporate values and business ethics. It is not easy to inculcate the highest levels of integrity in an organizational culture unless the tone is set at the top. The corporate board will have to mandate and monitor to ensure that such business values are internalized within the organization.

The tasks are undoubtedly daunting, but addressing them with single-minded focus is what will separate the success stories from the also-rans in the *post-reforms* era. Corporate boards that wish to stand up and be counted have no easy options and in fact no choice but to prepare themselves for the forthcoming struggle for survival and growth. The challenge laid down by economic reforms is clear: prepare, perform, and prosper, or else procrastinate and perish! The degree to which Indian companies as a whole take up this challenge to renew their governance structures and practices will impact not only the well-being of shareholders and stakeholders, but also development in India as a whole.

Notes

1. An instructive and impressive account of the history of corporations is available online at http://www.britannica.com/.

2. 'Too Much Corporate Power?', *Business Week*, 11 September 2000 is a representative essay that articulates some of these concerns.

3. Such concerns probably pre-date Smith. Consider, for example, Shakespeare's *Merchant of Venice* where the merchant was concerned about the safety of his argosies

sailing out of sight on the high seas, wondering how oversight was to be exercised, who should be running the venture, and so on! Refer R.I. Tricker (ed.), 'Introduction', in *Corporate Governance*, AQ 26.

4. *The Wealth of Nations*, Adam Smith (1776), Modern Library Edition (2000), edited by Edwin Cannan, Random House. Description of *directors* as *managers* is historical evidence of the confusion between the two functions insightfully brought out, among others, by Colin J. Coulson-Thomas in 'Creating An Effective Board', in *Corporate Boards and Governance*, (ed.) N. Balasubramanian, (1998), New Delhi: Sterling.

5. *The Modern Corporation and Private Property*, Adolf Berle and Gardiner Means, (1932), Macmillan.

6. 'Corporate Ownership Around the World', Rafael La Porta, Florencio Lopez-de-Silanes, and Andrei Shleifer (1999), *Journal of Finance*.

7. 'Disciplining the Dominant Shareholder', Jayanth Rama Varma, in *Corporate Boards and Governance*, (ed.) N. Balasubramanian, (1998), New Delhi: Sterling.

8. Governance codes, legislation, and best practices throughout the developed world (with developing countries following suit) seek a majority or at least a substantial proportion of directors of listed corporations to be independent and non-executive. The Derek Higgs Review of the Role and Effectiveness of Non-executive Directors, in the United Kingdom (January 2003) and the Naresh Chandra Committee Report on Audit and Governance (January 2003) in India, and of course the 2002 prescriptions of the Sarbanes-Oxley Act, SEC and NYE pronouncements in the United States are some of the recent developments in the field. Several influential pension funds and institutional investors, such as the California Public Employees' Retirement System in the United States, insist that such directors meet stringent criteria establishing their independence.

9. Credibility of audits and auditors as an independent reporting instrument of good corporate governance has of course taken a severe beating post-Enron 2001/02 in the US.

10. *Where Were the Directors? Guidelines for Improved Corporate Governance in Canada*, (1994), The Toronto Stock Exchange.

11. 'Isa Upanishad' in *Eight Upanishads*, Swami Gambhirananda, (1957), English translation, Advaita Ashram.

12. It is a different matter that apart from the possible exception of Jamnalal Bajaj, not many of his otherwise ardent supporters came anywhere near his expectations. See 'Economic Thinking of Gandhi', Shafiq Naqvi, in *Gandhi: Theory and Practice, Social Impact and Contemporary Relevance*, (ed.) S.C. Biswas, (1969), Indian Institute of Advanced Study.

13. *The Economic Structure of Corporate Law*, Easterbrook, F.H. and D.R. Fischel (1991), Boston: Harvard University Press.

14. *Ownership and Control: Rethinking Corporate Governance for the Twenty-first Century*, Margaret M. Blair (1995), Brookings Institution.

15. *Corporate Governance—Improving Competitiveness and Access to Capital in Global Markets*, (1998), OECD.

16. *Report of the Kumar Mangalam Birla Committee on Corporate Governance*, (2000), The Securities and Exchange Board of India.

17. 'A Stakeholder Theory of the Modern Corporation', R. Edward Freeman, in *The Corporation and its Stakeholders: Classic and Contemporary Readings*, (1998), (ed.) Max B. E. Clarkson, University of Toronto Press.

18. *The Corporate Board: Confronting the Paradoxes*, Ada Demb and Fred Nuebauer, (1992), New York: Oxford University Press.

19. The *Arthashastra*, (edited and translated) L.N. Rangarajan, (1992), New Delhi: Penguin Books India.

20. *Board Focus—The Governance Debate*, Sir Adrian Cadbury, (1997), Egon Zehnder International.

21. 'Corporate Stakeholders and Corporate Finance', Bradford Cornell and Alan C. Shapiro (1987), *Financial Management*, Spring 1987.

22. 'Stakeholder-agency Theory', C.W.L. Hill and T.M. Jones, (1992), *Journal of Management Studies*.

23. 'Corporate Governance, Reputation and Competitive Credibility', N. Balasubramanian and David Kimber, (2000), *IIMB Management Review*, June.

24. Quoted in *Watching the Watchers: Corporate Governance for the 21st Century*, Robert A.G. Monks and Nell Minow (1996), Blackwell.

25. 'The World's Most Admired Companies', Nicholas Stein (2000), *Fortune*, 2 October. The No. 1 rank remained the same in the previous year as well: see, Jeremy Kahn (1999), *Fortune*, 11 October.

26. *Wipro Corporate Overview 1999.*

27. *Competing Against Time*, George Stalk Jr. and Thomas M. Hout, (1992), New Delhi: The Free Press.

28. Regrettably, though, such bail-outs are still being made available to state-owned or controlled enterprises. The massive mutual fund, Unit Trust of India, that had to be bailed out twice in the space of four years, is a case in point.

29. The monopoly overseas communication giant *Videsh Sanchar Nigam Ltd.*, privatized in February 2002 with 25 per cent of equity holding and management control going to the Tata Group, is a recent big-ticket example. The January 2003 decision to disinvest equity in the two state-owned oil companies, Bharat Petroleum and Hindustan Petroleum (respectively Burmah-Shell and Standard Vacuum Oil prior to their nationalization several decades earlier), after prolonged inter-ministerial and intra-coalition-partners dissensions, is an example of consensus-building problems in democratic and coalition-dictated governments.

30. The extra-territorial demands towards this end in the Sarbanes-Oxley Act of 2002 in the United States is an extreme legislative example.

31. The steep fall in telecommunication rates in late 2002–early 2003 is an example of how even state-owned enterprises could not (earlier) resist the monopolistic temptation of charging exorbitant rates for these services.

32. A more detailed account is available in N. Balasubramanian's 'Corporate Governance: Some International Perspectives', a paper presented at a conference sponsored by the Malaysian Insurance Institute and the Malaysian Corporate Governance Centre in Kuala Lumpur in April 2000. For related information on this

and other aspects of corporate citizenry, see among others, 'Corporate Governance, Reputation and Competitive Credibility', N. Balasubramanian and David Kimber, (2000), *IIMB Management Review*, June.

33. *Report on Corporate Excellence on a Sustained Basis to Sharpen India's Global Competitive Edge and to Further Develop Corporate Culture in the Country*, (2001), Department of Company Affairs, Ministry of Law, Justice and Company Affairs, Government of India.

34. Civil service reforms in the United Kingdom are a case in point. See, *Report to the Prime Minister on Civil Service Reforms from Sir Richard Wilson*, Head of the Home Civil Service in the United Kingdom, (1999), British Cabinet Office.

35. *Corporate Governance—A Desirable Code*, (1998), Confederation of Indian Industry.

36. For a detailed critique see, 'Changing Perceptions of Corporate Governance in India', N. Balasubramanian, (1998), *ASCI Journal of Management*, vol. 27 (1 and 2).

37. *Report of the Kumar Mangalam Birla Committee on Corporate Governance*, (2000), Securities and Exchange Board of India.

38. The Companies (Second) Amendment Bill, 2000, pending before the Indian Parliament.

39. *Report of the Consultative Group of Directors of Banks/Financial Institutions*, (2002), Reserve Bank of India. This document is also referred to as the Ganguly Report, after its chairman, Dr A.S. Ganguly, a member of Reserve Bank's governing board.

40. *Naresh Chandra Committee Report on Audit and Governance*, (2003), Department of Company Affairs, Government of India.

41. Such transitions are already evident. The Chennai-based Murugappa Group, for example, a traditional family-managed company cluster is in the process of professionalizing its board of directors and executive management.

42. Finding such independent directors will not be easy given their very limited availability.

43. See, for example, Derek Higgs's *Review of the Role and Effectiveness of Non-executive Directors*, (2003), United Kingdom.

44. The regulatory body overseeing the audit profession is contemplating, post-Enron, tighter controls on audit practices and competencies, including peer reviews. Instances of audit committee chairs spending as much as two days a week on the job in some companies in the United Kingdom have been reported. See 'When the Numbers Don't Add Up', *The Economist*, 7 February 2002.

4

Economic Reforms, Corporate Philosophy, and Development

Anup Sinha

INTRODUCTION

In this paper I reflect upon how economic reforms are impacting corporate philosophy and whether the changes occurring in corporate philosophy are compatible with the traditional development goals of countries like India. At the outset I wish to clarify three issues regarding this short essay. First of all, this paper reflects on what the likely changes are in corporate philosophy in India brought about by economic reforms, which began in 1991. It is conceptual in nature, and not based on any case study or empirical survey. The second issue pertains to the debatable nature of what exactly is meant by corporate philosophy. Is a corporation like an individual? Can one assign moral agency to an organization? Can a business firm think and reflect? If a firm's only objective is to maximize profits, is it meaningful to talk about any other philosophy? Such questions are indeed problematic and can lead to a number of contentious arguments. However, I shall refrain from getting into this particular set of questions. I shall assume that the corporation represents an entity, which can embody and manifest the collective wisdom of people who run the organization. The term 'corporation' is used in a generic sense to include any business organization, independent of strict legal definitions. This is in keeping with much of the literature on business ethics. The third issue is about philosophy itself. Definitions of philosophy abound. I shall treat philosophy as thinking about thinking, indicating a second-order reflective trait. Philosophy, then, will be about formation of beliefs and claims to knowledge. Both beliefs and knowledge would then mould strategies and guides to actions.

THE ESSENCE OF REFORMS

India's economic reforms have, to a significant extent, changed the environment in which business corporations exist and function. The hallmark of the reforms process has been the reduction in government controls with greater freedom to respond to perceived market forces of demand and supply. Associated with reforms is the gradual opening up of the economy to foreign competition in terms of easier imports and investments. Indian firms are also, potentially, in a position to access wider markets abroad for financial capital as well as their products. The crucial aspects of the emerging market-friendly environment are increased freedom to operate in markets, greater reach in terms of global markets and associations with foreign firms, and finally, substantial uncertainty of outcomes in emerging markets with a rapidly changing global environment.

Corporations have obviously responded to the changing environment in terms of their own policies. There has been a good deal of re-engineering and restructuring. Strategies have been shaped and reshaped to cope with the new opportunities, as well as new threats of competition. Firms have downsized, diversified, and struck new alliances. Change has been substantial. Such change is obviously driven by new concerns about, and new assessments of, the business environment in India and the world. The assessments would obviously be different for different firms, depending upon their history of performance, size, the industry in which they are located, their financial strengths, and the technology they can access. Perforce, any such assessment must reflect a new way of looking at the world. It is in this sense that corporate philosophy is undergoing modifications and alterations.

The essence of reforms is based on three distinct but interrelated aspects, in terms of changes in business environment. The first of these is the greater *freedom* corporations have in deciding on matters involving production, pricing, and technology. This freedom, in turn, has two specific dimensions. Present decisions have to be made along with strategic corporate plans for the future. The second aspect relates to the greater global *reach* corporations have in relating to other corporations across the world, set in different cultural and social contexts. The third aspect, and arguably the most important one, relates to the increased *uncertainty* faced by corporations. This increased uncertainty has two dimensions. There is increased uncertainty about a firm's optimal structure, size, and strategy when the environment itself is not stable. There is also increased uncertainty about the policy regime in terms of when, and how, the residual agenda of economic reforms will be implemented. Similarly, global fluctuations and trends would have to be constantly tracked and analysed.

Corporate Philosophy

How would such changes influence the philosophy of a corporation? A corporation presumably works on a lifetime horizon far longer than the lifetime of people who run it. The *core* objectives are to survive, earn profits for its stakeholders, and grow. These objectives are the only ones that are unambiguously consistent with market-driven capitalism. Indeed, the process of market-friendly reforms is supposed to reinforce the core objectives. However, the underlying beliefs, claims to knowledge, and resultant strategies adopted to fulfil the core objectives, would be expected to alter as the business environment changes, new technologies become accessible, and social demands and perceptions alter. I shall take the three essential aspects of reforms, namely, freedom, reach, and uncertainty, and discuss how each of them affects the formation of beliefs, claims to knowledge, and corporate strategies.

Greater freedom to access markets comes in the form of positive freedom (freedom to do) over larger opportunity sets. It also comes in the form of negative freedom (not being constrained from) in terms of reduced government controls. Such freedoms require confidence to do new things, as well as a sense of responsibility to refrain from doing things that are socially perceived to be (de facto, though not de jure) unacceptable. It entails an enhanced self-knowledge that can translate into new visions. In other words, freedom affects forms of belief in terms of an altered vision of self.

Freedom also affects claims to knowledge. If a larger number of options become accessible, the organization must be able to know which of those are acceptable. Social acceptability becomes an integral part of feasibility considerations. In other words, the corporation's claim to knowledge is its understanding of its own responsibilities. An altered vision of self along with a better awareness of responsibilities together translate into a strategy of restructuring the organization and reassessing corporate values and ethics.

The opening up of markets to internal and external competition brings in new friends and foes for a firm or corporation. It has to constantly monitor a larger number of other corporations as competitors as well as potential allies. It generates a strong belief of tolerance in accepting specific differences and appreciating commonality in functioning. This also leads to new claims of knowledge in terms of heightened understanding of the 'other' in the realm of business cultures. Knowing the 'other' and knowing the 'self' are part of the same learning process. Corporations will be systematically re-evaluating their own cultures. The strategic response arising out of a cross-cultural sensitivity is a constant search for allies and a deeper analysis of business rivals and their behaviour.

Greater doses of uncertainty about markets and regulations lead to a stronger belief that though risks are inherent in business, they can, and must, be managed and reduced. The claim to knowledge is made in terms of acquiring a substantially wider information set, aided by modern information technology. Every single piece of information has to be collated with perceptions of risks and their reduction. The strategic response is to incessantly put information into a larger picture and comprehend a larger system. In other words, the people who run the corporations have to become attuned to what is called 'systems thinking'.

The above discussion is summarized in the following table.

	Formation of Beliefs	*Claims to Knowledge*	*Strategic Response*
Freedom	vision of self	social responsibility	restructuring
Reach	tolerance	knowing the other	looking for allies/locating foes
Uncertainty	risks can be reduced	information sets	systems thinking

It was mentioned earlier that new strategies which reflect new thoughts in changing environments must be consistent with the core objectives of a firm in a market economy. Greater freedom and the associated restructuring of organizations and their values help to promote growth and profitability in the long term. Greater reach, leading to systematic search for allies and rivals, helps protect profits in the short run. Greater uncertainty and the consequent strategy of systems thinking aid firms in striving for survival.

A Caveat

The above discussion highlights a few interrelated issues in corporate thinking and world views, in a stylized, conceptual framework. Actual changes in corporate philosophy are likely to be a complex process riddled with conflicts and ambiguities. It can happen quickly and decisively, though it is more likely to be slow and tortuous. Outcomes of reflective processes are hard to predict and not likely to be homogeneous across different firms with different histories and cultures. For instance, corporate ethics (as an important dimension of a larger corporate philosophy) can become more aggressively self-seeking, devoid of any serious moral agency, in a world of rising uncertainties and greater freedoms. Similarly, global reach may not always result in lasting relationships based on trust and respect. Quite often, such relationships can be marriages of convenience based on myopic considerations with painful long-term consequences. Such developments obviously forebode very negative consequences with respect to traditional development goals.

Modern corporations, the world over, are powerful and influential agents who affect social norms, government policies, and political processes. They can create economic and social needs; they can also change individual priorities. Thus, they have an awesome potential to influence the course of a society's development. Current global trends generated by mega corporations with closely guarded technologies and cornered markets are not always encouraging in terms of the development aspirations of countries like India. Some examples may help illustrate these trends.

Take, for instance, the philosophy of restructuring which is usually synonymous with downsizing. A political theorist from Princeton University has noted:

> When we reach a situation where the bottom 80 per cent—not the underclass, but most of the population—sees itself struggling to make ends meet, sees no gains from increased productivity, and sees an elite creaming (off) all the benefits of a transformed economy, trouble looms.
>
> Ryan. 1996

The observations are quite relevant in the Indian context, where a new corporate elite enjoys incomes and lifestyles completely out of tune with that of the overwhelming majority of the population.

Similarly, take the case of the worldwide wave of takeovers and mergers resulting in what is referred to as strategic alliances. Lee Iacoca (1987) observed some time ago:

> I see billions of dollars tied up in corporate debt to keep the raiders at bay while research and development go begging. I see billions going for greenmail that ought to be building new high-tech factories. I also see a huge share of America's best management talent wasted on takeover games when it should be devoted to strengthening the industrial base of the country.

UNDP in the Human Development Report (1999) observes:

> In defining research agendas, money talks louder than need—cosmetic drugs and slow-ripening tomatoes come higher on the list than a vaccine against malaria or drought-resistant crops for marginal lands. Tighter control of innovation in the hands of multinational corporations ignores the needs of millions. From new drugs to better seed for food crops, the best of the new technologies are designed and priced for those who can pay.

The vast majority of the world's population cannot pay for these wonders of science.

A recent survey conducted amongst college students in USA (Shaw, 1999) revealed that most young people identified themselves with the Michael Douglas character in the movie *Wall Street* and believed that a no-holds-barred, trample-over-anybody, get-what-you-want approach is the necessary and glamorous road to success. Some of the college students of today are the corporate leaders of tomorrow.

A business magazine (*Business Week*, 11 September 2000) made a cover story of a survey they conducted to gauge the power and influence American corporations exerted on the life of people. A large number of respondents (72 per cent) were of the opinion that business had too much power over too many aspects of American life. A similar percentage (74) was of the opinion that corporations had too much political influence. Eighty-two per cent of Americans felt that corporations moulded entertainment and popular culture for their own benefits. What is of the greatest significance is that 95 per cent believed that corporations ought to have a larger responsibility towards the community and wider body of stakeholders, and should make sacrifices in profits if necessary in carrying it out. The central issue is reconciling short-term profits with the creation of more enduring value in the longer run.

Social Responsibility as Corporate Strategy

This calls for a corporate philosophy that manifests social responsibility as an outcome of strategy. Social responsibility, in turn, involves three major components that inform action. First is the quality of engagement that a corporation has in dealing with human beings. This includes people starting from direct employees to shareholders, to a wider concept of stakeholders and, ultimately, society at large. The essence of the tension in this engagement is between ensuring economic efficiency on the one hand, and exhibiting care and compassion on the other. The second aspect deals with systems thinking. The corporation has to be able to take a holistic approach to business. It must constantly keep sharing individual learning, and build on the stock of knowledge accessible to the corporation. The essence of this aspect lies in going beyond the pursuit of pure profits, as well as the pursuit of ad hoc philanthropy, in a corporation's engagement with society. The third aspect lies in managing a broader portfolio of assets that include social investments in areas like education, health, community development, and environmental conservation. This is the core tension that has to balance short-term profitability with long-run social development. The issue of addressing social capabilities clearly involves going proactively beyond meeting the usual regulatory standards of emission controls or energy conservation. It entails the creation of sustainable strategies in all areas of business.

Yet, the recent events of corporate governance that have shaken the world hardly point to the direction of corporate philosophy being more committed to a wider body of stakeholders. If anything, the events have underlined relentless greed as dominating strategies and actions. There is a lesson, however, that goes beyond emphasizing the unremitting pressures to get the numbers; and get them by any means possible. The real lesson is that some of the 'best' firms in terms of corporate social responsibility were hit by scandals. For instance, Enron was included for three years in the list of one hundred best firms to work for in America. It had received half a dozen awards for being environmentally conscious. It issued triple-bottom-line reports. It had impressive policies on climate change, human rights, and anti-corruption. It indicates the inadequacy of assuming (as has been done in this paper at the outset) that a corporation's world view is the consequence of the collective wisdom of the people who run the organization. What goes on inside the organization is important, especially when opportunistic behaviour of senior managers is common. The lack of democracy *within* a corporation can undermine the effectiveness of corporate philosophy and the socially responsible strategies that can emanate from it.

The Indian Context

Prior to the economic reforms in the Indian economy initiated in 1991, the public sector undertakings (PSU) were treated as major instruments in the implementation of a planned national strategy of development. This strategy had at its core the mission of creating growth but with greater social equity. Public investment programmes were carried out through the PSUs. Private organizations were also controlled through policy instruments to align their purpose to the national objective. The public sector was not created to maximize profits. Their existence was planned to be consistent with the priorities of resource allocation, promotion of social equity, and the making of a regionally balanced economy. The corporate philosophy of the PSUs reflected the developmental concerns of the state.

Economic efficiency was compromised for meeting other social objectives like employment creation, granting of subsidies, locational strategies to stimulate growth in backward regions, and so on. However, over the years, the social and political objectives began to overwhelm the economic aspects of the PSUs. The public sector was caught in a contradiction between the 'rational' demands of planning efficiency and the 'irrational' intervention of political processes. The sector as a whole failed to address issues of wastage and inefficiency, the granting of subsidies in response to popular agitations, the location of projects on grounds of electoral convenience. The corporate philosophy of the public sector undertakings, the temples of modern India, as the nation's first prime minister had described them, degenerated from a deep social commitment to a position of 'anything goes' in meeting the political demands of special-interest groups and lobbies. The Indian history of public sector corporate philosophy is a clear example which indicates a failure to reconcile the core objective of being in business with the social commitment to harmonize development.

There is a hesitant, slow process of reinstating the core objective of economic efficiency in the PSUs, especially the larger ones with a national presence. There is a convergence of challenges facing all corporations, whether in the public or private sector. The emerging environment in which business now operates in India is far more competitive than ever before. Struggles for survival, and the pursuit of continuous growth seldom put social objectives in the forefront. Yet, more than ever before, forward-looking strategies require the creation of new skills, increased human capabilities, a cleaner physical environment and, above all, a need to be sensitive to social concerns and anxieties. Corporations that can respond fast to changing role expectation from its stakeholders are the ones that will succeed in the long run.

The changing role expectation comes forth from two distinct but interrelated sources. The first source is the sheer dimension of social and economic deprivation in India. The post-colonial Indian state never really believed that the problem could be tackled fully without the active support of business; hence the entire strategy of planning in a mixed economy with a large public sector and a tightly controlled private sector. This has failed to deliver what it had promised. Yet there continues to be a residual expectation of business having an *obligation* to address issues of employment generation and contributing towards the provision of services such as health and education. The second source comes from the fact that after the advent of market-friendly economic reforms, the domain of the state has shrunk, thereby affecting the social-sector services (albeit inadequate in quantity as well as quality) that used to be provided for by government at zero or subsidized costs. With a receding state that has begun to farm out some of the services that had come to be essentially associated with it, the pressures keep shifting to business to provide adequate and cheap services. On both these counts, people in India expect corporations to carry some of the responsibilities of government. Hence, the entire issue of corporate social responsibility as reflective of an inclusive forward-looking philosophy is so challenging. On the one hand, the social needs and expectations for responsible corporate citizenship are large and growing as a consequence of market-friendly reforms. On the other hand, the forces of global competition are threatening the survival of many corporations that feel relentless pressures to find the right numbers by any means. In such a situation, no step is deemed to be too brazen if it boosts the profit bottom line sufficiently. This is more so if it involves a question of survival.

Indeed, it is interesting to note that new organizations growing at impressive rates (especially the ones in the 'new economy' of information technology) are the ones that have had the vision of reaching out in the fields of education and the creation of human capabilities. This reflects a new image of self, a new evaluation of responsibilities, and a realization that social commitment need not necessarily go against creating profits in the long run. The strengths of corporate philosophy stem from confidence and access to real resources. Uncertainty and fear, which often grip corporations undergoing rapid internal restructuring (or when the external business environment changes), inhibit the articulation of forward-looking strategies. Little surprise that very few corporations in India reveal much depth in their philosophies. Some of those who do make a commitment to address social concerns often do so as a reaction to the growing trend in developed nations where corporate social responsibility has become big business in itself. Finally, as discussed in the earlier section, there could be serious opportunistic deviations between the stated corporate philosophy and the actions of individuals working in those organizations.

In the light of the above, PSUs in India (despite their notoriety for inefficiency), can set examples to reconcile social commitment with core business objectives. They can become successful precisely because of their long (but not always successful) history of being involved in the attainment of well-defined developmental goals. A survey conducted to identify India's most respected companies (*Business World*, 12 July 1999) showed that many of the large PSUs have been improving their position in the 1990s. The survey is conducted by the magazine every other year, and it takes into account hard business parameters like profitability, as well as broader indicators of ethics and community responsibilities.

Corporate philosophy is still in a state of flux given the environment of change and uncertainty. The possibility of a new order of social commitment cannot be ruled out, despite the ruthless pressures of competition. What is worth keeping in mind, however, is that in India the dimensions of social and economic deprivations are so large and complex, that the philosophy of corporate commitment alone is unlikely to be adequate.

A Hope

Corporate philosophy cannot be inconsistent with the core objectives of running a firm. Otherwise it will cease to exist. However, in today's world no corporation can openly deny the presence of a larger set of social obligations that emanate from the trust that society in general, and stakeholders in particular, place on them. The task of philosophy is to create spaces and guides to action that address this wider set of responsibilities, *without* compromising core objectives. The particular importance of corporate philosophy in the age of economic reforms lies in the fact that by incorporating a sense of social obligations it can indicate and exemplify possibilities for business having a positive developmental impact. Developing and implementing such a philosophy is undeniably a difficult and demanding task, one in which only a few organizations in the whole world have exhibited any significant competence or success. In correcting this trend, the purpose is obviously not about separating the good corporations from the bad. Rather, the task is to shape the forces that can act on *all* corporations.

Economic reforms are about facilitating markets to gain economic efficiency. Every successful society, however, has to go beyond economic efficiency alone. There has to be a shared vision of the 'common good'. Ideally, this shared vision is created through the institutions of democracy and individual empowerment. This 'common good' (even if defined imprecisely), can and must trump the narrow self-interest of shareholders and corporate managers if it comes to a crunch. Corporate philosophy is about imagining (and enabling) the structures that make this common good attainable—structures of decision making, structures of conflict resolution, structures of voice. Good management, like good politics, is all about the art of translating the seemingly impossible into tangible reality.

References

Business Week (2000). 'Too Much Corporate Power', Cover Story in Asian Edition, 11 September, pp. 52–60.

Business World, (1999). 'India's Most Respected Companies',12 July.

Iacoca, L. (1987). 'The Raiding Game', *Dollars and Sense*, 14 March.

Ryan, A. (1996). 'Too Nice To Win', *New York Review of Books*, 21 March. pp. 11.

Shaw, W. (1999). *Business Ethics*, Belmont, CA: Wadsworth Publishing House.

UNDP (1999). *Human Development Report*, New Delhi: Oxford University Press.

5

Corporate Financial Reporting

Asish K. Bhattacharyya[*]

Standard economic theory holds that economic growth (and development) comes about as a result of corporations being forced to provide goods and services under competitive market conditions. Recent economic reforms in India were intended to create more competitive market conditions. One critical condition for competitive markets is the supply of information to investors and potential investors. This paper examines a key area in the provision of information to investors, namely, financial reporting practices. It looks at such practices in the context of the recent changes in the economic and regulatory environments in India.

Introduction

Corporate financial reports aim at achieving the following twin objectives: (a) to evaluate management in its stewardship function; and (b) to provide information useful to investors in decision making. The board of directors, appointed by shareholders (owners), manages the company on their behalf. It has a fiduciary relationship with the shareholders of the company. Therefore, it is accountable to explain its decisions and actions, and their economic impact on the financial position and the performance of the company. The Companies Act, 1956, the statute that governs companies with limited liability, requires companies to place audited financial statements before shareholders at the end of each financial year. Similarly, the Securities and Exchange Board of India (SEBI) requires listed companies to publish abridged financial statements at the end of each quarter. These regulations aim at enforcing accountability of the board of directors to the shareholders

* The author acknowledges the suggestion received from Ms R Sadha Laxmi, fellow programme student at IIMC.

of the company. If shareholders are not satisfied with the performance of the incumbent management, they may replace it by a new management team. However, in practice, shareholders rarely spend time and energy to correct the management of the company, or to replace the incumbent management. They prefer to exit the company by trading their shares in the capital market.

The overriding objective of the corporate financial report is to provide relevant information to investors. Investors allocate their funds to different projects or firms based on their estimates of relative expected returns. A significant portion of those funds is invested in the corporate sector. Appropriate valuation of companies in the capital market is essential to ensure efficient allocation of funds available with investors. Moreover, appropriate valuation of companies in the capital market is important in developing a market for corporate control. The existence of an efficient market for corporate control improves the quality of corporate governance as it encourages management to perform at an optimum level so as to avoid losing control of the company.

The relevance of information in governance depends on the economic model that investors use to value companies. The contemporary literature on finance assumes that investors primarily use 'cash flow models' to value firms. Therefore, any information that has the potential to influence the projection of the amount, the timing, and the uncertainty of cash flows that the firm will generate in future is relevant to investors. Financial statements do not actually provide cash flow projections. They provide information that is historical in nature, but useful for projecting future cash flows. Financial reports include additional information that may facilitate the forecasting of the future performance of the firm.

Corporate financial reports assume special importance in publicly traded companies. Separation of ownership and control in publicly traded companies gives rise to the agency problem. In a publicly traded company, shareholders are primarily interested in the maximization of their wealth. Usually they enter and exit companies by trading their shares in the secondary market. They do not participate directly in the management of the company. In principle, they elect a board of directors that appoints management to manage the company. In practice, the incumbent management or large shareholders get their nominees elected to the board and control the board. Promoter-managers exercise control in much greater proportion than their voting rights should ostensibly allow. Professional managers exercise control even without voting rights. Agency problem arises, because the interest of management rarely converges with the interest of dispersed shareholders. Corporate governance systems aim at mitigating the agency problem. They focus on improving the supervisory function of the board and improving the quality of corporate financial reporting.

The information needs of investors depend on their relationship with the company. An investor, who has the right to seek information directly from the company, does not depend on the financial report for complete information. Similarly, an investor who has representation on the company's board may not look for complete information in the financial report. Therefore, a closely held company may not provide complete information in its financial report. On the other hand, a publicly traded company should provide complete information in its financial report, because widely dispersed shareholders have no right to seek specific information directly from the company. Thus, the ownership structure of a company is an important determinant of the quality of financial report. The quality of financial report is also determined by the standard of regulations and the efficiency and effectiveness of the monitoring system.

The quality of financial reports is measured in terms of the appropriateness of the accounting principles and methods used to measure assets and liabilities and the level of transparency and disclosure. Accounting standards regulate accounting policy by stipulating acceptable accounting principles and methods and thereby limiting the choice for individual enterprises. They prescribe mandatory disclosures. Regulators also prescribe disclosure requirements. For example, the Companies Act, 1956, provides the balance sheet format and stipulates requirements for the preparation and presentation of profit and loss account. It also prescribes minimum disclosure in the report of the board of directors. Similarly, SEBI stipulates disclosure requirements for companies listed in Indian stock exchanges. In addition to mandatory disclosures, companies voluntarily disclose additional information to improve 'transparency and disclosure' in their financial reports.

Transparency and disclosures in the corporate financial report are the cornerstone of good governance of publicly traded companies. Sloan (2001) describes explicit and implicit use of accounting information in corporate governance. Explicit use includes use in managerial compensation contracts and debt contracts. The implicit use of accounting information represents the most important role of accounting information. The terms on which investors are willing to part with their capital are a function of the informational efficiency and liquidity of capital markets. Corporate financial reporting practices directly influence the informational efficiency of stock prices. Stocks of companies pursuing good corporate disclosure practices are highly liquid and hence may have a lower bid-ask spread.

Patel et al. (2000) concluded that firms with higher transparency and disclosure are valued higher than comparable firms with lower transparency and disclosure. Choi and Muller (1986) have identified several environmental factors that have direct effect upon accounting development. These factors include the legal system, the political system, the nature of business ownership, difference in size and complexity of business firms, social climate, the level of sophistication of business management and of the financial community, the degree of legislative interference in business, the presence of specific accounting regulation, the speed of business innovations, the stage of economic development, the growth pattern of an economy, and the status of professional education and organization.

The structure of the board of directors has a bearing on the quality of corporate financial reporting. Chen et al. (2000) found a positive correlation between the proportion of independent directors on corporate boards and comprehensiveness of financial disclosures. However, this association is weaker for family-controlled firms compared to non-family-controlled firms. Xie et al. (2000) concluded that a management with a lower level of earnings is associated with greater independent outside representations on the board. They further concluded that more active boards and more active audit committees are also associated with management with a lower level of earnings.

The degree to which the economy in which companies operate is integrated into the global economy determines the quality of corporate financial reporting. Radebaygh (1993) observes that as the degree of internationalization of the economy increases, financial reporting systems tend to move towards internationally accepted benchmarks.

The Indian Economy—A Brief History

After independence, India followed a policy of central planning. The 'socialistic pattern of society' was the guiding factor. The government had complete control over the private sector. Industrial licensing, control over monopolies, control over capital issues, a ceiling on managerial remuneration, etc., were the hallmarks of the Indian economic system. High tariff and non-tariff barriers on imports, general discouragement of foreign investment, and price and distribution controls provided high level of protection to Indian business. Moreover, the government had complete control over the Indian finance system. Promoters could access public money through financial intermediaries like Development Financial Institutions (DFIs), and banks. They had no incentive to access public money directly in the capital market.

They could control companies without any significant investment of their own.

In the 1980s India initiated changes in the economic policy towards liberalization. Ghosh (1998:319) writes:

> While the specific expectations of trade and industrial policy liberalization surrounding the IMF loan did not materialise immediately, the 1980s were marked by a series of thrusts towards such liberalization. These became much more marked after 1985, but even before then a number of committees set up by the Government proposed measures of the de-licensing and de-control of both domestic economic activity and imports.

The change in government thinking resulted in initiatives to develop the capital market. In was in the late 1970s that the government, for the first time, offered sops to investors in equity securities.

Earlier, the capital market did not play the important role of channelling savings to the corporate sector. Before 1977, small investors did not show much interest in the capital market. The year 1977 was the watershed year for the Indian capital market (Bagchi 1998). In that year, the Reliance group raised far more capital through shares and convertible debentures than what was raised by practically all other firms or conglomerates in Indian history. However, the regulators had very little control over insider trading and other practices, which are subject to considerable regulations in the capital markets of advanced capitalist countries. The promoters had almost no accountability to shareholders for the utilization of funds mobilized by them through the capital market. In fact, SEBI was constituted only in 1988 to protect the interest of investors of listed companies.

Although the liberalization process started in the 1980s, until the year 1991, when India adopted some stabilization and structural reform measures, no significant change occurred in the Indian economic environment. The Indian economy was a closed economy with 'stifling constraints of the permit-quota raj'. In mid-1991, faced with the most serious balance of payment crisis since independence, India adopted some stabilization and structural reform measures of far-reaching consequences. Panda, et al. (1997: 27) describe the reform process as follows:

> While the short-run objective of these measures was to meet the payment crisis, the long-term objective was to put the economy on a higher growth path on a sustainable basis by enhancing the efficiency and productivity of the system. The major components of the reform process were:
>
> - Stabilisation of the economy so that balance of payments and inflationary pressures could be kept under control;

- Deregulation of the real and financial sector and removal of the licence and permit system that was prevalent in almost all spheres of production (except agriculture) and domestic trade to promote domestic competition and remove opportunity for rent seeking and its consequent distortion and inefficiencies;
- Liberalisation of international trade in various sectors to promote competition and efficiency by removing the high degree of protection enjoyed by the domestic industry; and
- Globalisation to attract international capital and modern technology and to take advantage of global division of labour.

With globalization and the unleashing of private initiative, foreign investment in Indian companies increased significantly. Foreign direct investment increased from US $97 million in 1990–91 to US $2155 million in 1999–2000. It reached the peak level of US $3557 million in 1997–98.[1] Foreign portfolio investment increased from US $6 million in 1990–91 to US $ 3026 million in 1999–2000. It reached a peak level of US $3312 million in 1996–97[2]. The new economic policy of 1991 provided a boost to the Indian capital market. The economic survey 2001-02 states: 'This suggests that for the largest firms, the securities market had become a major source of capital, and that they are able to disintermediate financial institutions by directly accessing the markets'.[3]

Traditionally, Indian companies have been managed by promoter-managers. Most companies belong to old, large business houses. There are a few exceptions. For example, in the 1980s the Reliance group emerged as a strong force in the Indian manufacturing sector. Similarly, Infosys presents an example of a highly successful venture of a new generation of entrepreneurs. With liberalization, new business opportunities have emerged in areas like information technology, telecom, media, and retailing. Lesser known business houses and first-generation entrepreneurs have emerged as winners in those sectors. In the new environment, many older business houses have not been able to retain their leadership position. Many of them have split into independent constituent units and many have sold or closed down some of the businesses in their fold.

In summary, before the 1980s, the Indian economy was a closed and centrally controlled economy. The business environment provided a high level of protection to Indian companies, who could access public fund through state-controlled financial intermediaries. Companies had no need to access capital market for funds. They did not have the opportunity to access international funds. During the 1980s, particularly in 1987, the government initiated a liberalization process. However, the change was not significant. In 1991, the government initiated stabilization and structural reform measures, which exposed Indian companies to global competition, and provided an impetus to private initiatives. With liberalization, new business opportunities have emerged. A new breed of entrepreneurs has emerged as winners over old business houses. Thus, in the pre-liberalization period, there was no incentive to the corporate sector for benchmarking corporate reporting practices with international practices. The situation is changing in the post-liberalization period.

THE REGULATORY FRAMEWORK

The Companies Act, 1956, governs the form and contents of balance sheet and profit and loss account of limited-liability companies. Section 211 of the Act requires that every balance sheet of a company shall give a 'true and fair view' of the 'state of affairs' of the company as at the end of the financial year. Similarly, every profit and loss account of the company shall give a true and fair view of the profit and loss of the company for the financial year. Schedule VI to the Act provides the form of the balance sheet and stipulates requirements for the preparation and presentation of profit and loss account. The Act does not define the term 'true and fair view'.

Until 1999, the Act had no reference to the term 'Accounting Standards'. In 1999, the Act was amended to incorporate the following provisions:

Every profit and loss account and balance sheet of the company shall comply with the accounting standards.

Where the profit and loss account and the balance sheet of the company do not comply with the accounting standards, such companies shall disclose in its profit and loss account and balance sheet, the following, namely:

- the deviation from the accounting standards;
- the reasons for such deviation; and
- the financial effect, if any, arising due to such deviation.[4]

Thus, until 1999, the government did not take into cognisance accounting standards issued by the Institute of Chartered Accountants of India (ICAI). In other words, the government took the view that the compliance with accounting standards was not necessary to provide a true and fair view of the performance and the financial position of the company. The changed position of the government is its response to the changing information needs of the new-generation investors and providers of international finance. In the pre-liberalization period, shareholder activism was totally absent, capital markets were not an important source of finance, and foreign capital was not available to Indian companies. The popular media did not take any interest in corporate financial reporting practices. It was only in the post-liberalization period that those Indian companies which had the potential to access international finance and the media propagated the need for benchmarking Indian corporate practices with international practices. All this created pressure on the government to recognize the need for elevating corporate practices.

Corporate annual reports contain a report by the board of directors of the company.[5] The Companies Act, 1956, requires that the report should cover the following:

(a) the state of the company's affairs;
(b) the amounts, if any, which it proposes to carry to any reserves in the balance sheet;
(c) the amount, if any, which it recommends should be paid by way of dividends;
(d) material changes and commitments, if any, affecting the financial position of the company which occurred at the end of the financial year of the company to which the balance sheet relates and the date of the report; and
(e) the conservation of energy, technology absorption, foreign exchange earnings and outgo, in such manner as may be prescribed.

The board report should deal with any material change which have occurred during the financial year: (a) in the nature of the company's business; (b) in the company's subsidiaries or in the nature of business carried on by them; and (c) generally in the classes of business in which the company has an interest. However, in instances where the board considers that a discussion on material changes will be harmful to the business of the company or of any of its subsidiaries, it may avoid dealing with those changes in its report. The board report also includes details of employees receiving remuneration of not less than Rs 12 lakh per financial year.

With effect from December 2000, the board's report includes a Directors' Responsibility Statement (DRS), indicating therein:

(a) that in the preparation of the annual accounts, the applicable accounting standards have been followed along with proper explanation relating to material departures;
(b) that the directors had selected such accounting policies and applied them consistently and made judgments and estimates that are reasonable and prudent so as to give a true and fair view of the state of affairs of the company at the end of the financial year and of the profit or loss of the company for that period;
(c) that the directors had taken proper and sufficient care for the maintenance of adequate accounting records in accordance with

the provision of this act for safeguarding the assets of the company and for preventing and detecting fraud and other irregularities; and

(d) that the directors had prepared the annual accounts on a going-concern basis.

Incorporation of the above provision is an important step towards raising the level of the corporate governance and the corporate financial reporting practice.

Accounting Standards

Accounting standards regulate accounting policy to ensure use of appropriate accounting principles and methods. They also ensure adequate disclosures in financial statements. Moreover, use of uniform accounting policy improves comparability. Therefore, the quality of accounting standards and the level of compliance are important determinants of the quality of the financial report.

From its early days the Institute of Chartered Accountants of India (ICAI) has issued, through its various technical committees, a number of documents which are variously styled as 'Statements' and 'Guidance Notes'. These documents deal with various issues covering preparation and presentation of financial statements and auditing of those statements. Statements are mandatory in nature. Auditors who are members of the ICAI have to examine whether the stipulations in the Statements are followed in the preparation and presentation of financial statements. Guidance notes aim at providing guidance to members on issues covering accounting and auditing. Guidance notes are not mandatory in the sense in which Statements are.

The ICAI decided to issue 'accounting standards' and constituted the Accounting Standards Board (ASB) in 1977. It was the response of the ICAI to the formation of the International Accounting Standards Committee in June 1973. Shah, et al., (2000) provides an account of the history of accounting standards in India. A meeting of former presidents, council members, and other prominent members of ICAI, under the chairmanship of Shri Gopaldas P. Kapadia, was held in December 1976. In that meeting it was strongly recommended that India should not follow international accounting standards, and India should formulate its own accounting standards. In the meeting, it was also decided that the ICAI would try to convince the government to make accounting standards mandatory. Accordingly, ICAI constituted the Accounting Standards Board (ASB) in 1977. The ASB, as a first step, issued the 'preface to the accounting standards' in 1979. It issued the first accounting standard in 1979, and another six by 1983. In order to improve compliance, it organized a workshop in 1983.

Shah et al. (2000) write:

ASB organised a Workshop in September, 1983, to hold a dialogue with the industry and other interested parties on the implementation of accounting standards. This workshop was attended by representatives of various bodies and the issues thrown open by them were discussed at the 107th Council meeting held in September 1983. After detailed discussions, the following recommendations of the ASB, based on the discussion at the above workshop, were accepted:

- To begin with AS-4 and AS-5 should be implemented in respect of accounts for periods commencing on or after January 1, 1985.
- The date of implementation of the remaining Standards already issued should be considered by the Accounting Standards Board.
- There should be a *recommendatory period of three years* (emphasis added) in respect of Accounting Standards to be issued in future.
- At the first stage, Accounting Standards should be made applicable to: (a) public sector companies; (b) private sector companies listed on the Stock Exchanges; and (c) large borrowers of funds from banks and financial institutions in the corporate sector.

Among the various alternative methods for implementation of Standards, the following were approved:

- Approaching banks and financial institutions and pointing out to them that adoption of accounting standards by their borrowers would be of great utility to them; and holding a workshop with representatives of leading banks and financial institutions as well as representatives of the Reserve Bank of India, the ministry of finance, and the Indian Banks Association.
- Approaching authorities for making compliance with the Standards a necessary requirement for companies listed at the various stock exchanges in the country.
- Requesting apex bodies of trade and industry like FICCI and ASSOCHAM to issue directives to their constituents for adoption of accounting standards in preparation of their accounts.
- Adopting the procedure followed by the Institute of Chartered Accountants of England and Wales whereby the accounting standards had been defined as describing methods of accounting for application to all financial statements intended to give a true and fair view of financial position and results of operations. Accordingly, any departure in financial statements from the applicable accounting standards should be disclosed and explained.

It was also decided that, besides the Company Law Department, representation should also be made to the Income Tax Department. The

Accounting Standards Board was authorized to take suitable follow-up action.

Between the period 1979 to 2002, ICAI issued twenty-eight accounting standards. If we divide the period (twenty-four years) in four-year blocks, the number of standards issued in each block is as shown in Table 5.1:

TABLE 5.1 *ICAI accounting standards issued (1979–82 to 1999–2002)*

Years	*Standards Issued*
1979–1982	6
1983–1986	4
1987–1990	1
1991–1994	3
1995–1998	1
1999–2002	13

The above shows that the pace of issuance of accounting standards was abysmally slow during the period 1983–98 (sixteen years). It is difficult to explain why ICAI went into slumber during the period 1983–98 after a good start during the period 1979–82. As a conjecture, we may assign two reasons for the same. One, the government's failure to support ICAI's efforts in improving corporate financial reporting killed the initiative. Two, after the 1983 workshop, intense pressure was created by the industry and members of the accounting profession to reverse its policy to regulate the accounting policy.

Issuance of thirteen accounting standards during the period 1999–2002 reflects the change in the environment. This is the period in which regulators initiated policy changes to raise the level of corporate governance. With globalization of capital markets, the urgency to harmonize Indian accounting standards with international accounting standards was felt by companies which have the potential to attract foreign capital. The pace of issuing accounting standards was accelerated due to pressure from SEBI, the Government of India, and emerging leaders in Indian business like Infosys Technologies Limited.

THE QUALITY OF FINANCIAL REPORTS AND COMPLIANCE WITH ACCOUNTING STANDARDS

Lal (1985) studied the disclosure practices by measuring the extent of disclosure in published corporate annual reports. He constructed an index of disclosure for his study. The index consists of fifty items of information (the fifty items with all possible sub-items are 104 in total). The items are relevant to investors in making investment decisions. The important conclusions drawn from the study are:

(a) A large number of items of information contained in the index of disclosure have not been disclosed in the annual reports covered by the study;
(b) The extent of disclosure in annual reports of sample companies increased over a period of time, that is, from 1965 to 1975;
(c) The association between the size of the company in terms of total asset and disclosure score was positive and statistically significant for the years 1965 and 1975; and
(d) Size of the company possessed a better association with the extent of disclosure than earnings margin, nature of industry, and association with 'large industrial house'.

Thus, the study finds that until 1975 disclosures in annual reports were inadequate, although the situation improved over the period from 1965 to 1975. The result of the study did not provide any surprises. It is natural that in a closed economy, where public money was being channelled to the corporate sector through intermediaries, the need for transparency and disclosure in corporate report was not felt either by the investors or by the companies.

Among various actions initiated by ICAI to improve the level of compliance, the most important were making certain accounting standards mandatory.[6] Generally, though, it appears that ICAI initiatives lacked conviction. In June 1990, however, the council of ICAI, in their 144th meeting, decided that the financial statements would not present a 'true and fair' view unless they comply with the mandatory accounting standards.

The lacklustre attitude of the ICAI at that time is reflected, for example, in the fact that accounting standards were made mandatory for the first time only in the year 1987 (and then only two of them[7]), even though it issued ten accounting standards between 1979 and 1987. The decision to make AS-4 and AS-5 mandatory was taken some time in 1985. It took two years to implement the decision. Moreover, the accounting standards which were left out[8] are more important than those which were made mandatory in 1987. Although there is no evidence to suggest that intense lobbying by the industry might have led to such an attitude, the possibility cannot be ruled out. It may not be wrong to conclude that in the 1980s, Indian companies were very reluctant to present a 'true and fair' view of their financial position and the performance of the company and to provide relevant information to investors. In this context, it is worth mentioning that until the year 2001, ICAI did not come out with an accounting standard on consolidated financial statements. Similarly, the Companies Act, even today, does not require presentation of consolidated financial statements of group companies in an environment in which cross-holding was a norm, rather than an exception. SEBI has recently made it mandatory for listed companies to present consolidated financial statements. Lal (1992) reported that 45 per cent of Indian investors disagreed that financial information given currently in company annual reports was adequate for investors.

There were other changes in the environment, which could have led to better compliance with accounting standards and better disclosure in corporate financial reports. The most important was the emergence of credit-rating agencies. In 1987 the first credit-rating agency, Credit Rating Information Service of India Limited (CRISIL), was formed. In 1991, the second agency, Investment Information and Credit Rating Agency (ICRA), was formed. Credit-rating agencies initiated services for rating fixed-income securities immediately after they came into existence. Among other factors, they took into account the level of disclosures in corporate financial reports. This improved the quality of financial reports of those companies which issued fixed-income securities. However, in the absence of statutory recognition, the emergence of credit-rating agencies could not improve the quality of corporate financial reports in general.

Compliance depends on the effectiveness of the monitoring system. The Companies Act provides a monitoring system to ensure, among other things: (a) that the company has not falsified its books of accounts; and (b) that the statutory auditors have carried out their duties properly, while certifying a true and fair view of the state of affairs of the company. Section 209A of the Companies Act, 1956, empowers the Registrar of Companies to undertake inspection of the books of accounts and other records of the company. Qualification in the auditor's report is one of the bases for initiating inspection under section 209A. However, the monitoring system did not work well. Companies did not bother much about auditor's qualifications, because the Registrar of Companies seldom initiated actions based on those qualifications.

Before 1990, private sector companies did not pay attention to corporate financial reporting. This is reflected in the fact that only a few private sector companies could be awarded prizes for best-presented accounts.[9] During the twenty-year period from 1971–72 to 1990–91 only the following companies in the private sector won prizes, either the first prize or the second prize (see Table 5.2).

TABLE 5.2 *ICAI prizes awarded to (private sector) companies (1971–72 to 1990–91)*

Company	*Number of times prize won*
Ashok Leyland Ltd.	1
Associated Cement Companies Ltd.	4
Britannia Industries Ltd.	4
Escorts Ltd.	6
India Cements Ltd.	2
Shaw Wallace and Co. Ltd.	1
Siemens Ltd.	1
Tata Iron & Steel Co. Ltd.	1

The above list does not include many good companies of that time. Practically there was no competition, only a few companies continued to bag prizes for a number of years. The reason might be that many good companies either did not participate in the competition or could not win prizes. This reflects that even good companies did not value quality of financial reporting because of small public holdings in those companies.

CORPORATE GOVERNANCE INITIATIVES

Since 1999, India saw significant policy initiatives to improve the level of corporate governance. A committee on corporate governance was set up in May 1999 by SEBI under the chairmanship of Sri Kumar Mangalam Birla. SEBI accepted the recommendations of the committee in January 2000.[10] It decided to implement the recommendations through the amendment to the listing agreement. The recommendations are applicable to:

(a) Companies seeking new listings after the amendment to the listing agreement;
(b) Companies falling in the 'A' Group of the Bombay Stock Exchange (BSE) or included in the S&P CNX NIFTY as on 1 January 2000 from the financial year 2000–01;
(c) Listed companies with a paid-up share capital of Rs 10 crore and above, or companies with net worth of Rs 25 crore or more at any time in the history of the company, from the financial year 2001–02; and
(d) Companies having paid-up capital of Rs 3 crore and above by the financial year 2002–03.

The important recommendations include:

(a) Not less than 50 per cent of the total number of directors should be non-executive directors. In case of a non-executive chairman, at least one-third of the board should consist of independent directors, and in case of executive chairman at least half of the board should consist of independent directors.
(b) A qualified and independent audit committee, consisting of non-executive directors, shall be set up. The committee should have at least three members, majority of whom will be independent directors. At least one director should have financial and accounting knowledge. The committee should meet at least thrice a year.
(c) Management discussion and analysis should form part of board of directors' report.
(d) There should be a separate section on corporate governance in the annual reports of the company.

The Companies Act, 1956, was amended in 1999 and 2000 to incorporate certain provisions to raise the level of corporate governance. The following are the important amendments relating to corporate governance:

(a) To include a directors' responsibility statement in the board's report to highlight the accountability of directors in good corporate governance;
(b) To provide that public listed companies with paid-up capital of Rs 5 crore or more shall set up an audit committee of the board of directors;
(c) To prescribe voting through postal ballot in case of important items with effect from such date as may be notified by the government;
(d) To provide that no person can hold the office of a director in more than fifteen companies at a time; and
(e) To provide that a shareholder of the company be disqualified for appointment as auditor of the company.

A committee, headed by Mr R.D. Joshi, was formed by the government in 2002 to suggest changes that might be urgently required in the Companies Act, 1956. The committee has proposed various measures to raise the level of corporate governance. One of the recommendation is that the management and the statutory auditors should be imprisoned for a period of not less than one year and not exceeding ten years, if they are found to have been involved in fraudulent accounting practices. Similarly, the government appointed a committee, headed by Mr Naresh Chandra to examine various corporate governance issues. Its focus was to improve the quality of audit and the quality of corporate financial reports. The committee has proposed various measures to enhance the independence of auditors and to strengthen the monitoring system.

Corporate Financial Reporting—Current Trends

The induction of independent directors, the formation of audit committees, and the flow of international finance into Indian companies have all had a positive impact on the quality of financial reporting by Indian companies. As already stated in the Introduction, empirical research shows a positive correlation between the level of disclosure and the presence of independent directors on the board, an audit committee and the internationalization of the economy. Corporate reporting practices of large companies have improved over the last couple of years. Patel et al. (2002) report an average transparency and disclosure score of forty against the Asia average of forty-three. However, China, Korea, Malaysia, and Thailand are ahead of India. This change is in conformity with the findings of the research referred to above.

In the 1990s, some Indian companies mobilized resources internationally through Euro issues. They issued Foreign Currency Convertible Bonds (FCCB), Global Depository Receipts (GDR), and American Depository Receipts (ADR). As per an NSE (2002) study, the extent of Euro Issues during the period 1992-93 to 2000-01 was as follows (see Table 5.3).

TABLE 5.3 *Euro issues by Indian companies (1992–93 to 2000–01)*

Year	*Amount (Rs Million)*
1992–93	7,020
1993–94	78,980
1994–95	67,430
1995–96	12,970
1996–97	55,940
1997–98	40,090
1998–99	11,480
1999–2000	34,870
2000–01	41,970

Indian companies, which either accessed or intend to access international finance, have raised the level of transparency and disclosure in their financial reports. They benchmarked their corporate financial reporting practices with international practices. This is reflected in the list of award winners for the best-presented accounts. In 1990, the ICAI instituted separate prizes for best-presented accounts for non-finance companies in the private sector. During the ten-year period from 1991–92 to 2000–01 the following companies won prizes, either the first prize or the second prize (see Table 5.4).

TABLE 5.4 *ICAI prizes awarded to non-finance (private sector) companies (1991–92 to 2000–01)*

Company	*Number of times prize won*
Cheminor Drugs Ltd.	2
Dabur India Ltd.	1
Global Tele-systems Ltd.	1
Hero Honda Motors Ltd.	1
I-Flex Solutions Ltd.	1
Indian Aluminum Co. Ltd.	2
Infosys Technologies Ltd.	6
Siemens Limited	2
Tata Press Ltd.	1

Almost all the companies listed above mobilized international finance. Moreover, the period for which they won prizes was the period in which they mobilized international finance. For example, Indian Aluminium Company, which won prizes in 1991–92 and 1993–94, issued GDR in 1994. Similarly, Cheminor Drugs Ltd., which won prizes in 1996–97 and 1997–98, privately placed equity shares with Schein Pharmaceuticals Inc., USA, in 1998. Global Tele-systems Ltd., which won the prize in 1998–99 issued FCCB in 1996 and privately placed equity shares with foreign investors in 1998.

Infosys Technologies Limited is the leader among the companies which have raised the quality of corporate financial reports. Narayanaswamy (1996) has identified the following factors that explain the company's decision to produce statements that use generally accepted accounting principles in the United States (US GAAP) as part of voluntary disclosure:

(a) The company made a private placement of equity in October 1994 with foreign institutional investors;
(b) The company derives a very large part of its software revenues from the US; and
(c) The company was seeking a NASDAQ listing in the future.

Other large and reputed Indian companies have also focused on improving their corporate financial report, especially increasing the quantum of voluntary disclosures. The most popular disclosures are the value of brand equity, the economic value added (EVA), and the value of human assets. Perhaps the emergence of knowledge-based companies, particularly in the IT sector, has raised the level of transparency and disclosure in financial reports of Indian companies. Companies, which have significant amounts of intangible assets, have an incentive to disclose intangible assets voluntarily as additional information, because those assets are not recognized in the financial statements. Similarly, companies have raised the quality of their financial report to attract foreign portfolio investment. Moreover, as a part of corporate governance reports, listed companies have started providing futuristic information in management discussion and analysis (MDA).

In the post-liberalization period, although the ownership of Domestic Financial Institutions (DFI) has come down significantly, promoter's ownership continues to be significantly high. One study (J. Sarkar et al., 1999) which analyses the equity ownership data as of 1995-96 shows that the sum of mean holdings by directors and relatives and by bodies corporate in private companies belonging to business houses was 41.9 per cent. Similarly, the sum of mean holdings by directors and relatives and by bodies corporate in private stand-alone companies was 40.10 per cent. The public holding was 34.5 per cent and 46.5 per cent in private companies belonging to business houses and private stand-alone companies respectively. Inclusion of holdings of bodies corporate to determine promoter's holding is important, because promoters control the management of a company through a system of complex cross-holdings.

A recent study by NSE (2001) revealed the shareholding pattern in June 2001 of companies listed in the NSE (see Table 5.5). The study indicates that the holdings of institutional investors (17.43 per cent) and the Indian public (17.53 per cent) are not large enough to provide adequate incentives to Indian companies to raise the level of transparency and disclosure in their financial report. Usually, institutional investors, including FIIs, do not deal with scrips of companies below B category. Therefore, it is unlikely that companies below B category have any incentive for improving corporate financial reports.

TABLE 5.5 *Shareholding pattern of NSE-listed companies (2001)*

Type of Investor	*Shareholdings (%)*	
Institutional Investors:	17.43	
Financial Institutions		7.99
Foreign Institutional Investors		4.61
Mutual Funds		4.83
Non-Institutional Investors:	34.20	
Indian public		17.53
NRI/ Overseas Corporate Bodies		1.46
Private Corporate Bodies		10.82
Others		4.39
Promoters:	48.36	
Indian Promoters		39.65
Foreign Promoters		5.39
Persons acting in concert		3.32

Thus, we may find wide variations in the quality of corporate financial reports in India. In fact, there will be a clear divide between top-rung companies and companies that are listed in capital markets but whose shares are not traded frequently. Top-rung companies will benchmark their corporate financial reporting practices with international practices. On the other hand, the second category of companies will try to circumvent new regulations. It is interesting to note that only 37 per cent of the companies listed on the Bombay Stock exchange (BSE) were traded in September 2001. CMIE (2002) reports:

There were 3705 companies listed on the BSE as of April 1996. These grew to peak at 6008 in January 1997. Since then, the number of companies listed on the BSE has declined to stabilise around 5800. However, the number of scrips traded is much lower than the number of scrips listed. Only about 65 per cent of the listed companies on the BSE were traded. This ratio rose to 82 per cent the first half of 1996. But, in 1998, it declined to less than 50 per cent and then to around 40 per cent. In September 2001, only 2174, or 37 per cent of the 5939 companies were traded.

CONCLUSION

Over the past three years, regulatory authorities have instituted mechanisms to improve corporate governance and to improve the corporate reporting practices in India. It is too early to evaluate the results of these new initiatives on corporate financial reports. There will be implementation problems.

Companies will find it difficult to identify the right persons for the position of independent directors. Many companies will not be able to attract the right individuals to head their audit committees. Therefore, it is unlikely that the system will work effectively for average Indian companies. However, the Government of India has initiated actions to train potential directors to create a pool of individuals, who will be available to act as independent directors.

The issuance of accounting standards by itself does not improve the quality of corporate financial reports. A recent study (Vijayalakshmi, 2003) that examined the segment-reporting patterns of Indian companies reported the following:

This study examined the top 200 Indian companies belonging to 10 industries. The findings indicate that overall the level of compliance is fairly high and only about 15 per cent of our sample companies failed to comply with the requirements. The bad news however is that many companies that have not followed segment reporting in the right manner are large companies like Telco, Bajaj Auto, Sterlite Industries, Wipro, HLL, Philips and Ranbaxy. For instance, the 13 companies, whose segment report are found to be inadequate, account nearly 30 per cent of the sales and profit values of companies that are disclosing segment reports. Many of these companies are one of three largest companies in their respective industries. Similarly, 18 companies, which claim to be single segment companies, have been found to be operating in multiple segments. These companies account for nearly 7 per cent of the sales and 15 per cent of profit of the sample companies that are not disclosing segment reports.

Compliance should be ensured by regulatory authorities through effective monitoring mechanisms, including audits. The audit is the cornerstone of good corporate financial reports. However, all the companies named above could receive clean report from their auditors. Therefore, there is a need to strengthen the auditing practices in India. The Naresh Chandra Committee has commended various steps to enhance the independence of the auditor. The ICAI has introduced the system of 'Peer Review'. Moreover, it has decided to constitute a 'Financial Report Review Panel'. The panel would suo moto look into the published accounts of different organizations. The government has decided to set up a Serious Fraud Investigation Office (SFIO). It is conceived as a multidisciplinary unit capable of investigating corporate white collar crimes. It is expected that all these steps will improve the quality of corporate financial reports in India.

The change in corporate reporting practices is clearly visible. Indian companies, particularly those attracting international finance, will achieve international standards within a short period. Companies which will continue to depend on local finance are not likely to benchmark their corporate reporting practices with international practices. As a result, Indian regulatory authorities must take steps to ensure that they achieve the acceptable level of transparency and disclosure. Such increased vigilance is essential if the Indian economy is to generate the growth that it needs.

Notes

1. Handbook of Statistics on Indian Economy, RBI (2000)
2. Handbook of Statistics on Indian Economy, RBI (2000)
3. Economic Survey 2001-02:109
4. Section 211 (3A) and Sec 211 (3B) of the Companies Act, 1956.
5. Section 217 of the Companies Act, 1956
6. An accounting standard is mandatory in the sense that it is the duty of the auditors to ensure that the accounting standard is implemented in the presentation of financial statements covered by their audit reports. Auditors should disclose deviations, if any, in their audit reports.
7. AS-4, Contingencies and Events After the Balance Sheet Date, and AS-5, Net Profit or Loss for the Period, Prior Period Items, and Changes in Accounting Policies.
8. AS-1, Disclosure of Accounting Policies; AS-2, Valuation of Inventories; AS-3, Cash Flow Statements; AS-6, Depreciation Accounting; AS-7, Accounting for Construction Contracts; AS-8, Accounting for Research and Development; AS-9, Revenue Recognition; and AS-10, Accounting for Fixed Assets.
9. Since 1958, the ICAI has been awarding prizes/awards for the best-presented accounts of the corporate sector. From 1990, ICAI instituted separate awards for public and private sector companies.
10. SEBI Press release No. PR-17/2000, dated 25 January 2000.

References

Bagchi, Amiya Kumar, (1998). 'Public Sector Industry and the Political Economy of Indian development', In *The State, Development Planning and Liberalisation in India*, (ed.) Terence J. Byers, Delhi: Oxford University Press.

Chen, Charles J.P. and Vikki Jaggi (2000). 'Association between independent non-executive directors, family control and financial disclosures in Hong Kong', *Journal of Accounting and Public Policy*, 19, pp. 285–310.

CMIE (2002). *Economic Intelligent Service July 2002*, Mumbai: CMIE.

Choi, Fredrick D.S. (1973). 'Financial disclosure and entry to the European capital market', *Journal of Accounting Research*, Autumn, pp. 159–175.

Ghosh, Jayati, 1998. 'Liberalisation debate', In *The Indian Economy: Major Debates Since Independence*, (ed.) Terence J. Byers, Delhi: Oxford University Press pp. 319.

Lal, Jawahar (1985). *Corporate Annual Report: Theory and Practice*, New Delhi: Sterling Publishers Private Ltd.

_____ (1992). *Understanding Indian Investors*. New Delhi: Global Business.

National Stock Exchange (2001). *Indian Securities Market: A Review*, Volume-IV, Mumbai: National Stock Exchange of India Ltd.

Narayanaswamy, R. (1996). 'Voluntary US GAAP Disclosure in India: The Case of Infosys Technologies Ltd', *Journal of International Financial Management and Accounting*, 7: 2, pp. 137–66.

National Stock Exchange (2002). *Indian Securities Market: A Review*, Volume-V, Mumbai: National Stock Exchange of India Ltd.

Panda, Manoj K. and Kirit S. Parikh 1997. 'Macroeconomic scene assessment and outlook', In *India Development Report 1997*, (ed.) Kirit S. Parikh, Delhi: Oxford University Press.

Patel, Sandeep A. (2002). 'Measuring transparency and disclosure at firm level in emerging markets', *Emerging Market Review*, 3, pp. 325–37.

Redebaugh, Lee H. and J. Gray Sidney (1993). *International Accounting and Multinational Enterprises*, 3rd edition, New York: John Wiley & Sons.

Sarkar, Jayati and Subrata Sarkar (1999). 'The Governance of Indian Corporate', In *India Development Report 1999–2000*, (ed.) Kriti S. Parikh, Delhi: Oxford University Press.

Shah, P.N., A.H. Dalal, and H.N. Motiwalla (2000). *History of the Accountancy Profession in India*, New Delhi: The Institute of Chartered Accountants of India.

Sloan, Richard G. (2001). 'Financial accounting and corporate governance: A discussion', *Journal of Accounting and Economics*, 32: 2001, pp. 335–47.

Vijayalakshmi, S. (2003). 'An Analysis of Segment Disclosures under AS 17,' Calicut: Indian Institute of Management, Kozhikode (unpublished paper).

Xie, Biao, Ravidson III, N. Wallace, R.A. Datt, and J. Peter (2002). 'Earnings Management and Corporate Governance: The Role of the Board and the Audit Committee', *Journal of Corporate Finance*, 150, (In press).

6

Institutional Investors and Nominee Directors

Jairus Banaji *

Over the last decade a clear consensus has emerged that a substantial reform of governance is necessary in the Indian corporate sector. There is much less clarity, however, about the paths along which reform should be pursued. Certainly, the most interesting development during this period has been the publication of the Security and Exchange Board of India's (SEBI) Code of Corporate Governance. In this chapter I examine whether the approach SEBI has taken to corporate governance reform is likely to be effective in terms of promoting transparent and responsible corporate governance. In taking up this task, however, I primarily limit myself to examining the recommendations concerning the role of one particular set of actors in the governance complex, namely, institutional investors. The aim is to map out a broad perspective for a stronger institutional role in the governance of private sector companies.

This chapter is based upon a series of approximately 160 interviews conducted between April 1998 and January 2000, mostly in Bombay. The interviews revealed that there is widespread support for institutional activism, but premised on the need for substantial changes in the governance culture of the institutions themselves, which are largely perceived as government entities subject to endemic pressures from both politicians and individual business houses. There is no evidence to suggest that a radical overhaul is currently under way in these respects, but even if it was, it may not be enough. In its existing form the Takeover Code has done little to encourage hostile

* This chapter is a compressed and slightly modified version of my contribution to the report published as Jairus Banaji and Gautam Mody, 'Corporate Governance and the Indian Private Sector', Queen Elizabeth House Working Paper Series, no. 73, Oxford University, 2001. I am especially grateful to Barbara Harriss-White and Gautam Mody for their stimulating discussions over several years.

takeovers and seems, in fact, to reflect a general aversion to them. I argue that a properly regulated market for acquisitions is the single most important condition for the success of any perspective that gives a stronger or more aggressive role to institutional investors.

INTRODUCTION—CORPORATE GOVERNANCE AND CORPORATE CODES

The dominant academic view frames the issue of corporate governance essentially as one of the 'agency costs' inherent in the separation of ownership and control. The assumption here is that the dispersal of shareholding in the large modern publicly quoted corporation created a power vacuum which was filled by the emergence of a cadre of professional corporate managers who came to form a powerful and unsupervised constituency in modern industry.[1] However, the assumption of dispersed ownership is seen to be limited in at least two ways once we extend this largely American model to the contemporary world and to corporate regimes outside the US and the UK. First, the dispersion of shareholding cannot be, and was never, a valid description of those situations, such as in Europe,[2] India, and East Asia,[3] where corporate ownership patterns have traditionally been highly concentrated, even as many of these companies have gone public and listed their shares on the stock exchange. Second, even in the Anglo-American markets, the last four decades of the twentieth century have seen a gradual but dramatic increase in the percentage of shareholdings under institutional ownership, leading to a significant *re*-concentration of capital in the hands of pension funds, insurance companies, and investment trusts, and through them of the fund management industry generally.[4] In fact, it is these latter developments which underpin the emergence of the contemporary debate on corporate governance and in particular the corporate governance platform of the 1990s, associated, in the public mind, with the Report of the Cadbury Committee in the UK, the activity of public pension funds in the US, and the sporadic upsurge of shareholder activism in various parts of the world.

The Cadbury Model

A major business innovation of the 1990s involved the rapid spread of codes of corporate governance worldwide, following the publication in 1992 of the report of the Cadbury Committee in the UK. The new feature of the Cadbury framework was that it provided a model where market-based regulation, institutional investors, and codes of best practice would work in synergy to produce greater transparency and accountability in business, boosting investor confidence and contributing significantly to the liquidity of the market. The market was seen as the general medium of accountability. However, it was also recognized that for the market to be able to exert accountability pressures on companies, it needed a benchmark. In Cadbury-style corporate governance that benchmark is a system of rules and principles of good corporate governance, which are expressed in a formal way in codes of best practice. Such codes are self-regulatory, with one important qualification, namely, that amendments are made to the listing agreement to create an obligation on companies to state how far they comply with the code. Secondly, Cadbury acknowledges the strategic disparity between classes of shareholders, namely, the ability of institutional investors to influence corporate behaviour by contrast with the relative apathy and or impotence of small shareholders. Finally, the codes themselves are largely about defining and formalizing management's accountability to the board, and, through the board, to the shareholders as a whole.

Central to the professional character and independence of boards is the role the independent non-executive directors are expected to play and the formal mechanisms (i.e. board committees) through which such directors are expected to supervise management. The existence of board committees controlled by independent directors creates a presumption of formality and transparency in the procedures for appointing new directors to the board and developing a policy on executive pay. Cadbury assigns special importance to Audit Committees, since a major part of the brief of independent directors is the ability to exercise financial supervision over companies and reassure investors that the company's 'financial controls and accounting systems are of a high standard'. Nomination Committees are also important because they ensure that the selection of the board is grounded in a formal and transparent procedure, and is independent of management. Independent directors are also expected to play a major role in establishing and reviewing the compensation of the CEO and senior management. It is now considered best practice for these three committees (Audit, Nomination, and Remuneration) to be staffed entirely or largely by independent directors, which raises the issue of who counts as an independent director, or how independence is construed.

Having summarized the prevailing Anglo-American approach to corporate governance in this way, one should note that Cadbury makes several assumptions. It assumes a corporate culture or system where there is *already* a widespread and well-established separation of ownership and control. Cadbury is not tailor-made to a context where dominant shareholders, e.g. promoters, control management and where the corporate governance problem is chiefly one of the protection of minority shareholder rights. The assumption of dispersed ownership explains why there is little emphasis in Cadbury on the equitable treatment of different groups of shareholders. Cadbury also assumes that supervision can effectively be exercised within the framework of a unitary board where independent directors are expected both to contribute to decision-making by the management and to monitor the decisions management makes. Third, the model assumes a powerful external shareholder base that is strongly motivated to monitor companies. Finally, of course, at the most general level, Cadbury assumes that 'accountability can be best achieved through a voluntary code coupled with disclosure'. Of course, compliance with the Cadbury Code 'is not entirely a matter of self-regulation', since, as we noted above, the listing rules of the London Stock Exchange 'provide important backing' in having the status of subordinate legislation.[5]

Now, self-regulatory structures are prone to a number of criticisms (even when one allows for the legal status of the listing rules). Among these, the most important, perhaps, are that 'they are designed with large, well-organised, well-resourced enterprises in mind and fail to deal with those who really need to be regulated'; 'they are low on accountability'; and, they 'tend not to enjoy public confidence'. Enforcement is particularly problematic: it is doubtful if most exchange authorities would seriously contemplate striking off any company for failure to comply with a code of best practice.[6] So the general issue here is whether self-regulation is a sufficient (and sufficiently strong) form of accountability.

The SEBI Code and its Limitations

Sensing this difficulty, the drafters of the SEBI Code of Corporate Governance (the Committee was headed by Kumar Mangalam Birla and published its report in January 2000) decided to divide their recommendations into two types, 'mandatory' and 'non-mandatory'. One is not aware of any other governance code which refers to any of its recommendations as 'mandatory', and indeed it is peculiar to describe a *recommendation* as mandatory, since a recommendation is by definition advisory in nature. This is primarily a matter of language, however, the key point being that the code adopted by SEBI describes itself as a 'statutory' code and wants the self-regulation of business to have the force of law.

More substantially, the actual provisions of the SEBI Code deviate from international best practice in important respects. This is particularly clear when the code is compared with other codes of corporate governance worldwide. One important area of difference relates to independence. Almost all codes are agreed on the need for the board to have a substantial degree of independence from management. Where they differ is in the details, and how tightly or loosely they define the independence of the so-called independent directors. SEBI's definition is rather loose because it restricts itself to only one feature, namely, whether directors have 'any material pecuniary relationship or transactions with the company, its promoters, its management or its subsidiaries' which (in the opinion of the board) may affect their independence of judgment. But if the issue is independence of judgment, this can surely just as well be affected by a director having no such relationship but being, for example, a former executive of the company or a member of the immediate family of an individual who has been an executive in the recent past. Contrast this with a best practice definition such as that proposed by The California Public Employees' Retirement System (CalPERS) in the US or the National Association of Pension Funds in the UK. The importance of this preliminary issue is that unless we construe independence in a sufficiently realistic way, none of the recommendations on the independence of the board, e.g. that the Chair of the audit committee should be an independent director, will have much meaning. This is why in the US the new audit committee rules pay special attention to this question, with both the New York Stock Exchange (NYSE) and The National Association of Securities Dealers (NASD) enhancing their definitions of independence.[7]

Secondly, almost every code recommends nomination committees to control the selection of the board. The SEBI Code omits any recommendation of this sort and does not even raise the issue, despite its own clear assertion that 'till recently, it has been the practice of most of the companies in India to fill the board with representatives of the promoters of the company, and independent directors if chosen were also handpicked thereby ceasing to be independent' (Code 6.4). This is one of the most interesting omissions in our code and will surely be looked at in any future review of the guidelines.

Third, almost every code recommends the setting up of remuneration committees so that the pay of CEOs and senior management is not self-determined and there is transparency in the policy governing executive pay. SEBI makes this a non-mandatory recommendation, i.e. desirable but not essential, although disclosure of the compensation package *is* mandatory. Again, this looks like a compromise between conflicting pressures.

Fourth, and most important for our concerns, is the issue of the responsibilities of institutional investors. Most codes agree that they should be encouraged to intervene, should exercise their voting rights, and should state their voting policies. For example, according to the UK Combined Code,

'Institutional shareholders have a responsibility to make considered use of their votes', while the recommendations of the European Association of Securities Dealers stipulate that 'Institutional investors acting in a fiduciary capacity for external beneficial owners should state their voting policies'. These are crucially important recommendations for they will determine the whole future course of how proficiently companies are run. Here, as is well known, the draft SEBI Code circulated in the last quarter of 1999 was more concerned with reducing the presence of institutional nominees on Indian boards, although the final version of the code took a more cautious and neutral stance, and suggested that the institutions 'should appoint nominees on the boards of companies only on a selective basis' (Code 7.4). Whatever the drawbacks of the institutional nominee system, the regulator should surely have sought to encourage a better quality of monitoring and concentrated on the issue of how that is best achieved. Indeed, there is not even a recommendation in the code that the institutions should state their voting policies. This contrasts sharply with the Cadbury recommendation that 'institutional investors should disclose their policies on the use of voting rights'.

NOMINEE DIRECTORS

A careful survey of the press would show that since September 1996 there has been a great deal of institutional pressure for reform of the governance culture of Indian businesses. That was when the financial institutions first mooted the idea of a block sale of their equity holdings to effect a management change 'if it is in the interests of the company'.[8] This extremely radical idea failed to get off the ground for a variety of reasons, which include a strong business lobby backlash that has chosen to make the issue of institutional nominees central to the debate on governance. Although contributions to this debate have ranged from the hysterical to the more considered and dispassionately argued, almost no attempt has been made to disentangle the different issues involved. Some of the distinct issues are: (a) whether institutional shareholders have a right to be represented on boards; (b) whether institutional shareholders should seek board representation; (c) whether the present nominee director system is the most effective and efficient means of institutional board representation; and finally (d) whether insider trading has any relevance to issues (a) and (b). Clearly (a) and (b) are different issues; the fact that shareholders may have a right to be on the board does not necessarily mean that they will want to, or see it as in their best interests to, exercise that right.[9] Moreover, there are different kinds of institutional investors and the strategic issue under (b) may have different kinds of resolution depending on the kind of institution involved.[10] We shall return to some of this later and concentrate for the moment on nominee directors.

The presence of institutional nominees is certainly the most distinctive feature of the Indian corporate governance system, and consequently the 'failure' of corporate governance in India is often seen as a failure of the institutions to safeguard the general shareholder and public interest. And of course, no feature of India's corporate governance has generated more controversy. Among the large number of business representatives we spoke to, there was a clear division of views on the issue of nominee directors, with widespread hostility among corporates but strong support among professionals and a few managements as well. The more critical responses consistently emphasized lack of contribution, occasionally also the low calibre of many nominees and their lack of competence in understanding the business. Respondents who were more sympathetic to the role played by nominees also evaluated that role in rather different terms, highlighting not their ability to contribute so much as the restraint imposed on managements by the presence of nominee directors. Several managements were extremely positive about the contribution of their institutional directors. Finally, the few nominees we spoke to emphasized the severe constraints within which they operated but, interestingly, interpreted these rather differently. The following excerpts from our interviews illustrate these diverse points of view.[11]

Lack of contribution was the most common complaint:

> I have in the last three years sat on so many boards, along with institutional nominees, and I don't think they take a stand or they speak up or do something like that. [That] is an idealised image of the institutional nominee director. (Non-executive director)

> Where there are representatives of the Indian development banks, which is in almost every company, board meetings that I've attended, when there's some kind of financial transaction to be done, they don't contribute at all. (Investment banker)

> ... at our board meetings the institutional shareholders hardly open their mouth. (Industrialist)

> For myself, over my eighteen-year span, I would argue strongly that they don't contribute. There may be exceptions. (Tata director)

> (What is your own experience of the kind of contribution that nominee directors make?) Very poor! (But why do you feel that is?) Number one, because they don't have any sense of responsibility or accountability, they have no stake, no professional stake in their role, and they feel it's just another job to be done. (MNC non-executive chairman)

(What about the nominees? How do you see their role?) I think there is no role that they have played at all. I don't see any purpose of these institutional directors. (But are you generalizing from your own experience?) I am generalizing from my own experience as well as all the other companies. (Industrialist)

Another concern was a lack of requisite skills in dealing with businesses:

You often go to companies where they have institutional nominees, they don't even have a clue about what the business is all about! (Head of investment banking division)

Even the kind of directors we have do not have the competence to really understand the balance sheets or understand the game. Their personal contribution cannot be substantial (Institutional nominee)[12]

Professionals who serve as non-executives were more supportive:

The financial institutions have their own cell, and they are in a better position to elicit more from the management rather than non-working directors like us, who merely attend board meetings .... I'm on quite a few good companies, where high-level executives are representatives of financial institutions. And they are quite vigilant. (Solicitor)

Even participation by institutional directors quite often acts as a very wholesome safeguard of the interest of the minority shareholders, as long as institutional directors are sincere, and not under the obligation and shadow of the Indian promoter; they can also act as a very important check against any abuses. (Solicitor)

The nominees themselves do not necessarily view their situation in exactly the same way. Two nominees who spoke with a degree of frankness expressed very different points of view. The older of the two, quoted above, complained of the hostility and isolation which such directors face:

Ultimately, an institutional nominee or director is not a welcome constituent on the board .... You are a lonely voice, you are not there to create unpleasantness

In contrast, a young ICICI manager thought the major issue was one of time and incentives:

Now I'm a nominee, many of my colleagues are. How much time do we have? It's not our main job .... I am in the position of an independent non-executive director. What incentive do I have? Why must I challenge executive management?... The question is that of time. I'm not a full-time board member, I'm a full-time employee somewhere else. Sitting fees are two thousand rupees ... How much can you pay? My time is worth, to my company, in lakhs. That is the value of my time to the company. Who is going to pay me that much money?... The compensation would have to be really large to get a truly competent guy.

The fact that a lot of our interviewees were critical of the nominee director system does not mean that these respondents were necessarily opposed to seeing institutional nominees on boards. Many felt there was no point in having institutional nominees if they were not going to be effective, and that nominees were there essentially to play a proactive role:

I think the institutions should, if they do nominate somebody, have a far more proactive role in understanding the business. (Head of investment banking division)

A nominee director has a very important role to play. In fact, right under their noses things are happening! (Private equity fund)

They (the institutions) are largely reactive. What I would like to see is the institutions getting very proactive, and, if that happens, my God, things will change! Change very rapidly. (Fund manager)

The underlying issues are much larger ones, of course. For nominee directors to play a more 'proactive' role, the whole culture of the boardroom has to change. Institutional heads have repeatedly complained that 'FI nominees on boards have little power as they are only updated on those matters of the company which are placed before the board'.[13] Secondly, with institutional governance policy largely driven by the government, it can always be argued that it was primarily up to the latter to enforce stricter standards of supervision. This change has only begun to come about in the last few years, under the pressure of global integration, the collapse of the primary market, and rising non-performing assets. Finally, there is the whole issue of whether the institutions should continue to depend on their own resources or outsource expertise. Data that we collected in the course of this research shows the staggering scale on which the public financial institutions have had to conduct monitoring. As of end-1999, we were reliably informed, IDBI had 470 nominees spread over 1026 companies, of which the majority, 364 nominees, were officials of the institution. In the same year, LIC had 124 nominee directors sitting on the boards of 171 companies. Half of these nominees were retired employees of the company. In ICICI, as of March 2000, there were 231 nominees supervising a total of 436 companies, with ninety-eight executives/officers and 133 outsiders. There is also strong evidence to suggest that the institutions have been debating a more viable threshold limit for the deployment of nominees.

Institutional Investors

Unlike the UK, where the dominant institutional shareholder is an arm's-length investor, in India the domestic financial institutions have always regarded themselves as 'committed' shareholders.[14] With large, illiquid stakes in many companies, the institutions are locked into their investments.

Consequently, the *potential* for institutional monitoring is distinctly greater than it is in the few markets dominated by arm's-length investors.[15] Press accounts also suggest that there has been a noticeable increase in institutional interventions in the last two years. On the other hand, there is a powerful business lobby that seeks to restrain the extent of institutional intervention. The clearest formal expression of this lobby was the CII's *Code of Corporate Governance*, published in 1998.

Both the CII and SEBI Codes claim descent from Cadbury,[16] but it is worth noting that their stances on the rights of institutional shareholders depart significantly from Cadbury's. Indeed, while in the UK the Institutional Shareholder Committee's Statement of Best Practice on the Role and Duties of Directors 'had a strong influence on the report of the Cadbury Committee' which provided an 'express endorsement of the ISC Code',[17] the CII, it is well-known, sought to circumscribe the rights of institutional investors, and the Kumar Mangalam Birla Committee failed to include even a single representative of any major financial institution.

The failure of the CII Code to gain wider acceptability may well have prompted the regulator to step in and fill the void. The author of the draft on which the Code is based stated at a CII roadshow that he was 'pained' by the lack of response to the Code.[18] Though the CII Code is littered with illogicalities, clearly this is not the place to delve into them. But taking its own cue from the Confederation, in the draft of the Code, SEBI came out with a controversial suggestion that 'the financial institutions maintain an arm's-length relationship with the company *by not seeking a seat on the board of a company*.' It was suggested instead that they would serve the cause of shareholders better by the use of their voting power at the General Body meetings (Draft Code 5.11). This was later retracted in the final form of the code where it is merely suggested that 'the institutions should appoint nominees on the boards of companies *only on a selective basis* where such appointment is pursuant to a right under loan agreements or where such appointment is considered necessary to protect the interest of the institution' (Code 7.3), and that where institutional directors sit on boards, the nominating institutions should ensure that effective safeguards exist to control the flow of price-sensitive information. SEBI abandoned its earlier stance largely under institutional pressure, agreeing to leave the matter to their discretion.

The new element in SEBI's suggestion, conspicuously missing in the CII Code, is reference to insider trading. Had the authors of the CII Code perceived this as a major risk, there is scarcely any doubt that it would have figured prominently in their arguments. Our own scrutiny of the press suggests that the insider trading argument first surfaced in the middle of 1999, in an editorial reacting to the CII's demand for evacuation of boards by nominees.[19] Be that as it may, our interviews show that the argument about price-sensitive information has had a considerable impact and is now widely accepted as the stock argument against institutional nominees. It is equally important to realize, however, that the *weight* one assigns to this argument is a matter of individual opinion, and that several respondents proposed persuasive counter-arguments. Following the publication of the SEBI draft code at the end of September 1999, most of the respondents we interviewed between October and January were asked, 'How do you react to SEBI's draft recommendation that the investment institutions withdraw their representatives from the boards of companies on the grounds that they are privy to price-sensitive information?' It would be useful to disentangle the various arguments on both sides of this important divide.

Arguments against Board Representation

The arguments against representation took three major forms: (a) nominees are privy to price-sensitive information and risk making their institutions insiders—Chinese Walls are a myth;[20] (b) term-lending institutions should not seek representation except in the case of an actual or potential default; and (c) there is an inherent ambiguity in the role of the institutional director which might involve a conflict of interest.

Some of the more interesting responses were as follows:

I believe very strongly that if you are a director, you *have* to be aware of price-sensitive information. And representatives of the institutions have to send periodical reports to the institutions. And how can they not report such price-sensitive information back to the nominating institution? So, if an institution is actively trading in the shares of a company, it would be wise for them *not* to put people on the board .... I think the institutions, which actively trade in the stock market, are taking an unnecessary risk in nominating their representatives on the boards of companies. (Of course, they claim that they have Chinese Walls in the organisation ....) They don't have Chinese Walls! No way, no way! (Non-executive director)

I do feel that entities, whether they're institutions or otherwise, who regularly trade in securities and will have access to special information, should not have nominees. (For example, the UTI should not have any nominees on the board? Is that what you're saying?) Or there should be some sort of a 'Cease & desist', that whatever information comes to them cannot be used as the basis for trading. I'm sure some way or the other it gets used. They should not then trade in the securities of those companies, but that defeats the whole purpose for an institution like UTI ... they are on the boards of a whole lot of companies whose shares they are buying and selling every day. Now they make this distinction between fund managers and people who are actually on the board. I don't know how far that really holds up, eventually. If you want to really test it, test it with a hard-nosed lawyer's approach, I think it'll just break down somewhere. You'll find that the top four or five people know everything. And the top four or five people are involved in the decision-making on what to buy and sell. I know from my experience that every major restructuring proposal that happens in India, the moment your thinking process is over, the first thing that you do is you go and talk to the IDBI, ICICI, and UTIs of the world and tell them that you're going to come up with this two weeks later and please bless this. Now that information is provided to the institutions, but from that date onwards, till the proposal actually gets announced trading goes on merrily ... it's very illustrative of the kind of special knowledge which institutions in the Indian environment (enjoy). They are far more powerful than similar institutions anywhere else. (Lawyer, on several corporate boards)

Why should they have a right to be on the board? (Well, as dominant shareholders?) Even in the United States, CalPERS doesn't have seats on any board—none of the financial institutions. Because you have a huge conflict of interest, you are privy to a lot of information which the ordinary shareholder isn't. And if you've got arms of those companies which are trading left, right, and centre, huge .... (So you think this does happen, despite all the Chinese Walls?) This Chinese Wall is a figment of people's imagination. I tell this to my investment banking friends from Goldman Sachs and Merrill Lynch and CSF: 'Don't give me all this rubbish about the Chinese Wall.' (Tata director)

McVea notes that the 'crucial question surrounding the Wall is the extent to which it can be "straddled" by top executives', but adds, 'To what extent this is a problem is uncertain and much will depend on the exact circumstances.'[21] This is clearly a huge area, and the best one can say for the moment is that *if* SEBI is convinced by the insider-trading argument as applied to institutions and their nominees, it should seriously consider establishing minimum requirements for Chinese Wall procedures.[22] The advantage of this would be that it would weaken the case for using the insider-trading argument to press for removal of institutional directors from boards.

The second argument against representation (see (b) above) is exemplified in the written responses submitted by the chairman of one of the country's most successful NBFCs. He stated:

Investment institutions may see board representation as a result of their debt exposure to the company. However, this representation should be triggered off by the happening of an event detrimental to the working of the company rather than as a matter of right.

The senior manager of a large business house took the same position:

We believe that institutions, merely because they have the financial exposure, should not have a place on the board. (By financial exposure you mean equity?) Equity as well as debt. (As well as debt?) Yes. Let's tackle the two things separately. As far as debt is concerned, we believe that until and unless there is a potential default or an event of default, not necessarily actual default of payments but let's say slippage on project milestones, etc., until and unless there is a significant event that affects the ability of the company to service its loan, the institutional lenders should not have a place on the board. And financial institutions, which are equity holders, merely because they are equity holders they should not have a place. (What's the logic behind this?) The logic is that in front of other stakeholders, these institutional nominees actually become institutional nominees, while the role of the board is actually a combined role.

Of course, the institutional response to the first part of this statement might be that their directors are frequently criticized for not being sufficiently 'proactive', whereas keeping representatives on hold, so to speak, until a default is *likely* to occur will only constrain their ability to act proactively even more.

The second part of the statement, with its reference to the 'combined role' of the board, takes us to the final argument against board representation (see (c) above) which is the most complex of the three. Thus one respondent argued:

As soon as the financial institution in its capacity as a *shareholder* wants a seat on the board, then it becomes answerable to the other shareholders. It cannot then say, I'm a shareholder, the board must be answerable to me. Because he's himself a part of that board. And, therefore, I would say that this is a tradition which is followed in the Anglo-American countries also: none of the big institutional investors in the US, for example, are represented on the boards of companies, because it affects their independence.

Here the argument seemed to be not that *lenders* did not have a right to appoint their nominees to the board, but that shareholders who did so or sought board representation would lose their independence and not be able to hold the board accountable. One can respond to this by saying that to be consistent it presumes boards which are totally independent of *all* shareholder representatives, which seems unrealistic, given that most boards in India do have a significant presence of promoter nominees. However, the issue is really whether accountability can work without making directors dependent on specific shareholders.[23]

Arguments for Board Representation

The counter-arguments were: (a) as major shareholders, institutions have a right to board representation; opposition to nominee directors is an infringement of their rights as shareholders and produces different classes of shareholders, some more privileged than others; (b) insider trading is more rampant among promoters; (c) the insider trading issue is irrelevant to the question of the rights of institutional shareholders; (d) Chinese Walls *are* in place in the investment institutions, ensuring that nominees are insulated from the fund management side, and, (e) for creditors, the point of having a financial monitor is lost if the company reaches a state where it risks defaulting on its loans.

The contrary position, defending the institutions' presence on the board, was largely made to hinge on an assertion of shareholder rights:

If the board is taken as the representative body of the shareholders, then every class of shareholder is entitled to have a representative on the board, who gets duly elected by the shareholders. (Institutional head)

How can you tell a shareholder 'You cannot be represented on a company'? (Institutional executive)

I think the financial institutions and banks which have a very large stake in these companies are bound to have a say in these matters, and I would not deny them that right, they must have that. (Former head of institution)

Most forcefully, perhaps, in the following statement:

(About this more specific recommendation that the investment institutions should withdraw their nominees?) It's a completely absurd provision! It's a completely self-serving provision, and it speaks volumes for the mindset of this Committee that they don't recognize the rights of the shareholders—when it's the whole purpose of corporate governance, one of the purposes, is that they recognize all shareholders as equal. (Private equity fund)

It was also claimed that insider trading was more rampant among promoters. The same respondent went on to say:

The insiders, the management is the principal culprit in insider trading, in India today! And here the onus is being put on investment institutions. I think it's absurd. The investment institutions must safeguard their responsibility. Often we've found it's the investment institutions that have safeguarded the rights of all small shareholders, not the managements.

One fund manager thought it was wrong to link the argument about insider trading with the issue of board representation:

Here I think the approach is wrong ... that because there are no proper checks and balances on insider trading, you don't want institutions to be a part of the board. That, I think, is probably a wrong argument. You should actually have proper checks and balances for insider trading, there is no substitute for that in a capital market. If you're saying, that is not there, therefore you should not have them, we're tackling the wrong end of the problem.

The argument that lenders should appoint nominees only if a default is likely was met with the reply:

This is funny—our nominee directors are there exactly to avoid default. After it becomes default and becomes an NPA, what is the use of that? That is something we don't agree to. Moreover, I have a responsibility to the public shareholder. Otherwise they have no forum. See, the whole institution of nominee director came that way. (Institutional manager)

And finally, there were professional non-executives who said they disagreed with the suggestion:

I have a bit of a dilemma that if I'm either a significant shareholder or a lender to you, I think I should be on your board, and the way to protect you and the company from price-sensitive information being issued is, I think, the company should enter into a covenant with such board members specifically .... That is one point that I disagree with SEBI. (MNC non-executive chairman)

(*Q*. on SEBI recommendation to remove nominees from boards) I would certainly oppose that. I don't know about the small companies, fortunately I'm on quite a few good companies, where high-level executives are representatives of financial institutions. And they are quite vigilant .... (Do you find it surprising that SEBI might actually come out with a recommendation of this sort? Does it surprise you?) It did ... when I read it in the papers, it surprised me. I don't know what motivated them to do that. (Lawyer)

The counter-response to SEBI's draft recommendation could then be summed up as follows. The issue of insider trading is logically independent of the question of board representation for institutional investors (or any other class of shareholders), in the sense that the latter is a question of principle and cannot be settled by looking at the effectiveness of the Chinese Wall in institutions that trade in equity. In fact, the efficacy of Chinese Walls is notoriously problematic, and full disclosure may well be the best antidote to the problem of insider trading.[24]

Foreign Institutional Investors

Besides domestic financial institutions, the other group of institutional investors who have had a significant impact on the Indian market are the so-called foreign institutional investors (FIIs). There was a widespread perception among respondents that much of the change in the market has in fact been driven by the FIIs through their pressure for a central depository, better standards of disclosure, regular interaction with managements, and the brute exercise of market force. FIIs look for companies which they feel are going to be internationally competitive and exert a diffuse pressure on Indian managements to build professionally run, transparent, competitive businesses, similar in many ways to the 'functional convergence' effect described by Coffee with respect to securities market integration and the influence of overseas listings.[25]

One of the most fascinating discoveries in the course of this study was the sheer extent of interaction between research analysts or fund managers and top management. Interviews with senior executives established that huge amounts of time are spent meeting with analysts and fund managers on a collective or individual basis. Even foreign subsidiaries with a low FII stake described themselves as devoting significant amounts of time to such meetings. '*A nuisance, but there it is, you can't turn them down and you can't tell them lies*', was how one managing director of an Indian company described his feelings about meeting fund managers the next day. Asked if integration into global financial markets had affected the climate of corporate governance in India, another CEO replied:

> I'm not very sure if it has affected corporate governance in India, but what it has affected is definitely the anxiety level of the CEOs .... Earlier I had to satisfy Mr ** and **, once a year, in the AGM. Today you have to satisfy every investor every day.

In the light of all this evidence, it would seem crass to imagine that the Indian market has not seen a dramatic transformation in the course of the 1990s which is closely bound up with the entry of international investors.

Having said that, it is much less easy to be certain about how far the FIIs will seek actively to shape the culture of accountability in the corporate sector. Fund managers see themselves as 'passive investors' who have the potential to influence corporate behaviour by dumping stock and affecting companies' ability to raise money in the market. (There are numerous instances of companies responding to institutional pressure in this form.) None of the fund managers we interviewed saw themselves taking board positions:

> We are not interested in a position on the board, we are just passive investors as far as the company is concerned. (Fund manager)

> We are not long-term strategic investors .... By and large you vote with your feet, you exit, dump the stock if you're unhappy with the management .... By and large we vote with our feet. (Fund manager)

> Foreign institutions don't want to sit on boards. They have the right in many cases and don't. (Consultant)

Nor is it clear that the mutual fund industry will make regular use of its voting rights to seek more forthright ways of influencing management. In a discussion with a group of fund managers at one of the Indian mutual funds it was said:

> We haven't got used to the idea of voting in a meeting yet. All these years we've never had a vote. Therefore, there have been many meetings which we've not attended, having nothing better to do. Now that we have the vote and we can exercise it, and our opinions will be heard, we are also looking at this much more seriously.

Of course, the trend internationally is for investor networks such as The International Corporate Governance Network (ICGN) to propagate the active use of voting rights by institutional investors and the lowering of barriers to cross-border share voting.[26] 'It is now widely accepted that the right to vote a share has an economic value.'[27] But with investment time-frames of twelve to twenty-four months, it is unlikely that there is a strong incentive in the Indian market to translate that kind of prescription into reality.[28] As one fund manager stated: 'We'll have to wait for long-term players with reasonably large exposures to India.'

Regulatory Intervention and Institutional Monitoring

Where, then, does the cutting edge lie? There is no doubt that company initiatives have played an important role in India and that a handful of corporates have gone out of their way to replicate best practice ideas in corporate governance.[29] This is obviously particularly true of the disclosure and reporting standards pioneered by Infosys and, to a lesser extent perhaps, the growing willingness among Indian companies to 'try out' US GAAP (Generally Accepted Accounting Principles). On the other hand, it still remains true that there are very few very good companies in the country, it is unlikely that their governance initiatives can be seen in isolation from their strong performance as businesses, and doubtful whether corporate governance elitism will make much difference to the mainstream of Indian businesses, large and small. There is also the wider (or deeper) problem of whether constructing a formal architecture of corporate governance does address the underlying issue of corporate accountability, in other words, the problem of the limitations of the Cadbury model.

There was a widespread view among our respondents that corporate governance should be left 'to the market'. However, most of our interviews were conducted in 1998 and 1999, during a downward phase of the business cycle, and one of the most perceptive points made in the discussions, especially by some fund managers, was doubting the efficiency of such a market as a measure of rewards to governance:

I don't know whether the market would have done the same thing when things were looking up. We saw preferential allotments by promoters at ridiculous prices, and at that time, when the market was moving up, most of the investing community took it, they didn't create much of a furore over that.

The general implication here is that the market is a rather blunt instrument of governance, conditioned as much or more by the state of the business cycle as by fund managers' perceptions of management quality and governance. Thus there is a need, and scope, for at least two other kinds of governance agendas, namely, regulatory intervention and institutional monitoring.

To take these points in reverse order, it was really quite striking how many respondents reposed faith in the possibilities of institutional activism, *despite* the severe criticisms meted out to the nominee director system. This was a genuine surprise, given the climate in which it was expressed, namely, the need to free business from controls, reduce government intervention, etc. It became apparent, however, that a rise in institutional activism was seen as premised on the growing autonomy of the institutions from government control and interference, their increasing professionalization, and their responsiveness to their own shareholders and the public at large. What was also striking was the considerable diversity of backgrounds from which the support for a more aggressive institutional role was expressed and articulated. It may be helpful to separate the two propositions before illustrating them, firstly, that institutional activism is inevitable in the long term, it is bound to come; and secondly, that the domestic financial institutions need to be more aggressive. Here are some responses:

(Are you even slightly optimistic about change in the level of activism or quality of activism from the FIs, that they will ...) I think it will come about, yes. I don't think this apathy can last forever. It should come, but I just hope it comes in the right manner. Until now, the biggest protest that an FI has done is probably abstain from voting, which is not really helpful, in the sense that if a motion is to be blocked, abstention from voting is not the answer. You should vote against the motion, so you have that solid 20 per cent or 30 per cent or 40 per cent going against that motion. (Fund manager in group discussion at an Indian mutual fund)

Shareholders like institutions *will* start asserting their rights .... Litigation, active involvement from institutions to protect their rights—these will be the driving forces today. (Private equity fund)

If, for example, in India you had the equivalent of CalPERS of the United States, and some of those pension funds, those pension funds are employing very capable accountants, lawyers, and business drivers on to the boards of companies, and I think that will come here, it's bound to come ... it has to come ... (Are you suggesting that the size of the institutions' stake in most private sector firms will make it difficult for them to actually just exit now, and they have to become more actively involved?) They can't just exit, they'll crash, and drag the market. (Managing director of a large business group company with a 24 per cent institutional stake)

The sheer size of domestic institutional stakes distinguishes the Indian corporate governance system in a remarkable way from most others in the world, and Coffee's assertion that 'as the scale of institutional holdings grows, the expected gains from activism should increasingly outweigh the losses' has an obvious relevance for India.[30] The general issue here is how the institutions can best exercise their governance responsibilities, and the most interesting responses were that they should use their voting power, not hesitate to bring about a change in promoters, and auction their holdings in the emerging market for corporate control. One's impression from these responses was that this would be the single most powerful means of reshaping the governance culture of family-owned businesses—more powerful than regulatory pressures, which can always be accommodated, and certainly more persuasive than a mere reliance on codes of best practice. It is worth re-emphasizing, however, that a perspective of this kind presupposes that the institutions are no longer government-directed entities, have the autonomy to make the best decisions in terms of their own interests as institutional shareholders and their responsibilities as trustees of public wealth, and have the professionalism and flexibility to combine a core portfolio with a trading component, concentrating professional monitoring skills on the former. Seen in this perspective, there is no need for institutional shareholders to overstretch their own resources in monitoring managements.

Several respondents suggested that they should rely primarily on a panel of non-official nominees, independent outside directors appointed at the behest of the institutions, who would act as representatives of the general shareholder interest. Such directors would be genuinely independent of management, both in the sense of having no affiliation with the company or group, and in the sense of being responsible to their appointers. They would function primarily in the huge grey area of Indian business which lies sprawling between the handful of genuinely professionally managed companies and the mass of family concerns where there is no significant public stake.

Here, then, are some of these responses:

Vote out the promoter directors! Put your own people in .... Where there's a will, there's a way. I think they are moving in that direction, I have to say to their credit, that they're moving in that direction, if for no other reason than the fact that they have to survive, and they have so much bad debt on their books .... (With institutions becoming more aggressive, how do you see them actually dislodging bad managements?) To vote against the resolutions for their re-appointment. (In other words, the AGM is the essential forum?) Absolutely! And if you've got 30 per cent, the other shareholders that come will muster 2 or 3 per cent, the promoter may have 10 or 15 or 20 per cent, you'll be able to knock them out. (Do you see them doing this in the next few years?) That's for you to ask them, I can't comment. (MNC chief executive)

If the institutions were to assert themselves a little more, and start selling companies, start changing managements, when they find underperforming or non-performing managements, I think we will see a sea change. Even today the perception is that the institutions dance to the tune of North Block. That has to change. (MNC director)

I think the public financial institutions hold a sizeable lot of shares in a large number of companies, and, irrespective of performance, they have continued to hold them, in the process destroying value for themselves. I would really say that bringing about a change in promoters and inducting a new set of promoters if the company is not performing is something which would really, to my mind, bring about far better results than any other form of corporate governance you may talk about. (But that presumes a takeover market, which doesn't exist at the moment?) Oh, there's plenty of it! Who says it doesn't exist? (You think there is a market?) There is a market in India and I think it's a question of freeing the institutions from a certain degree of political interference. (Same director, separate interview)

Financial institutions today have a large enough block where they can create serious damage to ... serious nuisance value they can create, by auctioning off their block to the highest bidder. (Former head of equity research)

Finally, and most revealingly:

(I suppose the standard argument there is that the takeover market acts as a sort of discipline on the under-performing companies ...) [Chairman] It will largely happen that way, but right now, of course, to put it politely or impolitely, you use your contacts, political and otherwise, etc., to see that takeover bids ... hostile takeover bids don't succeed, so you go along to the financial institutions, etc., whatnot, put pressure on government, it's happened in the past, it's likely to happen ... this takes its place .... [Jt managing director] the day the government lets loose these institutions, in terms of their control over them, you will certainly see a lot more aggressive activism from them. (Heads of a large business house)

The key issues here, of course, are the government's likely response to the prospect of Indian promoters losing control to more successful rivals, foreign and domestic, as well as the problem of the liquidity of large holdings in the Indian market. Institutional respondents were more sceptical about the chances of finding buyers in a corporate control market. What is clear, however, is that as a market for acquisitions develops in India, aggressive institutional players will have greater leeway in deciding what to do with sub-standard managements, if they have the freedom to make those decisions. Mergers and acquisitions will also speed up consolidation in fragmented industries and add scale to individual businesses.

The SEBI Code is clearly an attempt to replicate the form of the Cadbury Code in a context where the institutional presuppositions for 'self-regulation' are considerably weaker. The most damning criticism of the code in the course of our interviews came from two senior executives of one of the bigger multinationals. One of them argued:

> Before having a Nominations Committee and an Audit Committee, you need integrity of business, because otherwise I fear an even greater danger, that the people that want to be dishonest will do so despite having all the committees, and will in fact find the committees as an excellent subterfuge to get about what they want to do.

The argument here is one of form versus substance. Of course, whether the formal architecture of corporate governance will work towards fulfilling its stated aims (creating a more transparent and accountable business system) will have to depend largely on the rôle of the independent directors. But the Code abstains from prescribing Nomination Committees, espouses a narrow definition of independence, and fails to address the practical issues confronting most non-executives who wish to play a more active role, above all, lack of time. These are serious lacunas and reinforce the critique of a formalist subversion of the whole exercise:

> Actually, my great worry is that as soon as this SEBI Code comes on, there will be wholesale skulduggery with a great degree of aura of the Committee .... (In other words, formalism?) Yes, and everything will carry on and they will feel even more confident—because you will have an 'independent' director, in quotes, who will aid and abet you in all your ventures or adventures. (So, substantially, the degree of accountability won't necessarily be any greater?) It'll be far worse for independent third parties, and far better for promoter-shareholders. ([Second director] ... Our system has been built around the accountability and responsibility of promoters. On that system if you impose today the Audit Committees, the Nominations Committees, and the Complaints Committees or Grievance Committees, the net result would be that promoters' accountability would get substantially diluted.) They'll be delighted! .... All the Indian promoters will be absolutely delighted! (Could you very briefly explain why exactly this would be the case?) I've already explained it to you, Mr. Banaji. The fact is that you will continue to do what you do but you will have the complete shelter and umbrella of protection [from] these Committees, and the committees will be staffed by a whole series of people who are, in quotes, as I said, 'independent'. (It boils down to not having genuinely independent directors, is that

what you're saying?) Well, at the end of the day who will appoint them? Is the Central government going to sit and appoint the independent directors? .... And what can an independent director do? He would comment on what is brought to him, and that is where, at the heart of the issue, are the ethics and integrity inherent within a corporation, because otherwise you can comment on what is there for you to see. If you just .... I personally believe that in India we are totally hung up with form rather than substance.

The essence of this critique, then, is that the Code may lead to a dilution of the promoter's accountability through a process of window-dressing. Of course, there is no doubt that many of the better, more professionally run companies will use the opportunity to upgrade their systems of governance in the ways 'mandatorily recommended', and this will be a step forward. The issue raised by the mainstream of the business system is how the SEBI Code is going to impact the real integrity and culture of business in this country. Prima facie, the response is that the mandatory recommendations encourage corporates to adopt best practices. In reality the various committees may constitute an elaborate façade behind which many promoters continue to govern their businesses without any significant addition to integrity.

In short, a code of best practices will work best when reinforced by a new level of institutional monitoring and certainly should not be seen as a substitute for the role and responsibilities of the institutional shareholders, even if the occasion of a regulatory intervention was seen by many as being used to circumscribe rather than promote their rights. The two governance agendas have to work together in a kind of symbiosis, with much greater input from institutional investors into the drafting of regulations and self-regulatory exercises and a publicly transparent articulation of institutional policy.

Summary and Final Issues

There is now a clear consensus that a substantial reform of governance is necessary in the Indian corporate sector, but much less clarity about the paths along which this should be pursued. Certainly, one of the more interesting developments during the reform period has been the publication of SEBI's Code of Corporate Governance. A major criticism levelled at the code is that it is 'more about methods and procedures than about substance'. The fact that the Committee which drafted the code was headed by Kumar Mangalam Birla was surely intended as a signal to the leading family businesses that it was not the regulator's intention to question the legitimacy of promoter control of businesses, but rather to lay down a framework of rules and principles to encourage such businesses to operate in more 'accountable' and 'transparent' ways. The Code can be read as a response to the global pressures on Indian business to reform the system of governance around stronger, more professional boards, and to upgrade and internationalize its standards of disclosure and financial reporting. But it can also be understood as an attempt to allow Indian businesses to retain control over the sort of adjustments they will sooner or later have to make at *all* these levels.

There was a widespread recognition among our respondents that non-executive directors have been ineffective and do not contribute sufficiently to the exercise of independent supervision. Professionals, the category that in theory best approximates the ideal of the independent director, complain of lack of time, lack of training, 'subconscious' loyalty to management, poor structuring of agendas, and the fear of full liability under the law. The SEBI Code says nothing about any of these issues, apart from its general exhortation that independent directors should 'devote adequate time for meeting, preparation and attendance'. A crucial omission relates to the lack of any sort of recommendation for the introduction of Nomination Committees.

Institutional investors have a major role to play. The single most divisive issue we encountered in the course of this study was the whole question of the nominee director system and whether the public financial institutions should continue to retain a significant presence on boards. We have propounded the arguments for and against. We have suggested on the one hand that the promoter lobby has made a bogey out of a real problem (namely, the rampant nature of insider trading in the Indian market), seeking to use this to immobilize the institutions, while arguing on the other hand that the nominee system needs a complete overhaul, with the institutions relying largely on outside independent directors insofar as they choose to be on the boards of companies. It is also suggested that government control of the financial institutions has been a constraint on their monitoring capacity, in the sense that the *political* influence wielded by promoters has shielded them from accountability, despite the brazen plundering of many companies listed on the stock market. As the institutions evolve a more professional approach to issues of corporate governance, this should mean both less government interference (in the bad sense) and a stronger regulatory push in the direction of a more transparent articulation of institutional policy as well as better corporate governance in the banking institutions themselves.

Finally, a couple of other sets of issues are also worth reflecting on. The Cadbury-style corporate governance initiatives of the 1990s set out to revitalize the board, encourage greater activism by institutional shareholders, and improve disclosure standards. As the cornerstone of the Cadbury model is the board, the first set of issues we should address is Cadbury's belief in the efficacy of the board as a potentially powerful tool of supervision over management. Contrary to the faith placed by Cadbury in the board, however, the evidence seems to point overwhelmingly to the 'limited desire of boards to monitor management'.[31] This may be because non-executive directors share management's culture of limited monitoring.[32] In any case, it is clear from our own study that, even in the best of companies, boards are strongly driven by management. As one director of a Tata company put it, 'I'm not very sure if you can really uncouple the board and the management.' Thus, a first issue here is: *how effective can independent directors be*? And certainly, how effective can they be without a 'power base from which to insist on explanations or to impose appropriate remedies', e.g. a mandate from institutional shareholders who treat them as representatives of the general shareholder interest?[33]

A second set of issues relates to the nominee director system, which is surrounded by considerable confusion at the moment. On the one hand, among the Indian financial institutions, it is the investment institutions and not the term-lending banks that own the largest quantity of shares in private sector companies. On the other hand, the nominee director system evolved as an offshoot of the loan agreements of both term-lending and investment institutions, and the constitution of the panel of nominee directors was hemmed in by restrictions due to reservations from the private sector: for example, companies objected to the appointment of CAs as institutional nominees.[34] It is surely time that these confusions were removed by a clear statement of the rights of institutional investors as well as a clear definition of institutional shareholder policy and strategy.

There are several issues here. First, *how do we make the nominee director system more effective*? Should the institutions continue to appoint their own employees and retired officials as nominees? There is an attractive view that in future they would do best to rely primarily on a panel of independent outside directors who seek appointment at the behest of the institutions and see themselves as representing the general shareholder interest. Such directors could be drawn from a very wide range of backgrounds and may need to be equipped in governance by the requisite level of training.

Second, *should the institutions be prevented from trading in the shares of a company where they have such directors*? The head of one of the more reputable exchanges in the country raised this issue at a workshop in Bombay, stating that the institutions were being immobilized in their governance role by the fear of handling 'inside' information. He argued:

> If we really, all of us, believe that the institutions have a role to play, then we have to resolve this basic issue. If institutions really take interest in the company, can they be

totally prevented from market operations in that company because of the insider-trading problem? In the literature on corporate governance about the role of institutions etc., this point comes up frequently. If institutions cannot operate freely in the market, they will not take interest in corporate governance. They will have a purely free ride. And if a free ride situation develops, I think we as a democratic society will have a serious problem. Are we going to run corporate governance purely through the executives who run the company and shareholders have no say?

Finally, it has been argued that 'institutional investors have the potential to exert significant influence on companies via their voting rights, and this has clear implications for corporate governance'.[35] Moreover, it has been noted that in the US, 'There is a fairly widespread feeling that to vote blindly for management is essentially a violation of Employee Retirement Income Security Act's (ERISA's) requirements and may have a detrimental effect'.[36] So the last issue here is *how can institutional investors (of whatever type) be encouraged to exercise their voting rights and disclose their voting policies*? The SEBI Code is not sufficiently clear on this question.

Notes

1. A.A. Berle and G.C. Means, *The Modern Corporation and Private Property*, New York, 1932.

2. Julian Franks and Colin Mayer, 'Corporate ownership and control in the U.K., Germany and France', in *Studies in International Corporate Finance and Governance Systems*, (ed.) D.H. Chew, New York and Oxford: 1997, 281–96, e.g. 'large-block family ownership is a highly representative feature of the largest enterprises in Germany' (286).

3. E.g., Stijn Claessens et al., *Who Controls East Asian Corporations?*, The World Bank, Policy Research Working Paper 2054.

4. David Blake, *Pension Schemes and Pension Funds in the UK*, Oxford, 1995; OECD, *Institutional Investors in the New Financial Landscape* 1998.

5. B.R. Cheffins, 'Corporate governance in the UK: lessons for Canada', *Canadian Business Law Journal*, 28, 1997, 69 ff., at 82.

6. For these criticisms, see Vanessa Finch, 'Corporate governance and Cadbury: self-regulation and alternatives', *Journal of Business Law*, 1994, 51–62.

7. Gerald S. Backman, 'The new audit committee rules', *Securities Regulation Law Journal*, 28, 2000, 3–14.

8. 'FIs to put corporates who do not behave on notice', *Economic Times*, 9 September 1996.

9. The chairman of one of the largest institutions stated this in so many words: *whereas it is one thing to enjoy the right to appoint a person as a director, it's another to exercise that right.*

10. See John C. Coffee Jr., 'Liquidity versus control: the institutional investor as monitor', 1991, 91 *Columbia Law Review*, 1277, contrasting institutions with

long-term trading strategies (esp. pension funds) and active traders (notably, mutual funds).

11. The italicized responses are culled from approximately 160 interviews conducted between April 1998 and January 2000, mostly in Bombay.

12. Not a taped interview; transcribed from notes.

13. 'Montek wants FIs to take active role in company boards', *Economic Time*, 29 November 1996, reporting the views of S.H. Khan. *Cf.* similar observations in P.S. Subramanyam's speech to the CII workshop on corporate governance held in Bombay on 4 August 1999, arguing strongly that 'boards should be privy to information': author's notes at the workshop and 'UTI chief urges higher quality of disclosures', *Business Standard*; 5 August 1999.

14. For the UK, see G.P. Stapledon, *Institutional Shareholders and Corporate Governance*, Oxford, 1996.

15. Stapledon, *Institutional Shareholders*, 128, argues that in the UK 'most institutions consider it preferable to sell their shareholding where possible rather than undertake an intervention'. He states that 'the possibility of an alternative course of action to intervention is the greatest disincentive to an institution intervening' (129). Counteracting this is the fact that 'greater concentration of shareholding makes monitoring more rational for large shareholders', partly because it 'decreases the benefits from alternative courses of action' (256). In spite of this, however, in the UK at any rate, 'most large fund managers [are] still more likely to sell than intervene when serious managerial problems arise' (257). Stapledon then explains this in terms of what he calls a 'formidable set of obstacles to serious intervention by managers of external funds' (266), which include (a) collective-action and free-rider problems; (b) the way in which the performance of external fund managers is measured; (c) financial constraints; (d) the growing popularity of index funds (on which see Booth and Wrighton, 'Down, but not out', *Institutional Investor*, July 1999, 45–50), and the resulting absence of any significantly overweight holdings; and (e) 'structural conflicts of interest', namely, the fact that fund-management firms may be subsidiaries of merchant-banking companies or 'financial conglomerates' (see 255–66). This discussion is helpful because it shows how much stronger the potential for increased monitoring is in the Indian corporate governance system, insofar as none of the disincentives just listed apply, with the modified exception of a financial constraint, namely, a lack of high-quality or sufficiently qualified personnel to act as non-executive directors, either independently or as nominees. Disqualifying the factor (a) is the historical fact that the FIs have always worked through a coalition of institutional interests, sharing nominees, for example. The second factor, (b), has no bearing because it applies to the external management of funds, which is not the pattern in India. The fourth obstacle is likewise irrelevant since index funds have barely taken off, though the picture could change substantially in the future. Finally, domestic fund-management groups do not operate as part of larger financial conglomerates, so (e) fails to apply. On the other hand, it is probable that most of the disincentives described by Stapledon, and his general argument, *do* apply to the so-called FIIs.

16. The strength of this association was helped by Sir Adrian Cadbury's personal presence at the highly publicized meetings of the CII, where Indian business made its first public statements on the need for companies to take the issue of corporate governance seriously and institute minimal reforms in the functioning of boards and levels of transparency. The meeting received considerable publicity. See 'Corporate governance code proposed', *Business Standard*, 10 September 1996, 'Adrian Cadbury to help CII draft corporate governance', *Business Standard*, 30 October 1996, 'Corporate codes can't be imported, but evolved: Cadbury', *Economic Times*, 27 November 1996, 'Khan wants FIs' role in company boards redefined', *Business Standard*, 29 November 1996.

17. Paul L. Davies and G.P. Stapledon, 'Corporate governance in the United Kingdom', in *Aspects of Corporate Governance*, (eds) M. Issakson and R. Skog, Stockholm, 1994 55–81, esp. 72; also Stapledon, *Institutional Shareholders*, 67, where he states 'compliance by companies with the Cadbury Code is ... a measure—albeit an indirect one—of institutional influence in UK corporate governance.'

18. The author of the draft stated at a CII road show that he was 'pained' by the lack of response to the code. What cannot be said, of course, is that the comparative failure of the CII Code was due to an excess of rigour. Contrary to best practice, even in India, the code rules out the need for nomination committees, disingenuously suggesting that 'securing the services of professionally competent directors' does not necessitate having such committees. It recommends that 30–50 per cent of the board should consist of 'independent, non-executive directors', without advancing any definition of 'independent'. (In our study we found that most managements automatically regard their non-executives as 'independent', so adding this epithet to 'non-executive' does not make a substantial difference unless one has something more in mind.) The code also rules out remuneration committees, although these had been part of the recommendations of the draft report (see 'Companies under fire over selection policy for non-exec directors', *Economic Times*, 3 February 1997, where the draft is said to recommend that 'listed companies should also have remuneration committees consisting of the CEO and three to four non-executive directors'). Most significant, perhaps, is its conception of the role of the 'independent' director as consisting, in part, of 'appreciating the issues put forward by management'. It was left to a company secretary to point out: 'The committee's assessment of the role of such professionally independent directors does not seem to be correctly expressed. The role of the independent directors is to act as a foil to the management .... The use of the words "appreciating the issues put forth by the management" is therefore misplaced and should be read as "independently assessing".' (B.J. Shah, 'The cover and the pages within', *Economic Times*, 16 May 1997.) If, in spite of these obvious concessions, the code failed to inspire the mass of the Indian business community, the experience should prompt us to ask whether it makes sense to conceive of self-regulation purely and simply as an *alternative* to stronger regulatory intervention.

19. See 'Unfair demand', edit., *Economic Times*, 31 May 1999, where the argument runs: 'There seems no reason why institutional shareholders should be treated differently from any other class of shareholders. It is doubtful whether the

CII would demand that other shareholders with, say, 15 per cent of the equity of a company should not seek a place on its board. Why then should such a demand be made from the institutions, especially when all of them put together often hold as much as 40 per cent? *One reason could be that by virtue of their presence on the board, they would be privy to information that they could use to their advantage as players on the stock market. But this would be just as true for all members of the board.*'

20. 'Chinese Walls' are a self-regulatory device to stop the flow of price-sensitive information within a corporate entity through compartmentalization. The most extreme form of such segregation is the creation of separate subsidiaries within the group. See Harry McVea, *Financial Conglomerates and the Chinese Wall: Regulating Conflicts of Interest*, Oxford, 1993.

21. McVea, *Financial Conglomerates*, 133. The local head of a British banking group who argued that 'Chinese Walls are certainly not a myth in well-run companies' described the position in his bank as follows:

> At the working level, our experience is that Chinese Walls work extremely well. At the very senior level—and this could only cover normally in a company not more than ten people—they are (the jargon is) 'above the Wall', because they have to take decisions about what the investment bank can do. And they are people that are aware of the damage that could come to an investment bank if the view in the market was that information which shouldn't be was leaking and the company was taking advantage of it. And it would quickly become apparent because you couldn't: in an institution like this, if you're going to take a position, it's got to be a big position to make any difference, and you can't hide that from the market. So I think in the trading aspects Chinese Walls do work.

22. Again, *cf.* McVea, *Financial Conglomerates*, 125, stating: 'Recently in the USA there have been calls to outline criteria for minimum Wall procedures.'

23. *Cf.* Paul L. Davies, 'Institutional investors in the United Kingdom', in *Contemporary Issues in Corporate Governance*, (eds) D.D. Prentice and P.R.J. Holland, Oxford, 1993, 69–96, esp. 93, arguing that true independence of management 'can only be achieved in a reliable way by making the non-executives dependent on another powerful group within the company'; supported by Stapledon, *Institutional Shareholders*, 145–6, 293.

24. See McVea, *Financial Conglomerates*, 214ff. and 227ff. for each of these assertions.

25. John C. Coffee Jr., 'The future as history: the prospects for global convergence in corporate governance and its implications', 1999, 93, *Northwestern University Law Review*, 641.

26. See T. Baums and E. Wymeersch, (eds), *Shareholder Voting Rights and Practices in Europe and the United States*, Kluwer Law International, 1999.

27. Department of Trade and Industry, *Modern Company Law 5: Developing the Framework*, DTI, March 2000, 86. The full statement reads: 'It is now widely accepted that the right to vote a share has an economic value and that those who hold voting rights on behalf of others have a fiduciary responsibility to consider whether (and if so how) to vote.'

28. See the survey of institutional investors in Dewe Rogerson, *Findings of Perspective India III: General Section*, June, 1998. I am grateful to Rosie Catherwood for permission to cite the general section of this valuable survey.

29. Note Cadbury's recently stated view: 'The drive to produce codes of good governance came from different groups in different countries. In the UK it was the financial sector, in France and India it was companies themselves, in Hong Kong the accountants took the lead, in Spain it was the government, (etc.)', in Sir Adrian Cadbury, 'The corporate governance agenda', *Corporate Governance*, 8, 2000, 7ff., at 9.

30. Coffee, J.C. Jr., Liquidity Versus Control: The Institutional Investor as Monitor, 1991, *Columbia Law Review*, Vol. 1277.

31. Sigurt Vitols et al., *Corporate Governance in Large British and German Companies*, London, 1997, who also note: 'In all companies in both countries...the initiative clearly lies with top management' (at 15).

32. Davies, 'Institutional investors in the United Kingdom', 93f.

33. Parkinson, *Corporate Power*, 194.

34. These remarks are based on a presentation made by Dr R.H. Patil at a workshop organized in Bombay by Queen Elizabeth House, University of Oxford, in September 2000.

35. Chris A. Mallin, 'The voting framework: a comparative study of voting behaviour of institutional investors in the U.S. and the U.K.', *Corporate Governance* 4, 1996, 107ff.

36. Mallin, 'Voting framework', 110, referring to The Employment Retirement Income Security Act, which established fiduciary standards for private pension funds in the US.

7

Corporate Governance and Development in India

A Survey

Sanjoy Mukherjee

INTRODUCTION

Since the start of the most recent wave of economic reforms in India in 1992, a significant amount of attention has been paid to issues of corporate governance (CG). This situation is not unique to India but reflects a trend in the larger global economy, one which has been induced by the interrelated processes of economic liberalization and changes to corporate structures that are commonly referred to as globalization. The basic promise of the new, global economy, of course, is that it will provide all countries increased economic opportunities. For developing countries like India, this promise is embedded in a decades-long discourse on development and the problem of how to best organize the economy to meet the needs of millions of unemployed, underemployed, and unemployable people, many of whom are in constant risk of illness, violence, hunger, and death.

In effect, the recent changes in economic policy, including the emphasis on CG, represent a new development strategy for India and scores of other developing countries. At the base of this new development strategy is a strong emphasis on markets, property rights, and the dynamism of corporations, factors most commonly associated with an Anglo-American model of CG. The underlying presupposition of the reforms has been that if corporations are freed from government restrictions, they can more effectively serve as engines of growth and produce a greater economic development impact (which will then have spin-offs in other areas such as education, health, etc.). Corporations are understood to achieve this development impact unintentionally for the most part. Under conditions of competitive markets, the development impact primarily comes about as a result of corporations pursuing profits for their shareholders (though corporations can, of course, also contribute more directly through social and economic development programmes). As standard economic theory tells us, however, in order for this development impact to occur, corporations need to act in accordance with norms of responsible CG, out of either some moral commitment to such norms, or enlightened self-interest, or market pressures. To the extent that corporations do not abide by such norms, the development impact of their activities will be greatly reduced.

It was in this context that a group of researchers from York University in Toronto and the Management Centre for Human Values of the Indian Institute of Management Calcutta undertook a research project to study the relationship between CG, economic reforms, and development. Their concern was to examine the likely development impact of the recent economic reforms in India as they induce (or fail to induce) changes in the practices and structures of CG in India.

As part of this project, a survey of leading corporations in India was undertaken. The survey was primarily intended to investigate the potential development impact of CG reforms as they occurred through corporations' contributions to economic growth, rather than through social and economic community development programmes (this latter information was available from other sources, such as the surveys by Partners in Change). The focus then was to understand if the economic reforms were inducing corporations to practise more responsible CG and whether such reforms could be sufficient to achieve this goal or whether they would also require some new commitment on the part of corporate leaders and boards to act more responsibly. It is on the results of this survey that this chapter reports.

Designing and Administering the Survey

The basic goals of this survey were two. The first was to investigate whether there were changes occurring that were leading to more responsible CG. More specifically, the concern here was to determine whether boards and senior management had been instituting changes at the firm level on their own accord and/or whether policy changes were inducing them to practise more responsible corporate governance. The second basic goal of the survey was to understand how senior management views the reform process and its impact on CG. Of concern here was how senior management understands what responsible corporate governance entails, whether it thinks government reform efforts have been (or are likely to be) effective and whether there are any significant differences among senior management on these questions. Of particular concern for our team was the understanding by senior management of its own role and that of the board in promoting responsible corporate governance, including whether directors need to show greater moral leadership and responsibility in fulfilling their roles.

In order to fulfil the basic goals outlined above, a two-part survey instrument—a questionnaire—was designed.[1] The first part of the questionnaire was intended to gather information on the profile of the firms under investigation (Questions 1–8) and the nature of their boards (Questions 9–32). The second part was designed to capture information on the views of senior executives about what responsible CG entailed and how it could be effectively promoted (Questions 33–45), as well as about their understanding of the effectiveness of recent policy reforms in promoting more responsible corporate governance (Questions 46–54). The questionnaire contained a total of fifty-four questions, many of which had multiple parts.

The questionnaire was sent out to the entire list of companies on the *Business Today 500* (BT-500), addressed to the CEOs/managing directors. Following the initial mailing, the questionnaire was mailed again to firms that did not respond. Over the course of the year 1999, eighty complete and valid responses were received of which forty-five were from the Indian private sector (IPR), twenty-three were from multinationals (MNC), and twelve were from public sector undertakings (PSU). A series of follow-up interviews was held with a smaller number of MDs/CEOs surveyed, in order to help clarify the issues and delve a little more deeply into their understandings of responsible CG and how it might be more effectively implemented.

Part One of the Survey: Company and Board Information

Section A: Company Profile

The first section of the questionnaire, consisting of eight questions, was designed to gather basic information about key aspects of the company such as ownership structure, areas of activity, and financial health. The basic purpose for collecting such information was to determine whether and how these features of the company correlate with governance practices and structures and with the opinions of the firm's leadership on issues of CG and economic reform.

The first question in the survey asked firms to identify the main sectors of the economy in which they were active. There was a wide distribution of activities across such sectors as automobiles, textiles, paper, chemicals, tyres and tubes, mineral products, basic metals, machinery and equipment, electronics, and food, beverages and tobacco. The second and third questions asked for the size of the paid-up capital of firms and the annual turnover, while the fourth question asked companies to indicate the profit before tax over the years 1995–1997. There were no statistically relevant correlations between answers to these questions and subsequent questions on CG practices and the opinions of senior executives.

Where statistically significant differences between firms would primarily arise was on the basis of the nature of the ownership structure of the firm (Question 7). These differences can best be captured by distinguishing between the Indian private sector (IPRs)—which primarily included large, family-controlled business houses, multinational corporations (MNCs), and public sector undertakings (PSUs). In addition to board practices and the opinions of senior executives, discussed below, differences between these different types of firms were evident with respect to such issues as the tax status and remuneration policies. As Table 7.1 indicates, for example, a significant number of IPRs (22 per cent) were listed as zero-tax companies, while only one MNC and no PSUs belong to this category (Question 6). This question was inserted due to the association of this category with efforts by firms to evade taxes (Mukherjee Reed, 2001). While being in this category does not necessarily mark a firm as a tax evader, given the historic experience of firms in this category, a large number of zero-tax companies might serve as an indicator of potential irregularities in a given sector, irregularities which would undermine overall development impact.

TABLE 7.1 *Tax status of respondents (no. of respondents)*

Status *Firm Type*	*Zero-tax company*	*Not zero-tax company*	*Not disclosed*
IPR	10	34	1
MNC	1	20	2
PSU	0	11	1

Another important difference that emerged between different types of companies relates to remuneration. In particular, as Table 7.2 indicates, there was a very large discrepancy between the income distribution of PSUs vis-à-vis the private sector, with none of the PSUs reporting a ratio of more than 20:1 between the highest- and lowest-paid employee (Question 8). Among the other two sectors, MNCs had the highest propensity towards large salary differentials between the highest- and lowest-paid employees, though the IPRs were not far behind in this regard. It should be noted that these figures only indicate differences in salaries. When non-voucher payments and stock options are added in, the differences would be significantly greater. In contrast to such countries as Japan and Germany, such large income differentials have been common in the United States for some time. More recently, it seems not only has the trend been exacerbated in the US, but has become increasingly prominent in both other developed countries and developing countries as well. To many, such figures are alarming, especially when viewed in the context of issues of board control. The concern here is that the figures do not reflect the performance of senior management as much as they do the ability of such officials to set their own salaries. To the extent that this is the case, the development impact of the firms in question is adversely affected.

TABLE 7.2 *Salary ratios of the highest- and the lowest-paid employees*

Ratio / *Firm Type*	*10:1 or less*	*10:1 to 20:1*	*20:1 to 50:1*	*50:1 to 200:1*
IPR	3%	40%	30%	27%
MNC	0%	33%	22%	35%
PSU	90%	10%	–	–

Section B: Board Characteristics

Questions in this section were intended to generate an understanding of current governance practices among firms operating in India. Of interest here was the degree to which practices differ across different types of firms and the extent to which firms operating in India measure up to accepted international norms and best practices. The questions cover such issues as board composition, the nature of board meetings, and board sub-committees, as well as initiatives to promote more responsible CG.

Board Composition

A key issue in CG is the composition of the board of directors. One of the key roles of any board of directors is to serve as an oversight committee of the firm's management. In the Anglo-American model of CG, the primary responsibility of the board in this regard is to make certain that management runs the firm in the interests of the shareholders (i.e. to minimize the agency problem). In order to fulfil this role it is generally thought that the board must be independent from management (Tricker, 1994).

Determining the independence of the board from management can be a complicated task. One commonly cited criterion of independence is the ratio of external to internal directors on the board. With regard to this issue, our survey (Question 9) indicated a significant difference between IPRs and MNCs on the one hand and PSUs on the other. On PSU boards, executive (whole-time, inside) directors typically comprise more than 50 per cent of the membership, whereas most of the IPRs and MNCs have a majority of non-executive directors on their board. The latter practice is in conformance with the CII recommendations and the new SEBI guidelines. It is, however, an open question as to whether a simple majority of outside directors is an indication of board independence (especially given the influence that managers and minority owners are frequently able to assert over the selection of outside board members).

Another common concern that arises in relationship to the independence of the board has to do with the background of the chairperson or the president of the board. A couple of issues arise here. One has to do with what is termed chairperson-CEO duality (Kesner and Dalton, 1986). It is increasingly being advocated that, in the interest of independence, the chairperson and CEO/MD positions should not be held by a single person and, more specifically, that the chairperson should be an outside director. Our survey (see Table 7.3) found that among IPRs and MNCs this was the practice in 60 per cent or more of the cases (Question 10). In PSUs, by contrast, the incidence of chairperson-CEO duality remained extremely high at 80 per cent. Again, whether or to what degree non-duality is a good indicator of independence is open to question, given that boards can still be effectively controlled by management or minority owners without the use of duality (Kaufman et al., 1995).

TABLE 7.3 *Background of chairperson/president of the board*

Background / *Firm Type*	*MD/CEO*	*Executive Director (other than MD/CEO)*	*Non-Executive Director*
IPR	30%	10%	60%
MNC	28%	6%	66%
PSU	80%	0%	20%

Another concern that arises in relationship to the independence of the board, especially with regard to IPRs, has to do with the relationship of the chairperson and/or MD to the founder of the corporation. While in the West, the agency problem is typically conceived of in terms of a struggle between management and shareholders, in India (and many other developing countries) the primary agency problem has been between minority (but dominant) owners and small shareholders (La Porta et al., 1996). Such dominant minority owners have been able to maintain control of firms through a variety of devices, including stacking boards, the uses of cross-holdings, etc. (Mukherjee Reed, 2001). As Table 7.4 indicates, in 50 per cent of the cases in IPRs the chairperson is or is related to the founder of the company, while in another 45 per cent of the cases the MD/CEO is or is related to the founder of the company (Question 11). This is in contrast to only 16 per cent of the cases in MNCs for the chairperson and another 16 per cent for the MD/CEO. Such figures tend to confirm the continued ability of Indian business families to maintain control, even in the absence of significant shareholdings.[2]

TABLE 7.4 *Frequency of relationship of chairperson/senior executives to the founder*

Related to Founder *Firm Type*	*Chairperson*	*MD/CEO*
IPR	50%	45%
MNC	16%	16%

In addition to the background of the chairperson and the MD/CEO, other potential indicators of agency problems involve the backgrounds of non-executive directors and the ratio of executive to non-executive directors. Of concern here is the possibility that senior management or minority owners might be able to stack the boards in ways that allow them to run the firm in their own interests rather than those of the (majority of) shareholders. Again, our survey found significant differences between different types of firms. With respect to the background of board members, the performance of MNCs seemed to be generally in line with norms designed to ensure the independence of non-executive directors. As Table 7.5 shows, only 16 per cent of the MNCs had non-executives directors who are former employees and 16 per cent had non-executive directors who are related to the chairperson or the senior executive (Question 14). In IPRs, by contrast, the situation was quite different, with the corresponding numbers for former employees and relatives of the chairperson and CEO/MD being 30 per cent and 40 per cent, respectively. To the degree that the independence of such outside directors is subject to question, these boards are obviously compromised.

With respect to the relationship of inside to outside directors, most of the IPRs and MNCs have a greater number of non-executive directors on their board, approximating conformance to the CII recommendations and the SEBI guidelines (Question 9). Here, the biggest contrast is with PSU boards, where typically more than 50 per cent of the board comprised executive (whole-time, inside) directors.

TABLE 7.5 *Background of non-executive directors*

Background *Firm Type*	*Former* *Employee*	*Related to* *Chairperson/MD/CEO*
IPR	30%	40%
MNC	16%	16%

In some non-Anglo-American countries, such as Germany, financial institutions play a major role in corporate governance, both through their direct shareholding and through influence they exert in other ways (e.g. through debt, influence over other stakeholders, etc.). In India, as is well known, financial institutions have also had a formal role in the governance of firms through the institution of the 'nominee director'. Historically, both investment institutions (e.g. UTI, LIC, GIC) and term-lending institutions (ICICI, IDBI, IFCI) have had nominee directors in IPRs, while in PSUs, government agencies have typically had nominee directors (Gupta, 1989). Since the 1992 reforms, the desirability of having nominee directors has increasingly been called into question by many private sector firms (as well as by many, though not all, of the financial agencies nominating such directors). The standard assumption among these firms is that India is adopting an Anglo-American model of governance and in this model strong financial markets make the role of such directors superfluous. Many senior managers in the PSUs would also like to reduce if not eliminate the role of nominee directors, though for different reasons. The primary concern here has been that nominee directors from government agencies often place (unwarranted) political considerations above economic rationality in the decision-making process. Despite this opposition from both the private and public sector, as Table 7.6 indicates, the institution of nominee directors was still very prominent in 1999 (Question 15).

TABLE 7.6 *Percentage of companies with nominee directors (by constituency)*

Constituency *Firm Type*	*Banks and Financial Institutions*	*Employees*	*Government Agencies and Others*
IPR	40%	0%	10%
MNC	33%	0%	0%
PSU	10%	0%	90%

In addition to nominee directors, our survey (Question 16) indicated that most companies (40 per cent of IPRs, 50 per cent of MNCs, and 90 per cent of PSUs) had functional directors, who had special responsibilities for a particular area of the firm's operations (e.g. finance, research and development, personnel, production/operations, marketing, etc.). The lower figures for IPRs may support a common criticism that has been made of such boards about a lack of professionalism (i.e. being dominated by family, friends and associates, or the controlling family rather than highly qualified experts in different fields or of relevance to firm performance).

Board Meetings

An issue that receives much attention in the literature on CG is the nature of board meetings (Lorsch, 1995). If boards are functioning as effective decision-making bodies (and not merely rubber-stamping decisions that have already been made), this activity is likely to be reflected in the organization of board meetings. One area where this might be indicated is in the frequency of board meetings. The CG requirements indicate that meetings should be held at least six times a year. Our survey (Question 17), however, indicates that IPRs and MNCs typically do not meet this frequently (Table 7.7). PSUs have a tendency to meet more regularly, a fact that might be due in part to their larger proportion of inside directors facilitating more frequent meetings. Some might argue, however, that more frequent meetings are not necessarily helpful if they are primarily formal in nature, without clarity of roles, objectives, and agenda.

Other potentially important indicators of responsible and effective decision making in meetings include their length (Question 18) and the opportunity that directors have to provide input, viz., propose agenda items (Question 19) and prepare themselves for the meetings (Question 20). Here, our survey found few differences across the different types of firms. Typically, meetings lasted between two and four hours, directors were solicited to provide agenda items two weeks before the meeting, and they typically received the agenda one to two weeks before the meeting.

TABLE 7.7 *Frequency of board meetings*

Frequency / *Firm Type*	*4–5 times/year*	*6–9 times/year*	*10–12 times/year*
IPR	50%	40%	10%
MNC	90%	10%	0%
PSU	20%	50%	30%

Board-Level Committees

Advocacy of board committee as a means of promoting more responsible CG has grown tremendously in recent years (Cadbury Report, 1992). A frequent correlative is the notion that such committees should be dominated by outside directors. Our survey (Table 7.8) showed that while a significant number of corporations, especially IPRs (75 per cent), had instituted audit committees (Question 21), none of the three sectors had given much attention yet to nomination or remuneration committees (Questions 22 and 23). Even when such committees were present, typically they were not dominated by non-executive directors (Table 7.9). This situation calls into question the likely independence and effectiveness of such committees in protecting shareholder (and stakeholder) interests.

TABLE 7.8 *Existence of audit, nomination, and remuneration committees*

Committee / *Firm Type*	*Audit*	*Nomination*	*Remuneration*
IPR	75%	20%	20%
MNC	50%	–	22%
PSU	40%	–	–

TABLE 7.9 *Percentage of non-executive directors on committees*

Committee / *Firm Type*	*Audit*	*Nomination*	*Remuneration*
IPR	40%	55%	20%
MNC	55%	–	22%
PSU	66%	–	–

In addition to the three mentioned above, various other committees were also common. IPRs frequently report the existence of management committees, finance committees, investment committees, and share transfer committees. Among MNCs and PSUs only share transfer committees were in evidence. The existence of these committees, however, probably indicates concern around issues of market capitalization (especially MNCs and PSUs), rather than any strong commitment to norms of responsible CG.

Other Initiatives to Promote Responsible CG

Another potentially important indicator of good CG is the existence of formal policy, such as codes of ethics, mission statements, and CG statements. Our survey found (Table 7.10) that the vast majority of all types of firms have had formal mission statements for some period of time (Question 26). Our survey also revealed that many firms had recently adopted codes of the ethics as well, especially IPRs (Question 25). Only a small number of firms, however, (20 per cent of IPRs, 16 per cent of MNCs, and no PSUs) had developed a separate statement on CG (Question 27). This relative lack of attention to CG also gets reflected with respect to efforts undertaken to educate board members, e.g. through seminars and workshops on CG issues, either within or outside the organization (Question 30). On an average, only 30–40 per cent of the IPRs and MNCs had undertaken any such initiatives, while among PSUs the figure was only 20 per cent.

TABLE 7.10 *Existence of codes of ethics, mission statements, and CG statements*

Document / *Firm Type*	*Code of Ethics*	*Mission Statement*	*CG Statement*
IPR	65%	75%	20%
MNC	55%	90%	16%
PSU	40%	100%	–

In terms of content, the above statements typically addressed the responsibilities of the firm with respect to a variety of groups and issues (Question 28), including shareholders, local communities, employees, stakeholders, consumers, the environment, etc. Correspondingly, most firms also indicated (Question 29) that they provide financial support for a range of activities such as education, sports, culture, and community development (though not typically scientific research and religions activities). It is interesting to note that while most MNCs explicitly addressed the subject of corrupt practices in their statements, statements from many IPRs and PSUs contained no reference to this issue.

Another important issue for responsible CG involves the ability of shareholders (aside from the AGM) and stakeholders, including employees, to have access to the board and board committees and provide input (e.g. suggestions, grievances, concerns) for their deliberations (Question 31). Here, our survey (Table 7.11) indicated that employees were generally more likely to have such access to the board than either shareholders or other stakeholders. It also showed that PSUs tended to be better in providing access for all three categories of interested parties.

TABLE 7.11 *Existence of processes for providing access to the board*

Access by Firm Type	*Shareholders*	*Employees*	*Other Stakeholders*
IPR	35%	50%	35%
MNC	32%	55%	44%
PSU	40%	100%	60%

One final question in this section (Question 32) attempted to determine whether, since the start of reforms in 1991, there has been an increase in shareholder activism and/or increased efforts by boards to address governance issues, viz., by increasing disclosure norms and the percentage of outside directors. As Table 7.12 indicates, between 40 and 50 per cent of firms in all three categories report increased shareholder activism. Also, 30–35 per cent of IPRs and MNCs have increased the ratio of non-executive to executive directors, while the corresponding figure for PSUs was 50 per cent. (This figure may reflect government requirements more than any initiative on the part of boards to promote responsible CG.) With respect to disclosure, there has been more significant change across all three sectors, with 50–60 per cent of the organizations having increased their norms. While it is not clear from these numbers whether any causality is implied, follow-up interviews with a select number of CEOs/MDs did indicate that stakeholder pressure did contribute to some degree in encouraging boards to initiate changes.

TABLE 7.12 *Recent changes in governance policies and shareholder activism*

Activity Firm Type	*Increased Ratio of Non-executive to Executive Directors*	*Increased Disclosure Norms*	*Increased Shareholder Activity*
IPR	30%	50%	42%
MNC	33%	50%	45%
PSU	50%	60%	50%

PART TWO OF THE SURVEY: VIEWS ON CORPORATE GOVERNANCE

Section C: Understanding of Responsible Corporate Governance

This section was designed to elicit the understandings of MDs/CEOs about what responsible CG entails and how it can be most effectively promoted. In this section, participants were asked a variety of questions on such topics as the roles of directors, the effectiveness of different factors in contributing to responsible CG, the (potential and actual) contributions of different actors to responsible corporate governance, etc. Respondents were asked to rank each factor on an ascending scale of 1 to 5, with 1 being the least important and 5 being the most important.

In Question 36, participants were asked to rank five possible roles of non-executive directors, including: (a) providing expert/professional advice to the MD/CEO on specific matters; (b) acting as watchdogs against managerial abuse; (c) acting as a friend, philosopher, and guide to the MD/CEO; (d) generating pressure to drive the executive management to greater effort; and (e) ensuring social responsibility. As Table 7.13 indicates, across all different firm types, most respondents thought that the most important role of non-executive directors was providing expert/professional advice to the MD/CEO. Among MNCs and PSUs, the most common perception of the least important role was acting as a friend, philosopher, and guide to the MD/CEO, while for IPRs it was acting as watchdogs against managerial abuse.

TABLE 7.13 *Roles of non-executive directors*

Firm Type	*Most Important Role*	*Least Important Role*
IPR	▸ Providing expert/ professional service to the MD/CEO (40%)	▸ Watchdogs against managerial abuse (30%)
MNC	▸ Providing expert/ professional service to the MD/CEO (56%)	▸ Friend, philosopher, and guide to the MD/CEO (28%)
PSU	▸ Providing expert/ professional service to the MD/CEO (44%)	▸ Friend, philosopher, and guide to the MD/CEO (44%)

Question 37 asked respondents to rank the contribution of the following factors in ensuring responsible CG: (a) the personal commitment of the

MD/CEO; (b) company policy (e.g. codes of ethics, mission statements, etc.); (c) regulatory bodies (SEBI, etc.); (d) company law; and e) market pressure. Here, the personal commitment of the MD/CEO was most often seen to be the most important factor, while company law and market pressure were typically viewed as the least important (see Table 7.14).

TABLE 7.14 *Factors contributing to responsible CG*

Firm Type	*Most Important*	*Least Important*
IPR	▸ Personal commitment of CEO/MD (42%)	▸ Company Law (15%) ▸ Market Pressure (25%)
MNC	▸ Personal commitment of CEO/MD (62%)	▸ Market Pressure (50%)
PSU	▸ Personal commitment of CEO/MD (45%)	▸ Company Law (45%)

In Question 38 participants were asked to rank the following in terms of their importance as responsibilities of good CG: (a) maximizing shareholder value; (b) ensuring the long-term financial health of the company; (c) providing fair wages and safe working conditions to employees; (d) ensuring input by employees in company decision making; (e) protecting the interests of other stakeholders in the company (e.g. suppliers, distributors, the local community, etc.); (f) ensuring environment-friendly production/marketing practices; (g) providing consumers with quality products at competitive prices; (h) respecting the spirit of the law with respect to lobbying activities, political donations, tax laws, etc.; and (i) contributing to the socio-economic development of the local community. Here, all three types of firms gave high rankings to ensuring the long-term financial health of the company (see Table 7.15). Interestingly, PSUs also placed stress on providing quality products whereas MNCs gave more emphasis on maximizing shareholder value (with both being emphasized by IPRs). Typically, contributing to socio-economic development and ensuring input by employees were viewed as the least important responsibilities.

In Questions 40 and 41, respondents were asked to rank the potential and actual contribution of the following factors to responsible CG: (a) strategic plans and management policies and practices (e.g. TQM); (b) the corporate culture; (c) regulatory bodies (SEBI, etc.); and (d) company law. Uniformly across the different sectors, corporate culture and strategic plans were seen as making the greatest contribution (both potentially and actually) while regulatory bodies and company law were seen as contributing the least (both potentially and actually).

TABLE 7.15 *Responsibilities of good CG*

Firm Type	*Most Important*	*Least Important*
IPR	▸ providing quality products at competitive prices (90%) ▸ ensuring long-term financial health of the company (88%) ▸ maximizing shareholder value (80%)	▸ contributing to socio-economic development
MNC	▸ ensuring long-term financial health of the company (83%) ▸ maximizing shareholder value (72%)	▸ contributing to socio-economic development ▸ ensuring input by employees in company decision making
PSU	▸ ensuring long-term financial health of the company ▸ providing quality products at competitive prices	▸ ensuring input by employees in company decision making ▸ contributing to socio-economic development

Similarly, in Questions 42 and 43 respondents were asked to rank the potential and actual contribution of the following actors to responsible CG: (a) the MD/CEO; (b) the chairperson of the board; (c) executive (inside) board members; (d) non-executive (outside) board members; (e) nominee directors from financial institutions; (f) institutional investors; and (g) other shareholders. Again there was consistency across the different types of firms with all three giving the highest importance (both potentially and actually) to the commitment of the MD/CEO (followed by the chairperson), while 'other shareholders' were viewed as having the least importance (both potentially and actually). The widest gap between potential and actual frequencies was for non-executive or outside board members, followed by institutional investors—the obvious implication being that these groups could be playing a much bigger role than they currently are.

Question 44 inquired after the (potential) importance of the following tools for promoting responsible CG: (a) an audit committee composed only of non-executive directors; (b) a nomination committee composed only of non-executive directors; (c) a remuneration committee composed only of non-executive directors; (d) a company code of ethics (or mission statement); (e) workshops, seminars, etc., for senior management on business ethics and corporate governance; (f) more attention to issues of corporate governance and business ethics in the educational system (especially management schools); and (g) functional (non-executive) directors with specific responsibilities (e.g. financial, personnel, etc.). Across different types of firms, a company code of ethics was seen as the most important contributor, while the existence of a remuneration committee composed of non-executive directors was seen to be the least important. The second potentially most important tool turned out to be 'more attention to CG issues in management education'.

The last question in this section (Question 45) asked participants to assess the role of the following factors in inhibiting more responsible CG: (a) lack of will (moral leadership) on the part of managing directors to address issues of responsible CG; (b) lack of independent non-executive directors; (c) lack of active shareholder involvement; (d) insufficient liberalization of the capital markets; (e) inadequate revision of company law; (f) lack of cooperation by labour unions; (g) increased competitive pressures accompanying liberalization; (h) general cultural milieu of business; (i) changes in (traditional) societal values in recent years; (j) government interference (e.g. through nominee directors); and (k) lack of attention to issues of values and corporate governance in business schools and universities. Lack of moral leadership on the part of MD was viewed as the most significant inhibitor by PSUs and MNCs and the second most significant by IPRs. The IPRs rated lack of active shareholder involvement as the most inhibiting factor. Increased competitive pressures turned out to be the least inhibiting factor.

Section D: Impressions on Economic Reform and Corporate Governance

The purpose of this section was to survey the opinions of MDs/CEOs on the appropriateness and (potential and actual) impact of policy reforms on CG practices. Respondents were asked to rank the importance of different factors on an ascending scale of 1 to 5, with 1 being the least important and 5 being the most important.

In Question 48, respondents were asked to indicate whether they thought the following three policies were more likely to have a positive or negative impact on responsible CG: (a) share buy-backs; (b) the issuing of non-voting shares; and (c) group resource companies. Across all three sectors, share buy-backs were considered most likely to have a strong negative impact with regard to the promotion of responsible CG, while group resource companies were viewed as likely to have a moderately negative impact and the issuing of non-voting shares only a slight negative impact.

In Question 49, it was asked whether the CG practices of multinationals operating in India had significant 'demonstration effect' on initiating better

CG among other Indian companies. Respondents from all three sectors did not believe that there was any significant 'demonstration effect'.

In Questions 50 and 51, respectively, participants were asked to comment on whether the following SEBI policies were effective and whether they were too lax or too strict: (a) guidelines for disclosure and investor protection; (b) prohibition of insider trading regulations; (c) rules for annual statements of accounts and records; (d) foreign institutional investor regulations; (e) venture capital funds regulations; (f) mutual funds regulations; and (g) substantial acquisition of shares and takeover regulation. Across the three sectors, respondents found that the guidelines for disclosures and investor protection were the least effective, while prohibition of insider trading regulations and mutual funds regulations were considered to be highly effective. Overall, respondents believed that the SEBI guidelines were generally on target (neither too lax nor too stringent), except that among IPRs in particular it was felt that the 'substantial acquisition of shares and takeover regulations' were a bit too lax.

Similar to the previous two, Questions 52 and 53 inquired whether the following set of proposals were potentially important for promoting responsible CG and whether they would be effective if implemented: (a) the requirement of special shareholder approval (e.g. for buy-backs, the offering of shares at a premium, loans to directors, etc.); (b) increased compensation to non-executive directors; (c) increased non-financial disclosures (e.g. relatives of directors, interests of directors, directors' shareholdings, loans, etc.); (d) increased financial disclosures; (e) the requirement of audit committees for large firms; and (f) the provision for (optional) postal ballots. Generally, it was held that the provision for postal ballots and increased compensation to non-executive directors are the most potentially important proposals and could be very effective, while the requirement of audit committees for large firms was considered of least importance.

The final question on the survey (Question 54) asked whether the participants thought there had been significant changes in the following areas since the start of economic reforms in 1992: (a) more independent non-executive directors on boards; (b) a greater use of board committees dominated by non-executive directors (e.g. audit, remuneration, and nomination committees); (c) more extensive disclosure of information due to increased competition in the (primary) capital market; (d) more responsible governance due to more competitive (secondary) capital markets and the possibility of hostile takeovers; (e) increased pressure on Indian firms to be more responsible towards consumers (and investors) due to more competitive product markets (resulting from FDI, trade liberalization, etc.); (f) an emergence of more active and better-educated domestic investors; (g) substantial pressure from (foreign) institutional investors on domestic firms to improve their CG practices; (h) increased competitive pressures have led to a significant professionalization of management among family business houses; (i) a stronger ethical orientation among professional managers. For the most part, CEOs/MDs did not indicate that the above measures had a significant impact on promoting responsible CG, especially such measures as increased disclosure and pressure from institutional investors.

Interpretation and Reflections on the Survey Results

In examining the results of the survey, the discussion can be organized around three basic areas. The *first* of these involves the current state of governance practices. At issue here is the degree to which governance practices in India are approaching best practices and whether progress in this area has been sufficient to ensure the independence of boards and reduce (if not eliminate) agency problems. Our survey has showed that there has been moderate movement on a variety of fronts, with different types of firms more closely approximating best practices in different areas. With respect to such issues of board structures as the ratio of outside to inside directors and chairperson-CEO duality, for example, MNCs seem to be leading the way, followed by IPRs, with PSUs lagging significantly behind. In other areas, such as the existence of audit committees and ethics codes, IPRs seemed to be more advanced, followed by MNCs and PSUs. For their part, PSUs seem to have a better record with regard to the frequency of board meetings and participation by non-executive directors on audit committees. In all of these areas, however, all three types of firms still have far to go in approaching best practices. The levels reached so far, while they represent improvement from the start of the reform period, do not clearly indicate a situation of board independence. This lack of independence is most apparent with respect to outside directors in IPRs.

In the Anglo-American model, the independence of the board is generally considered important because of the conformance roles of the board, which are designed to help eliminate agency problems. While there is a school of thought—stewardship theory (Donaldson and Davis, 1994)—that holds the incidence of agency problems as exaggerated, there is little evidence, in the Indian case at least, to support this view. Historically, agency problems in India have been most noticeable between large (minority) shareholders and small shareholders in IPRs. Agency problems have also been evident in MNCs, but typically these have involved a conflict between management (and foreign shareholders) and domestic (i.e. Indian) shareholders. Insofar as the reform process has not yet engendered truly independent boards, the potential for agency problems remains high (and is likely to be exacerbated by the continuing presence of weak financial markets and an inefficient legal system). Such potential clearly has implications for investor confidence (which remains low in India), which in turn is likely to affect growth rates and the potential development impact.

The *second* key area of investigation involves the views of CEOs/MDs on CG. Our survey has shown that all sectors of the corporate economy in India support an Anglo-American model of corporate governance. This is indicated by their understanding of the primary roles of boards as well as by their rejection of non-Anglo-American elements (e.g. a role for nominee directors). In favouring an Anglo-American model of CG, however, CEOs/MDs have a particular conception of the role of boards in such a model. More specifically, they tend to emphasize the performance roles of boards (e.g. providing expert advice) rather than conformance roles (oversight of management and responsiveness to shareholders). Moreover, when it comes to understanding how responsible CG is best promoted, they tend to minimize the role of financial markets, company law, and the legal system, while emphasizing the importance of CEOs/MDs. In doing this, they are to some degree downplaying the significance of agency problems and/or the prospects for effective public policy solutions to such problems. What they see as more important in this regard is the moral leadership of the CEO/MD and a stronger emphasis on education around such issues.

The views of CEOs/MDs on CG, especially the role of the CEO/MD, are comprehensible, given their own experience in positions of power of being able to make a significant impact on the nature of corporate performance, including the promotion of responsible CG. It is also the case that if CEOs/MDs did consistently demonstrate moral leadership, there would be fewer agency problems and greater investor confidence, which in turn would help stimulate growth and development impact. However, while it is encouraging that the CEOs/MDs who responded placed such importance on moral leadership, there is some concern that they are not entirely representative in their views. In follow-up interviews, most of the CEOs/MDs were quite clear in expressing the view that the goal of more responsible corporate leadership remains an important challenge to the corporate sector in India. Thus, while moral leadership may be the most effective way of ensuring responsible corporate governance when it is present, the prospects for promoting moral development among business leaders remains an open question. What this means is that while it is important to emphasize moral leadership, this cannot be an exclusive focus, not only for pragmatic reasons, but also for moral reasons. Most significant in this regard is the concern that an emphasis on this strategy shifts the balance of risk to the shareholders (and stakeholders). If relatively little emphasis is placed upon company law, making the legal system more effective and strengthening financial markets, the plight of shareholders (and stakeholders) is largely dependent upon the moral character of individual corporate leaders. If these people prove untrustworthy, not only do shareholders (and direct stakeholders) have little or no effective recourse, but the entire population suffers through detrimental effects on growth, employment, etc.

The *final* area of investigation has concerned the views of corporate leaders on the reform process. Generally, the CEOs/MDs surveyed have been supportive of the reforms made by SEBI. They have, however, tended to prefer—and view as more effective—efforts that do not impinge on the autonomy of CEOs/MDs, while doubting the efficacy of efforts that place more constraints (e.g. the establishment of independent audit committees). Again, what is evident here is the belief that CEOs/MDs are the most important actors in promoting responsible CG and that they can, generally, be relied upon to do this. Other factors normally emphasized in the literature (e.g. the role of financial markets, the legal system, shareholder rights, etc.), while not neglected, are downplayed.

In conclusion, then, the survey has shown a distinct preference by the corporate sector for minimal amounts of restrictions on corporate activities (and the role of CEOs/MDs in particular) and a relative lack of emphasis on the role of financial markets and company law in promoting corporate governance. Rather, corporate leaders have shown a strong belief in the ability of CEOs/MDs to promote responsible CG. Till now, however, this potential has been largely unfulfilled (though there are many notable exceptions). If corporations are to realize the potential that many of their senior executives believe exists, they will have to develop a value-based organizational culture with a long-term development perspective. This will require a much greater emphasis on education, training, and development than has been evident in the past. In the meantime, many in society will remain sceptical of such efforts and will understandably want to strengthen other disciplinary tools (e.g. financial markets, company law) in order to protect the interests of shareholders, stakeholders, and society as a whole. The challenge to boards and senior executives, then, is to prove the sceptics wrong and demonstrate that they can provide moral leadership that will make corporations work in the interests of all society—a task that will still probably be best facilitated by the existence of strong financial markets and more stringent legal protection for shareholders and stakeholders.

Notes

1. For detailed survey form, write to Sanjoy Mukherjee at sanjay@iimcal.ac.in or sanjoy_m@hotmail.com.

2. This is, of course, not to say that there are not agency problems in MNCs. Here, however, the agency problems are more typically between management and shareholders.

References

Cadbury Report (1992). *The Financial Aspects of Corporate Governance*, London: Gee and Co. Ltd.

Donaldson, L. and J.H. Davis (1994). 'Stewardship Theory and Agency Theory: CEO Governance and Shareholder Returns', In *International Corporate Governance: Text, Readings and Cases*, (ed.) R. Tricker, NY: Prentice Hall, pp. 124–34.

Gupta, L.C. (1989). *Corporate Boards and Nominee Directors*, Delhi: Oxford University Press.

Kaufman, A., L. Zacharias, and M. Karson (1995). *Managers vs Owners: The Struggle for Corporate Control in American Democracy*, New York: Oxford University Press.

Kesner, I.F. and D.R. Dalton (1986). 'Boards of Directors and the Checks and (Im)Balances of Corporate Governance', *Business Horizons*, 29 (5), pp. 17–24.

La Porta, R., F. Lopez-de-Silanes, and A. Shleifer (1996). 'Law and Finance', National Bureau of Economic Research Inc., Working Paper 5661.

Lorsch, J.W. (1995). *Pawns or Potentates? The Reality of American Corporate Boards*, Boston: Harvard Business School Press.

Mukherjee-Reed, A. (2001). *Perspectives on the Indian Corporate Economy: Exploring the Paradox of Profits*, London: Palgrave.

Tricker, R. (ed.) (1994). *International Corporate Governance: Text, Readings and Cases*, NY: Prentice Hall.

8

Corporate Governance Reforms and Corporate Sector Development in India

Jayati Sarkar and
Subrata Sarkar

INTRODUCTION

In recent years the issue of corporate governance reforms and the design of appropriate governance mechanisms that aid corporate sector development have become important subjects of academic research and policy discourse in both developed and developing countries. The increasing importance of governance mechanisms comes from a large body of empirical and theoretical research that highlights the significant impact an economy's corporate governance system can have on the profitability and growth of corporations. The recent east Asian crisis is a case in point where the existing ownership structure and corporate governance system has been considered to be 'one of the main culprits for the crisis and the weak performance of corporations' (Claessens et al., 1999).[1]

Corporate governance systems are considered to influence output and investment decisions of firms through several channels that include ownership and control structure, development of financial intermediaries and capital market, corporate financing and investment patterns, investor protection and creditor rights, and the like. All these are likely to impact on the willingness of investors to finance companies and hence on the price at which capital is provided to the firm.

The recognition of the importance of corporate governance for development has concomitantly focused attention on the issue of reforming extant governance systems. This has been the case not only with respect to many transition and emerging economies with relatively underdeveloped governance systems, but also with respect to several developed countries with substantially matured governance institutions. For instance, calls for corporate governance reforms have been 'reverberating' throughout Europe, one of the sources of reform pressure being the ongoing integration of European capital markets and the perception that differences in corporate governance patterns inhibit investors from taking advantage of a single market (Berglof, 2000).

In emerging economies like India, the importance of undertaking corporate governance reforms has especially dawned in the light of the increasing exposure of these economies to domestic and international competition after decades of protectionism and regulation of corporate sector activities. In spite of the existence of important governance institutions for a long time, corporate governance was not considered an important policy issue in India, until the adoption of the structural adjustment and globalization programme by the government in July 1991. Since then, the increasing integration of the Indian economy with the global economy has led to the explicit realization that good corporate governance was absolutely essential for Indian companies to survive in the deregulated and liberalized environment.

Evidence of the integration of the Indian economy in general, and the Indian corporate sector in particular is apparent from several statistics presented in Tables 8.1, 8.2, and 8.3. Such integration has occurred in terms of the proportion of FDI flows to GDP, portfolio equity flows, share of foreign trade in GDP, value of cross-border mergers and acquisitions, and number of foreign collaborations (Table 8.1), as well as in terms of increasing involvement of foreign entities in corporate control and governance (Table 8.2). Additionally, Indian companies have been allowed to seek listing in international stock exchanges and also raise funds abroad through American Depository Receipts (ADRs) and Global Depository Receipts (GDRs) (Table 8.3).

The initiatives for governance reforms in India have come from both the government as part of a macro-strategy of building industrial capabilities of domestic firms, and the companies themselves at the micro level to compete effectively with their foreign counterparts. In subsequent years, reforms in governance in turn have furthered the process of integration of India with the world economy that in turn has spurred more policy changes. One example of this phenomenon of mutual reinforcement is the initial relaxation of controls on foreign direct investment which led to a sharp inflow and increase of foreign investment, triggering off the need for incorporating best practices

TABLE 8.1 *Some indicators of globalization of the Indian economy: 1990–91 to 1997–98*

	1990–91	*1991–92*	*1992–93*	*1993–94*	*1994–95*	*1995–96*	*1996–97*	*1997–98*
Cross-Merger and Acquisitions Sales ($M)								
(i) Majority[1]	52	13	105	327	148	45	194	782
(ii) Total	213	262	1854	2880	3311	3768	2855	1954
Total no. of foreign collaborations	976	1520	1476	1854	2337	2303	2335	NA
Total no. of collaborations with foreign financial participation	298	736	762	1054	1355	1555	1690	NA
FDI inflows ($M)	97	129	315	586	1314	2144	2821	3557
As percentage of GDP	0.03	0.06	0.14	0.21	0.41	0.61	0.72	0.90
Portfolio equity flows ($M)	6	4	244	3567	3824	2748	3312	1828
FDI inflows as percentage of gross fixed capital formation	0.14	0.28	0.63	1.00	1.87	2.53	3.23	4.09
Exports ($M)	18145	17865	18537	22238	26331	31795	33470	35006
Imports ($M)	24073	19411	21882	23306	28654	36675	39132	41485
Total Foreign Trade ($M)	42218	37276	40419	45544	54985	68470	72602	76491
Total Foreign Trade/GNP (%)	14.14	17.80	18.05	16.29	16.77	19.33	18.48	19.32
GDP at market prices ($M)	298514	209439	223959	279551	327912	354162	392825	395836
Exchange Rate (Rs/US $)	17.94	29.45	31.52	31.37	31.65	34.39	35.89	39.50

[1]Majority refers to business combinations of which the investor acquires more than 50 per cent voting securities of the resulting business. Exchange rates for 1990–1 and 1991–2 are the averages for the entire financial year. Exchange rates for other years, are March averages.

Source: World Investment Report 1999, UNCTAD.

TABLE 8.2 *Number of financial collaborations with India by top five countries in various equity ranges: 1997*

Name of the country collaborating	*Total no. of collaborations*	*No. of collaborations according to percentage of equity of the company held by the collaborator*					
		0–25%	26–39%	40–49%	50–59%	60–74%	> 74%
USA	310	23	20	49	49	22	147
Germany	162	13	10	32	39	16	52
UK	131	8	5	26	23	10	59
Mauritius	129	15	11	31	18	17	37
Japan	88	12	10	23	14	9	20
Total	820	71	56	161	143	74	315

Source: Computed from the Handbook of Industrial Policy Statistics, Government of India, 1998.

in securities-market regulations and other measures of investor protection. This in turn further encouraged additional foreign investment and sustained the process of globalization. Attempts by Indian companies to list in American and European stock exchanges and to conform to international best practices in accounting norms and corporate governance in order to qualify for listing, serve as other examples of how globalization has brought about greater integration of corporate practices.

TABLE 8.3 *Euro issues and FII investments: 1992–93 to 1999–2000*

Year	*Number of Euro Issues*	*Quantum of Euro Issues (Rs Crore)*	*Net Investments by FIIs (Rs Crore)*
1992–93	2	702.32	4.27
1993–94	27	7897.82	5444.58
1994–95	31	6743.23	4776.59
1995–96	5	1296.69	6735.01
1996–97	16	5594.27	7444.07
1998–99	7	4009.46	5972.96
1999–2000	3	1147.78	–806.56

Note: FIIs were allowed to invest in the Indian securities market from September1992. Their investments include both debt and equity.

Source: Handbook of Statistics of Indian Economy, 1999, Reserve Bank of India.

This chapter discusses the important corporate governance reform initiatives in India and analyses some of the significant developments in the Indian corporate sector. To put the analysis in perspective, the chapter draws upon the burgeoning theoretical and empirical literature on the channels through which corporate governance reforms can impact overall corporate sector development and development of the economy at large. The chapter is organized as follows. Initially, we discuss the corporate governance system and the quality of governance institutions in India in a comparative institutional perspective. Next comes an outline of the important corporate governance reform initiatives taken in India in the 1990s. Then we analyse some major developments in the corporate sector in the 1990s in the light of the governance reforms, focusing specifically on emerging corporate financing patterns, ownership and control structures, changing corporate strategies, the functioning of board of directors, and the role of large shareholders in corporate governance. Finally comes the conclusion.

Corporate Governance in India: A Comparative Perspective

The Governance System in India

In the literature one can identify several institutional parameters around which governance systems can be defined. One distinction between governance systems is made in terms of the traditional market-based/bank-based dichotomy, with the former represented by the Anglo-Saxon system of the US and the UK and the latter by the systems of Japan and Continental Europe, particularly Germany. The Anglo-Saxon 'market-based' system is generally characterized by the existence of a widely dispersed shareholder base, liquid capital market, and a fairly vigorous market for corporate control. In this governance system, the securities market occupies the centre stage in terms of channelling society's savings to firms, exerting corporate control, and easing risk management. In this system, underperforming management is disciplined through the 'exit' option—shareholders dissatisfied with company performance offload their shares in the securities market making the company susceptible to a takeover.

In contrast to market-based governance, the bank-based system is characterized by less liquid markets, relatively inactive takeover market, and a greater concentration of shareholder power with banks, non-financial corporations, and the government. Under this system, banks play a leading role in mobilizing savings, allocating capital, overseeing investment decisions of corporate managers, and providing risk management (Demirguc-Kunt and Levine, 1995). Here, the 'voice' option gains precedence over the exit option, with the various stakeholders trying to forge long-term relationships with management and for whom 'collective achievement' and 'consensus' are the keys to long-term success.

While cross-country comparisons are somewhat difficult given that the reporting of equity ownership data is not uniform, some broad comparisons with the two main prototype governance systems suggest that the Indian corporate governance system defined from the perspective of equity ownership of companies is by and large a hybrid of the 'outsider systems' of the US and UK, and the 'insider systems' of continental Europe and Japan (Table 8.4). Equity holdings by non-financial corporations, which are primarily inter-corporate cross-holdings, are much higher in India than in the US and the UK and are more comparable to that in Germany and Japan. However, at the same time, the participation of the small investor in corporate equity is at comparable levels with the US, with India having the largest number of listed companies in the world. In addition, while different types of financial institutions separately hold much smaller blocks of equity in comparison to that in other countries, given that nearly all of these institutions are government controlled and fall under the aegis of the ministry of finance, together they form a much bigger homogeneous block in India than that in other countries. The participation of institutional investors like mutual funds and insurance companies which are nearly fully owned by the government in India is also significant, and comparable to the extent of their participation in Japan and Germany, but much less in scope than that in the US and the UK.

TABLE 8.4 *Characteristics of equity ownership and shareholder rights in India and select countries*

	India[1] *(1996)*	*US (1993)*	*UK (1993)*	*Germany (1993)*	*Japan (1993)*
I. Distribution of shareholding (%)					
(i) All corporations	33.6	46	64	68	69
(ii) Financial institutions	9.8	46	62	29	45
– Banks/lending institutions	3.6[2]	–	1	14	22
– Insurance companies	2.1	5	17	7	17
– Pension/investment funds	–	26	34	–	1
– Mutual funds	4.1	11	7	8	3
– Others	–	4	3	–	1
(iii) Non-financial corporations	23.8	–	2	39	24
(iv) Individuals	40.9[3]	49	18	17	24
(v) Foreign	10.1	5	16	12	7
(vi) Government	–	–	1	4	1
(vii) Others	15.4[4]	–	2	–	–
(viii) Ownership by three top shareholders in the ten largest non-financial firms (%)					
– Mean	40	20	19	48	18
– Median	43	12	15	50	13

(Contd)

	India[1] (1996)	US (1993)	UK (1993)	Germany (1993)	Japan (1993)
II. Anti-director rights of minority shareholders[a] (scale of 6)	5	5	5	1	4
III. Per capita GNP ($) (1993)	300	24,740	18,060	23,560	31,490

Notes: [a] Anti-director rights measure how strongly the legal system protects minority shareholders against dominant shareholders in the corporate decision-making process, including the voting process. For details, see from La Porta et al. (1998).

1. Data based on the study sample of 1567 companies from the Prowess database.
2. Includes commercial banks, government owned/promoted term-lending institutions, and financial corporations.
3. Individuals include top-fifty shareholders. Others include shares held by directors and relatives.

Sources: Data on Distribution of shareholding (i)–(vii) for US, UK, Germany, and Japan from OECD, 1995. Data on I (viii), II, and III for all five countries pertain to the year 1993 and are from La Porta et al. (1998), Table 7 and Table 5. Table reproduced from Table 2 in Sarkar and Sarkar (2000).

The relative importance of stock market versus banks in corporate governance in India can also be evaluated from a corporate finance perspective at the macro level by examining the relative importance of bank vis-à-vis equity markets in corporate sector financing over the years. The trends in financial development and the evolving financial structure in India since the 1990s are presented in Table 8.5. This table is constructed following the work of Demirguc-Kunt and Levine (1999), who document the relationship between financial structure and economic development (as captured by per capita GDP) using a large cross-section data for 150 countries.[2] In terms of financial structure, the banking sector in India is relatively more important than the stock market as judged by its relative size, but the latter's presence is not insignificant. According to the classification by Demirguc-Kunt and Levine (1999) India's financial structure can be classified as underdeveloped and still largely bank-based.[3] The relative size of the banking sector decreased in the initial years of the reforms programme, but its importance has again increased in the later years. In terms of activity, however, there is a clear declining trend in the activity of the banking sector relative to that of the stock market during almost the entire period. Analysis of efficiency indicators, namely, the turnover ratio for the stock market and the net interest margin for the banking sector, also suggest that the efficiency of the banking system relative to the stock market has not shown much improvement since the initiation of the reforms.

An issue that is important in a discussion of governance reforms and its development implications is whether a particular governance system is superior to others in promoting growth. While some have argued theoretically the superiority of a bank-based governance system over a market-based one, there are arguments to the contrary too.[4] While, the bank versus market dichotomy has been the conventional perspective in governance debates, in recent years, however, two other perspectives have emerged in the literature that depart from such a dichotomy and instead focus attention on the broader institutional framework within which corporate governance systems are themselves embedded. One of these is the 'financial services view' (Levine, 1997), which stresses the need to create an enabling environment for both banks and markets to provide sound financial services at different stages of development. Thus, this view does not consider markets and banks necessarily as alternative governance institutions, but complementary ones. At the same time there is potential for competition between the banks and the securities market for corporate control, with the latter, by offering alternative means of financing investment, possibly reducing the harmful effects of excessive bank power (Stulz, 2000). The other analytical perspective in evaluating different governance systems, is the 'legal view' articulated by La Porta et al. (2000a) which 'unconditionally rejects the bank based versus market based debate' and argues that since finance is a set of contracts, the effectiveness with which such contracts can be defined is of paramount importance. Thus, it is the legal system that would determine the financial and governance structure, and that the century-long debate concerning bank-based and market-based financial systems is 'analytically vacuous'. Recent empirical evidence based on a cross-section of forty-eight developed and developing countries with widely varying financial structures and legal systems finds no support for either the bank-based or market-based financial and governance systems but seems to confirm the financial services and legal view (Demirguc-Kunt and Levine, 1999; Levine 2000).

The Quality of Governance

The quality of corporate governance institutions in India relative to some developed and developing countries is presented in Table 8.6. This table is compiled from a series of research papers by La Porta, et al. (1998, 1999a, 1999b, and 2000b), and shows the relative ranking of countries in terms of important elements of corporate governance system, namely, the extent of shareholder protection, creditor rights, and the efficiency of legal institutions.

Table 8.6 shows India to be very much at par with developed countries, especially with the English-law countries, with respect to the rights of minority investors and creditors. What is especially interesting from the point of view of minority investors is the comparable rank of India with that of the US and the UK with respect to anti-directors rights and oppressed minority mechanisms. With regard to creditor rights, India is at par with the UK and has more protective laws in the books than either the US, Japan, or Germany. The fact that many of the important governance institutions are at par with other common-law countries is not surprising given the long history of governance institutions in India dating back to the mid-nineteenth century and the fact that most of the related legislations were fashioned around the English law.

The relatively favourable ranking of Indian governance indicators seems to be inconsistent with the general perception in the country that minority investor rights as well as creditor rights are weak in the country. It is also hypothesized that the concentration of ownership and control that one finds in countries like India has been mainly in response to the existence of weak minority investor rights (La Porta et al., 1999a). However, the inconsistency can be resolved by noting that while important investor protection legislations are in paper, their implementation leaves much to be desired relative to international best practices. As is evident from Table 8.6, what is clearly lacking is in the area of implementation of governance regulations as is evident from the low score that India has with respect to the rule of law, corruption, risk of expropriation, and weak accounting standards.

Corporate Governance Reforms in India

Corporate governance reforms in India have involved a wide range of institutional and corporate initiatives that include (i) improving the functioning of capital markets, (ii) ensuring more effective protection of minority investors through promoting greater transparency of operations and higher standards of information disclosure, (iii) reforming company board structure and operational systems to make the board of directors more accountable to the shareholders, (iv) reforming governance mechanisms of financial institutions, and the like. Corporate governance initiatives have come from the government via government legislations involving several amendments of the Companies Act, 1956; from the organizations regulating capital market, notably the Securities and Exchange Board of India (SEBI), in the form of statutory regulations; and through self-disciplining and voluntary initiatives taken by the industry chambers and business associations, professional bodies, and the companies themselves.

TABLE 8.5 *Trends in financial development and financial structure*

	1990–91	*1991–92*	*1992–93*	*1993–94*	*1994–95*	*1995–96*	*1996–97*	*1997–98*
Stock Market Development								
Market Capitalization to GDP	0.206	0.574	0.324	0.456	0.456	0.470	0.346	0.377
Value Traded to GDP	0.081	0.098	0.098	0.232	0.157	0.187	0.458	0.581
Turnover Ratio	0.395	0.171	0.301	0.509	0.344	0.397	1.323	1.541
Banking Sector Development								
Bank Assets to GDP	0.645	0.677	0.681	0.653	0.661	0.631	0.616	0.649
Bank Credit to GDP	0.209	0.196	0.206	0.175	0.192	0.201	0.192	0.199
Net Interest Margin	0.026	0.028	0.021	0.023	0.026	0.028	0.029	0.027
Overall Financial Development								
Bank Assets plus Market Capitalization to GDP	0.851	1.251	1.005	1.109	1.117	1.101	0.962	1.027
Bank Credit plus Value Traded to GDP	0.290	0.294	0.304	0.407	0.349	0.387	0.650	0.780
Financial Structure								
Bank Assets to Market Capitalization	3.131	1.179	2.101	1.430	1.450	1.343	1.777	1.721
Bank Credit to Value Traded	2.580	2.000	2.102	0.754	1.223	1.074	0.419	0.343

Source: Constructed using data from Reserve Bank of India Report on Trends and Progress in Banking, 1998-99; Reserve Bank of India Report on Currency and Finance, 1998-99; and Emerging Stock Markets Factbook, IFC, 1999.

Notes: Bank assets and net interest margin are calculated using data on both scheduled commercial banks and all-India financial institutions. Bank credit includes credit by scheduled commercial banks only.

TABLE 8.6 *A comparative assessment of the quality of corporate governance institutions in India vis-à-vis major developed countries in the 1990s*

Country	*Legal Origin*	*Legal Variables*					*Variables Representing Shareholder Protection**							*Variables Representing Creditor Rigths***				
		Efficiency of the Judicial System (1)	*Rule of Law (2)*	*Corruption (3)*	*Risk of Expropriation (4)*	*Accounting Standards (Rating) (5)*	*One-Share, One Vote*	*Proxy by Mail Allowed*	*Shares Not Blocked before Meeting*	*Cumulative Voting*	*Oppressed Minorities Mechanism*	*Anti-Director Rights (6)*	*Mandatory Dividend*	*Restrictions for Going into Reorganization*	*No Automatic Stay on Secured Assets*	*Secured Creditors First*	*Management Does not Stay in Reorganizations*	*Creditors Rights (7)*
US	English Origin	10.00	10.00	8.63	9.98	71	0	1	1	1	1	5	0	0	0	1	0	1
UK	English Origin	10.00	8.57	9.10	9.71	78	0	1	1	0	1	5	0	1	1	1	1	4
Germany	German Origin	9.00	9.23	8.93	9.90	62	0	0	0	0	0	1	0	1	1	1	0	3
Japan	German Origin	10.00	8.98	8.52	9.67	65	1	0	1	1	1	4	0	0	0	1	1	2
India	English Origin	8.00	4.17	4.58	7.75	57	1	0	1	1	1	5	0	1	1	1	1	4

1. Scale from 0 to 10, with lower scores showing lower efficiency levels.
2. Scale from 0 to 10, with lower scores for less tradition of law and order.
3. Scale from 0 to 10, with lower scores for higher levels of corruption.
4. Scale from 0 to 10, with lower scores for higher risks.
5. The score is given on a scale ranging from 0 to 100, with higher scores showing more stringent accounting standards.
6. The index ranges from 0 to 6, with higher values signifying stronger 'Anti-director Rights'.
7. The index ranges from 0 to 4, with higher values signifying stronger 'Creditor Rights'.

* Except for 'Anti-Director Rights', a value of 1 shows the presence of the relevant feature (i.e. implying that investor protection is in the law).

** Except for 'Creditor Rights', a value of 1 shows the presence of the relevant feature (i.e. implying that creditor protection is in the law).

Compiled From:

1. La Porta, R., F. Lopez-de-Silanes, A. Shleifer, R. Vishny, (1999a). 'Corporate Ownership Around the World', *Journal of Finance*, 54, 471–517.
2. La Porta, R., F. Lopez-de-Silanes, A. Shleifer, R. Vishny, (1998). 'Law and Finance', *Journal of Political Economy*, 106, 1113–1155.
3. La Porta, R., F. Lopez-de-Silanes, A. Shleifer, R. Vishny, (1999). 'The Quality of Government', *Journal of Law, Economics and Organization*, 15, 222–279.
4. La Porta, R., F. Lopez-de-Silanes, A. Shleifer, R. Vishny, (2000b). 'Agency Problems and Dividend Policies Around the World', *Journal of Finance*, 55, 1–33.

Amendments to the Companies Act, 1956

With regard to legislative initiatives, the Government of India has sought to amend from time to time, the Companies Act, 1956, to ensure that the interests of shareholders and creditors continue to be protected in a changing economic environment. Several amendments have taken place in the 1990s, with the most recent ones coming through the Companies (Amendment) Act, 2000 and the Companies (Amendment) Act, 2001. These amendments have been introduced, while a substantially revised version of the existing Companies Act, 1956, namely the Companies Bill, 1997, is awaiting the approval of the Parliament. The Bill seeks to streamline the existing Act by reducing 658 sections and fifteen schedules to 458 sections and three schedules, and ensuring that the new provisions accord flexibility, greater disclosure and self-regulation of Indian companies operating currently in a liberalized, fast changing, and highly competitive environment.

Some of the most recent amendments that have important implications for corporate governance and corporate sector development are listed below:

The Companies (Amendment) Act, 1999

Buy Back of Shares: Subject to certain provisions, a company may purchase its own shares or other specified securities (hereinafter referred to as "buy-back") out of (i) its free reserves (ii) the securities premium account or (iii) the proceeds of any shares or other specified securities.

Issue of sweat equity shares: Notwithstanding anything contained in Section 79, a company may issue sweat equity shares (equity shares issued by the company to employees or directors at a discount or for consideration other than cash for specialized services provided) of a class of shares already issued subject to certain conditions

Establishment of Investor Education and Protection Fund

Liberalization of Inter-corporate loans and investment norms

The Companies (Amendment) Act, 2000

Penalties increased by almost ten times for non-compliances.

The offer of any securities to more than 50 people in one financial year will be treated as a public offer. Provision not applicable to NBFC's and public financial institutions.

Equity capital of the company can be now issued either with voting rights or with differential rights as regards to dividends, voting rights or otherwise.

The concept of postal ballot introduced to pass resolution instead of transacting the business in general meeting subject to certain provisions.

Board Report should include Directors Responsibility Statement requiring the disclosure of various information and making the directors responsible for the disclosures.

The observations or comments of the auditors which has adverse effect on the functioning of a company should be written in thick type or in italics in the Auditors' Report (Section 227).

A public limited company which has paid up capital of at least Rs 5 crore and at least 1000 small shareholders should have at least one director elected by such small shareholders.

The maximum number of companies in which a person can be a director has been reduced from 20 to 15.

The Companies (Amendment) Act, 2001

Liberalization of buy-back norms: If buy-back was to the extent of or less than 10 per cent of the total paid up capital and free reserves of the company and such buy-back had been authorized by means of a resolution passed at its board meeting, such buy-back shall not require special resolution. Further, the Act seeks to provide that no offer of buy-back shall be made within a period of one year reckoned from the date of the preceeding offer of buy-back. It further seeks to reduce the time limit from two years to six months for issue of the same kind of shares.

These include, among others, buy-back of securities, relaxation in norms relating to inter-corporate loans and investments, setting up of investor education and protection fund, compliance of accounting standards in preparation of annual accounts, provision for postal ballot, audit committee, directors responsibility statement, secretarial compliance certificate, a tenfold increase of fines, and the option for election of a director by small shareholders.

Capital Market Regulations

As in most countries, the capital market regulating agency, which in India is the Securities and Exchange Board of India (SEBI), has been responsible for a large proportion of the initiatives aimed at ensuring better governance by shareholders and in developing an efficient capital market. The key measures instituted by the SEBI in this respect have been the introduction of disclosure norms for issuers, strict entry point criteria for public offers, automation of all stock exchanges, modernization of market microstructures, and strengthening regulations for mergers and takeovers. Various legislations enacted in recent years in this connection are listed below:

1. SEBI Act, 1992
2. SEBI (Merchant Bankers) Regulations, 1992
3. SEBI (Stock brokers and sub-brokers) Rules, 1992
4. SEBI (Insider Trading) Regulations, 1992
5. SEBI (Registrars to an Issue and Share Transfer Agents) Rules, 1993
6. SEBI (Underwriters) Regulations, 1993

7. SEBI (Portfolio Managers) Rules, 1993
8. SEBI (Appeal to Central Government) Rules, 1993
9. SEBI (Bankers to an Issue) Regulations, 1994
10. SEBI (Foreign Institutional Investors Regulations), 1995
11. SEBI (Prohibition of Fraudulent and Unfair Trade Practices Relating to Securities Market) Regulations, 1995
12. SEBI Appellate Tribunal (Procedure) Rules, 1995
13. Delegation of Powers to SEBI under The Securities Contracts (Regulation) Act, 1956, Notification, 1996
14. The Depositories Act, 1996
15. SEBI (Depositories and Participants) Regulations, 1996
16. SEBI (Custodian of Securities) Regulations, 1996
17. SEBI (Mutual Funds) Regulations, 1996
18. SEBI (Substantial Acquisition of Shares and Takeovers) Regulations, 1997
19. SEBI (Venture Capital Funds) Regulations, 1996
20. SEBI (Buy-back of Securities) Regulations, 1998
21. Employee Stock Option Scheme and Employee Stock Purchase Scheme Guidelines, 1999
22. SEBI (Collective Investment Schemes) Regulations, 1999
23. SEBI (Credit Rating Agencies) Regulations, 1999
24. SEBI (Foreign Venture Capital Investor) Regulations, 2000

Source: www.sebi.com

While all the various legislations enforced by the SEBI have important implications for the functioning and development of the corporate sector, some of these have quite far-reaching consequences for corporate governance. Among these are the SEBI (Substantial Acquisition of Shares and Takeovers) Regulations of 1997, the SEBI (Buy-back of Securities) Regulations of 1998, the Employee Stock Option Scheme and Employee Stock Purchase Scheme Guidelines of 1999, and the implementation of the recommendations of the Kumar Mangalam Birla Committee on Corporate Governance set up by the SEBI in 1999.

The takeover regulations of 1997 have sought to ensure greater transparency in the market for corporate control and to facilitate the process by which an underperforming management can be replaced through takeovers. Prior to the economic reforms, regulatory bodies like the Monopolies and Restrictive Trade Practices (MRTP) Commission placed several hurdles in the way of takeovers, mergers, and amalgamations. Moreover, in the event of a hostile bid for a company, incumbent managers had the power to refuse transfer of shares to the bidder if the transfer was against the interests of the company or against public interest. Current regulations, by making disclosure of substantial acquisitions mandatory, have sought to ensure that the equity of a firm does not covertly change hands between the acquirer and the promoters. Moreover, the rights of existing management to withhold transfer of shares have been withdrawn, although under Sections 250 and 409 of the Companies Act, target companies can shelter against raiders if the proposed transfer prejudicially affects the interests of the company.

Governance Initiatives by Banks and Financial Institutions

An integral aspect of financial sector reforms in India has been the banking sector reforms. Banks, both scheduled commercial and development financial institutions, have traditionally been an important source of working finance and investment capital for the Indian companies. Some of the reforms, such as interest rate and entry deregulation, the contraction of subsidized and captive sources of funds, and encouraging banks to access the equity market through partial divestment of government equity (see Sen and Vaidya, 1998 for details) have subjected banking institutions to the pressures of the market and created incentives for them to become more profitable and efficient. The divestment of government equity from Industrial Development Bank of India (IDBI) and the Industrial Finance Corporation of India (IFCI), for example, have implied that these Development Financial Institutions (DFIs) themselves needed to perform well in order to be able to raise funds from the market.[5] The performance of the DFIs in turn is largely a function of the quality of their loan portfolio and the extent to which companies honour loan repayment commitments. With increasing competition among financial intermediaries, both domestic and foreign, DFIs have been feeling the pressure to adopt efficient loan assessment and risk management techniques as well as effective corporate control mechanisms to monitor the companies.

One of the channels through which DFIs and institutional investors exert a voice in corporate governance is through having nominee directors on company boards as in the case of Germany and Japan. Almost all DFI debt contracts have carried a covenant that it will be represented on the board of the debtor company through a nominee director (CII, 1998). Notwithstanding the significant voice DFIs and institutional investors potentially have by virtue of being investors and creditors, these institutions have been perceived by and large to be extremely passive in corporate governance. Attention has been drawn to this problem by several committees, including the Bhagwati Committee on takeovers, and several committees on corporate governance.

In the past few years, signs are increasingly emerging of a more proactive policy stance on the part of the financial institutions. DFIs have been asked by the finance ministry to take 'full responsibility' of corporate governance in companies where they have substantial stakes. The objective is to boost investor confidence and pep up the capital market. The government has issued a four point directive to DFIs directing them to insist on (i) making adequate disclosures, (ii) moving towards internationally accepted accounting standards, (iii) maintaining distance between the CEO and chairman where applicable, and (iv) holding regular board meetings with proper recording and dissemination of proceedings. The DFIs have also implemented new norms for appointment of nominee directors, which have drastically cut down the total number of such directors on company boards. According to the new criteria for nomination, financial institutions are required to place their nominees only in companies where their *combined* exposure, i.e. debt plus equity, is above Rs 50 crore, or their shareholding is above 26 per cent, or in the event of the company showing signs of problems such as defaults on loans.

A core issue in designing an effective bank based governance mechanism is with regard to bankruptcy laws. Insolvency laws in India, derived largely from English law, is contained in the Companies Act, 1956, but there has been very little revision of the provisions relating to corporate insolvency all these years. The Companies Bill of 1998 proposes to amend the law of corporate insolvency and is awaiting the approval of the Parliament. In the meantime, the Recovery of Debts due to Banks and Financial Institutions (Amendment) Bill has been approved by Parliament on 15 March 2000. The amendment allows summary attachment of property of defaulting borrower at the time of filing the complaint and empowers the Debt Recovery Tribunals to distribute sales proceeds among secured creditors, and other mechanisms intended to speed up recovery of debts and thereby help reduce non-performing assets (NPAs). However, as a report by World Bank (2000) observes, such amendments have to be followed up with greater vigilance on the part of financial institutions, and amendment in bankruptcy and liquidation laws, particularly the Sick Industrial Companies Act (SICA) under which borrowers can continue to avoid repayment by declaring their companies 'sick'.

Corporate Governance Codes

The first formal attempt at introducing a code of corporate governance came from the Confederation of Indian Industries (CII), which in 1998 published the Desirable Code of Corporate Governance (CII, 1998). The CII document outlines several policies that can be adopted by Indian companies in line with international best practices. Further, several Indian companies voluntarily initiated in-house reviews of their existing governance practices, particularly their board structures, operational mechanisms, and information disclosure norms. Notwithstanding these initiatives, the implementation of which was largely voluntary in nature, the need was increasingly being felt that some statutory governance codes be put in place in view of several malpractices, like insider trading, preferential allotment of shares at preferential prices, improper market valuation of shares, etc., being pursued by a large number of companies, that inflicted losses on small investors and undermined investor confidence in capital markets. It is in this context that the SEBI set up the Kumar Mangalam Birla Committee on Corporate Governance (KMCCG) in May 1999 to suggest measures to improve the standards of corporate governance of listed companies in India, particularly with respect to disclosure of material, financial, and non-financial information, and responsibilities of independent and outside directors on company boards, and to suggest safeguards against insider trading. Further, the Committee was given the responsibility of drafting a code of best practices, some of which would be mandatory, and some voluntary.

The KMCCG targeted its recommendations (SEBI, 2000) primarily towards three major constituents: the shareholders, the board of directors, and the company management, and accordingly sought to identify the rights, duties, and accountability of each of these constituents. Based on the KMCCG's recommendations, SEBI has made certain provisions *mandatory* and certain provisions *recommendatory* for listed companies through the route of the listing agreement (see SEBI, 2000 for details). Accordingly, Clause 49 on corporate governance has been inserted by the stock exchanges in their listing agreement.

Along with initiating several legislative amendments in the Companies Act, 1956, the department of company affairs (DCA) of the Government of India set up a study group in May 2000, following the KMCCG's recommendations, with the objective of further operationalizing 'the concept of corporate governance/excellence on a sustained basis to sharpen India's global competitive edge and to further promote and develop corporate culture in the country' (DCA, 2000, p.1). Like the KMCCG, the study group came up with a concrete set of recommendations and advised the phased implementation of the essential measures. While recognizing the need for self-regulation and self-discipline in complying with governance norms, the study group advised, like the KMCCG, that till the market and the economy reach a certain level of maturity, the recommendations should be made statutory through appropriate legislative and regulatory support with a provision for review after three years.

What is notable among the different governance codes that have been formulated by the three distinct entities, namely the CII, the department of company affairs, and the SEBI, is the broad consistency and consensus in their recommendations for better governance. To begin with, all the three codes subscribe to maximization of shareholder value as the fundamental objective of corporate governance reforms as has been the case in a majority of countries. This is different from the strict stakeholder view adopted in countries like France and Germany. All the three codes have also highlighted the importance of the board structure, particularly the role of non-executive and independent directors and proper board functioning through regular meetings and deliberations in protecting shareholder value. All the three codes have stipulated that the number of directorships that a person can hold in listed companies should be reduced from the current limit of twenty to ten. Further, the importance of having different sub-committees like the audit committee and the remuneration committee based on the 'fundamental premise of independence and expertise' has been highlighted in the codes. Finally, all the three governance codes have emphasized on developing market-based institutions of governance through smoothening the function of the capital market and the market for corporate control, through stringent listing agreements, and through better disclosure and transparency of information including standardization of accounting methods.

There are some differences, however, in the recommendations of the three committees regarding the role of nominee directors of financial institutions in company management. With regard to the presence of nominees of creditor institutions in company boards, the KMCCG recognizes, contrary to the view taken by the CII code, that there may be a case for having nominee directors of lending institutions on the boards to protect the interests of the creditors. The DCA does not take a firm position on this issue although recognizing at the same time like the KMCCG report that there could be potential conflicts of interests in having representatives of financial institutions who are equity holders to sit on company boards. With regard to institutional shareholders like mutual funds, the KMCCG strongly recommends that unlike present practices, these institutions should not seek participation at board level through nominee directors, but maintain an arm's-length relationship with management. The institutional shareholders, by virtue of being block holders of equity can potentially affect management decisions through their voting power.

Corporate Sector Development in the 1990s

Corporate sector development in the 1990s is best evaluated in the context of the continuing liberalization of the Indian economy and the continuing initiatives in governance reforms. This section analyses some important features of corporate sector development, particularly those that have relevance for corporate governance.

Sources of Finance and Corporate Governance

As indicated in the section on corporate governance in India, the overall financial structure of India can be termed as bank-based, though the importance of the stock market has been increasing over the years. Some additional insights into how financing patterns have changed at the micro level are presented in Table 8.7. The table is based on an analysis of the financing patterns of a panel of 786 companies observed over the period 1989–90[6] to 1998–99 (see Sarkar and Sarkar, 2001 for details).

Table 8.7 indicates a clear break in the amount of funds raised by Indian companies at two points of time. First is the increase of nearly 33 per cent in the year 1991–92 which is maintained for the two subsequent years, and then a sharper rise of nearly 50 per cent in the year 1994–95 which is maintained for the next three years, before declining in 1998–99, the last year covered under the study. Regarding the sources of funds, Columns 3 and 4 of Table 8.7 give the percentage break-up of total funds according to internal and external sources. The proportion of external funds increased in the year 1992–93, the first full year after the reforms were initiated, and then again in the years 1994–95 and 1995–96, by about 8 per cent compared to the pre-reforms years. However, since 1996–97, the proportion of external funds has shown a steady decline. In fact, the average proportion of funds raised from external sources in the last three years covered by this study (around 45 per cent) has been lower than the proportion observed just before the reforms were initiated (around 55 per cent).

With regard to the relative importance of different external sources of funds, Table 8.7 shows that the proportion of external funds obtained from the capital market (through new equity issues, debentures, and fixed deposits) increased significantly during the period 1992–93 to 1994–95 when capital market reforms were in full force. However, in 1995–96, the importance of the capital market as a provider of external finance fell sharply, a fall which is largely attributed to the lack of proper institutional and regulatory mechanisms to screen companies entering the market, as well as political instability. Since then, the contribution of the capital market has remained at the low level of around 15 per cent.

TABLE 8.7 *Corporate financing patterns in India in the 1990s*

Year	*Sources of Funds* Amount (Rs Crore)	Internal (%)	External (%)	*Percentage of external funds from* Capital Market	Borrowings	Current Liabilities and Provisions	*Major share of borrowing from* Financial Institutions	Commercial Banks
1989–90	22.44	0.48	0.52	0.14	0.39	0.47	0.13	0.26
1990–91	22.70	0.44	0.56	0.12	0.45	0.43	0.17	0.28
1991–92	30.26	0.43	0.57	0.15	0.38	0.47	0.15	0.16
1992–93	31.69	0.38	0.62	0.21	0.46	0.33	0.09	0.29
1993–94	33.30	0.50	0.50	0.3	0.33	0.37	0.13	0.11
1994–95	47.34	0.35	0.65	0.23	0.36	0.41	0.04	0.27
1995–96	43.85	0.36	0.64	0.13	0.47	0.40	0.09	0.31
1996–97	47.77	0.50	0.50	0.15	0.33	0.52	0.07	0.13
1997–98	48.87	0.51	0.49	0.16	0.62	0.22	0.11	0.39
1998–99	41.86	0.58	0.42	0.17	0.47	0.36	0.14	0.25

Source: Authors' calculation based on a balanced panel of 786 listed private manufacturing companies from Prowess database created by the Centre for Monitoring Indian Economy (CMIE).

Financial institutions and commercial banks one of the two major sources of borrowings, the others being commercial paper, debentures, and fixed deposits.

Coming to other sources of external finance, one observes that borrowings have always played an important role in the provision of external finance to Indian companies and its importance has not changed much over the post-reforms years. A large part of borrowings are from commercial banks and is for working capital. Bulk of the remaining borrowings is from the development financial institutions. Though the importance of this source had declined in the initial years of the reforms as companies increasingly accessed funds from the capital market, there is a clear discernible trend of the increasing importance of borrowings from development financial institutions in the later years covered by this study.

The trends in corporate financing pattern support our earlier observation at the macro level that the financial structure of India is largely bank-based. This in turn implies that governance mechanisms that emphasize the role of banks and financial institutions in monitoring company performance are likely to be important for overall corporate sector development in the future. Regarding this, an emerging area of concern has been the problem of accumulation of non-performing assets (NPAs) by DFIs. A large proportion of these NPAs have originated in the corporate sector and debt recovery has been lax. As of end-March 2001, the gross NPAs of public sector banks and all-India financial institutions had reached a high of Rs 71,928 crore and this has been largely attributed to weak credit management and creditor oversight with regard to the disbursement and recovery of loans.[7] Despite attempts to recover bad loans through a settlement process and despite giving chief executives and the board of directors of the institutions considerable flexibility on the issue, little progress has been made. That growing NPAs are increasingly affecting the health of the DFIs is apparent from the recent erosion of the net worth of IFCI and its subsequent government bail-out, as well as the fact that the shares of the DFIs, notably IDBI and IFCI, are trading considerably below par in the stock market.

The potentially debilitating effect that NPAs can have on financial sector stability and corporate sector growth is evident from the fact that such NPAs were instrumental in magnifying the east Asian crisis and were largely attributed to poor oversight by financial institutions and crony capitalism. While as is shown in Table 8.6, creditor rights on books in India are substantial, in practice, it has been difficult for borrowers to credibly discipline underperforming management. In this context, the recent initiative taken by the RBI in publishing the list of defaulting companies, including the identity of the board of directors, and encouraging banks to share this information is a welcome step.

Corporate Ownership and Control Structure

One of the important findings in the literature is that the structure of equity ownership can have important implications for corporate governance and company performance. It differs depending upon whether equity ownership is concentrated among a few large shareholders or is diffused, and in the former case, who the large shareholders are. Table 8.8 provides snapshots of equity holding pattern in Indian corporates for the years 1996 and 2000. The principal holders of corporate equity in India are (i) directors and their relatives, (ii) corporate bodies, (iii) foreign investors, (iv) term-lending institutions primarily comprising the three government-controlled/promoted development financial institutions (DFIs) and state finance corporations, (v) institutional investors, namely, the government-owned mutual fund—the Unit Trust of India, and three government-owned insurance companies, and (vi) the public. Of the six groups, the first five can be considered as large shareholders or block holders. Also, as the table shows, companies in India can be broadly classified into several ownership groups, namely, (i) private companies belonging to business groups, (ii) private stand-alone companies, (iii) foreign companies belonging to business groups, and (iv) foreign stand-alone companies.

It is evident from the table that the ownership structure has become more concentrated over the years. Dispersed shareholding, that is shareholding by the public, has reduced from 40 per cent to 33 per cent during the period. The composition of shareholding pattern by block holders has also gone through interesting changes. There has been a significant increase in equity holdings by directors and relatives, while holdings by corporate bodies have reduced. However, the reduction by the latter has been relatively low, with the result that the aggregate holdings by these two groups have increased. Holdings by institutional investors, predominantly the mutual funds, have declined, but those by financial institutions have increased. Finally, there is no noticeable change in foreign equity holdings.

The extent of increase in holdings by directors and relatives has been highly correlated with ownership types. The increase has been significantly higher for group companies than for stand-alone companies. Within group companies, those belonging to Indian business groups show very sharp increase, much higher than the rest. The holdings by directors and relatives in Indian group companies have increased to almost similar levels with those in stand-alone companies. This is a significant increase in concentration, given that group companies are about three times in size than stand-alone companies.

TABLE 8.8 *Shareholding pattern in the Indian corporate sector: Years 1996 and 2000 averages*

	All Companies		Indian Group Companies		Indian Stand-alone Companies		Foreign Group Companies		Foreign Stand-alone Companies	
	1996	*2000*	*1996*	*2000*	*1996*	*2000*	*1996*	*2000*	*1996*	*2000*
Number of shares (million)	14.324	21.288	22.943	34.649	6.907	8.571	48.326	63.763	15.307	24.868
Market capitalization (Rs Billion)	1.1091	4.2491	2.1519	6.714	0.1604	2.1643	4.4517	9.3849	2.1239	4.1426
Shareholding Pattern (%)										
Directors and relatives	15.37	27.80	8.59	29.72	21.69	30.23	0.93	10.88	3.73	8.90
Corporate bodies	23.70	19.46	32.62	21.60	18.73	19.29	18.25	17.06	15.29	11.19
Foreign bodies	10.38	10.85	8.85	7.79	7.13	6.49	39.66	35.75	41.36	44.80
Institutional investors	6.46	3.99	10.68	5.75	3.31	2.37	12.65	5.80	6.66	5.37
Financial institutions	3.65	4.51	4.15	6.39	3.40	2.95	5.17	9.29	2.02	4.01
Public/Dispersed	40.46	33.39	35.11	28.74	45.73	38.68	23.35	21.21	30.94	25.73

Source: Authors' computation based on 1422 listed manufacturing companies in 1996, and 1352 listed manufacturing companies in 2000 for which shareholding data are available from CMIE's Prowess database. Stock market data are also from the same source.

The consolidation of ownership pattern that is clearly evident between 1995–96 and 1999–2000 has taken place in the context of increased takeover and merger activities since the mid-1990s. Given the greater institutionalization of the market for corporate control, and the need for expansion and diversification in a competitive environment, the data on ownership changes suggest that promoters of business groups, for fear of losing control over their companies, may have taken towards consolidation of their equity holdings. Mechanisms such as creeping acquisitions and share buy-back have in all probability facilitated such consolidation.

That takeovers and merger activities have significantly increased since the reforms is evident from the fact that while 121 takeovers and mergers occurred between 1988 and 1992, 166 companies have been acquired between 1993 and 1997, with nearly 85 per cent of the acquisitions taking place between 1995 and 1997. This increasing trend seems to have continued and gathered momentum, given that between 1997 and January 2002, the total number of open offers for takeovers and substantial acquisitions have totalled 262 (Table 8.9).[8] What is of more significance is the dramatic rise in the proportion of open offers that been motivated by the need to take control of management. This clearly reveals the increasing role of the 'market for corporate control' in corporate governance through providing a credible threat to underperforming management. Such increasing takeover activity also explains the desire for consolidation of ownership by incumbent management, as is being revealed by the ownership changes in the last five years and by the fact that the motives for consolidation and substantial acquisition have also been behind several open offers made in the last few years.

TABLE 8.9 *Cases of substantial acquisitions of shares registered with the SEBI: 1997–98 to 2000–01*

Year	*Change in Management Control*	*Consolidation Holdings*	*Others*	*Total*
1997–98	20	10	13	43
1998–99	29	25	12	66
1999–00	44	9	23	76
2000–01	70	5	2	77
Total	163	49	50	262

Source: Computed from Data on Takeovers, SEBI, 2002.

Consolidation of ownership by insiders per se need not be value-reducing for outside shareholders. Several studies have shown that increased holdings by insiders, above a threshold, may align incentives of managers with those of outside shareholders and increase firm value (see for example Morck et al., 1988 and Sarkar and Sarkar, 2000).

In the study by Sarkar and Sarkar, (which was based on 1995–6 data on a sample of manufacturing sector firms in India), it was found that both directors and relatives and corporate bodies start monitoring the company after their shareholding reaches a threshold of 25 per cent.[9] An implication of this result put simply is that the benefits of concentrated ownership by directors and relatives and corporate bodies outweigh its costs when ownership becomes substantial. Notwithstanding this, however, as Stulz (1988) has argued, consolidation of ownership may also reduce firm value by reducing the success probability of value-enhancing takeovers from taking place. This is especially relevant in India where financial liberalization and removal of restrictions have shifted the growth frontier in most industries. However, domestic companies may be slow in exploiting all investment opportunities due to lack of adequate financial capital and could be under threat from foreign firms that have better financial access. Under such circumstance, even relatively better performing domestic companies can use consolidation to prevent value-enhancing takeovers which can reduce company value in the long run, especially for minority shareholders. What the net effect of the recent consolidation in insider holdings is remains an open empirical question.

While the alignment of managerial and shareholder interests is possible through higher shareholding by corporate insiders, expropriation of minority shareholders becomes an issue in cases where the control rights of insiders, particularly those of company promoters, are disproportionately more than their cash flow rights. This is an important feature of corporate ownership structure in India, as it is in many other Asian countries, where family-owned business groups are prevalent (see for example, Claessens et al., 2000). These business groups are conglomerates of firms, with a holding company at the top and a string of subsidiaries at different levels. Typically, business groups in India, which account for around 60 per cent of private sector assets in manufacturing, are organized as stock pyramids or as cross-ownership structures which enable a shareholder or a group to obtain complete control of a company with control rights disproportionately more than cash flow rights. While the existence of such pyramids is widely acknowledged, it has been difficult to come across general estimates of pyramiding in Indian business groups. However, some estimates specific to some groups are available and are illustrative of how pyramiding works. Bebchuk et al. (1998), citing a Forbes document (1998) reports that the Godrej family business group in India holds, through its privately held company Godrej and Boyce Manufacturing, 67 per cent of Godrej Soaps limited, whose shares are traded on the Bombay Stock Exchange. Godrej Soaps Ltd., in turn, owns 65 per cent of an agriculture product company, Godrej Agrovet, and together with the Godrej Group, holds 65 per cent of a food-processing company, Godrej Foods Limited.

Control structures in the form of pyramids and cross-holdings have implications for the quality of corporate governance. As has been discussed extensively in the literature, particularly with respect to the east Asian crisis, such control structures considerably increase agency costs in corporations (Bebchuk, et al., 1998), and in less developed countries with poor investor protection, these can be used by controlling shareholders to gain private benefits by expropriating minority shareholders (Wolfenzon, 1999). This form of expropriation is termed in the literature as 'tunnelling' (Johnson et al., 2000).

Tunnelling is usually manifested through loans at high or low interest rate, selling of inputs or purchase of outputs from group companies at non-market prices, leasing of assets, and the like. As Bertrand and Mullainathan (2000) argue, tunnelling, notwithstanding some of its attributes for minimizing transaction cost, may raise a serious barrier to financial development as expropriation of outside shareholders would lead to the thinning of capital markets and drying up of low-cost equity-financing options for companies. While empirical estimation of the extent of tunneling has been difficult due to its opacity and 'illicit' nature, there is evidence, based on data from 1989 to 1999 that there is substantial diversion of value to inside shareholders through tunnelling in India (Bertrand and Mullainathan, 2000). The diversion of resources is found to follow the lines of ownership, moving from firms near the bottom of a pyramid to firms near the top of the pyramid.

Consolidating the findings from the various ownership and performance studies, one can conclude that while insider block holders with substantial ownership and control rights may have a positive role in mitigating managerial agency problems in the presence of weak legal protection in line with the predictions of La Porta et al. (1999a), the problem of expropriation of minority investors becomes particularly pertinent, as Bertrand and Mullainathan (2000) have demonstrated in the case of India, and Claessens et al. (2001) in the case of eight east Asian economies, when control rights are in excess of cash flow rights. Given this, the urgency of providing legal protections to minority shareholders and placing reputational constraints on controlling families for curbing opportunistic behaviour (Bebchuk, et al. 1998) cannot be overemphasized. In this context, the recommendations of the KMCCG and other committees on corporate governance with regard to making the operations and accounting practices of Indian business groups more transparent through segment accounting, consolidated balance sheets, and greater disclosures assume importance.

The Functioning of Company Boards

Along with the structure of ownership, the structure of company boards has a significant bearing on how companies are managed and controlled. The primary responsibilities of any company board are to evaluate proposals put forward by the company management and to honestly discharge their fiduciary responsibilities towards the company's investors.

Several aspects of board structure and composition become relevant in the context of corporate governance and performance. These are, the size of the board, the composition of the board in terms of the break-up between executive, non-executive, and independent directors, and the issue of multiple directorships and board interlocking. The relevance of these factors in the context of corporate governance lies in the fact that these determine the ability of the board to perform its fiduciary responsibilities and have implications for corporate performance (see for example, Yermack, 1996 and Keister, 1998).

General estimates in India of the average size of the board as well as the constitution of the boards in terms of its break-up between executive and non-executive directors are difficult to come by. However, a recent study on board structure and the phenomenon of interlocking directorates in India based on a sample of group-affiliated companies of the top eighty-nine business groups in India for the year 1999–2000 estimates that the average board size across these groups is about eight (Table 8.10) (De, 2001). While estimates for other countries are not strictly comparable, Table 8.10 presents some broad cross-country statistics. As is evident from Table 8.10, while the average board size in India is the lowest, the magnitude of interlocking as given by the cumulation ratio is the highest. What is particularly interesting is the distribution of multiple directorships in Indian companies compared to other countries. While the proportion of directors holding two positions is significantly lower in India, the proportion of directors occupying more than four seats is much larger. An analysis of the raw data for India shows that persons with a larger number of multiple directorships are mostly the corporate heavyweights like the prominent family members of the leading business families of India.

TABLE 8.10 *Interlocking directorates in India: Comparison with Hong Kong, Great Britain, United States, and Thailand*

		Hong Kong (Top 200 firms)	*Great Britain (Top 250 firms)*	*United States (Top 250 firms)*	*Thailand (Top 200 firms)*	*India (Firms belonging to the Top 89 Business Group = 895 firms)*
Total Number of Directors		1628	2682	3108	1511	4930
Total Number of Director Seats		2105	3091	3976	1833	6823
Average Board Size*		10.53	12.36	15.90	9.17	7.62
Number of Positions Per Director (Cummulation Ratio)**		1.29	1.15	1.28	1.21	1.38
Total Number of Multiple Directors		276	282	564	213	893 ***
Proportion of Multiple Directors		17%	11%	18%	14%	18% ***
Number of Director Seats Held by Multiple Directors****	2	61%	69%	64%	69%	53% ***
	3	25%	21%	24%	19%	21% ***
	4	6%	6%	8%	8%	11% ***
	5	5%	3%	3%	3%	6% ***
	>5	3%	1%	1%	1%	9% ***

Sources: The data for India are taken from De, Bikram (2001), *The Incidence and Performance Effects of Interlocking Directorates in Emerging Market Business Groups*: *Evidence from India*. Working Paper. The data are for the year ending March, 2000.

The data on Hong Kong firms are from Au, Kevin, Mike W. Peng, and Denis Wang (2000), 'Interlocking directorates, firm strategies, and performance in Hong Kong: Towards a research agenda', *Asia Pacific Journal of Management*, 17 (1), 28–47. The data are for the year 1996.

The British and the US data are from Stokman, F., R. Ziegler, and J. Scott, (eds.) (1985), *Networks of corporate power: A comparative analysis of ten countries*, London: Polity Press, p. 22–7. The data for Great Britain and the United States are for the year 1985.

The data on Thailand are from Peng, Mike W. and Au. Y. Kevin (2001), 'Interlocking Directorates as Corporate Governance in Third World Multinationals: Theory and Evidence from Thailand', *Asia Pacific Journal of Management*, 18, p. 161–81.The data was for 1994–1996.

Notes:

* Average Board Size is computed as (Total Number Director Seats)/(Total Number of Firms in the sample).

** Cummulation Ratio is calculated as (Total Number of Director Seats)/(Total Number of Directors).

*** Multiple Directorships are calculated with respect to the number of positions held *within* a particular business group.

**** The percentages in this field are computed as proportions of the total number of multiple directors.

The above analysis reveals that the phenomenon of interlocking, while prevalent in India, is not particularly high compared to other countries and the incidence of high level of multiple directorship is restricted to a few prominent business groups. In the latter case, there is select evidence based on a case study of nine prominent Indian business groups for two points of time, 1990 and 1997, that group ties manifested through board interlocks, sharing across group activities, etc., which facilitate intra-group information exchange in groups, have strengthened during this period (Khanna and Palepu, 1999).

A relevant issue in view of the recommendation of all the corporate governance committees of putting an upper limit to multiple directorship is whether there is a negative effect of increased interlocking through multiple directorships on company performance. Recent empirical analysis for companies belonging to the top eighty-nine business groups for the year 1999–2000 has shown that interlocking has a positive influence on firm performance as measured by the return on assets (De, 2001). This result, consistent with the evidence that Keister (1998) obtains for Chinese business groups, suggests that the positive effects of interlocking in terms of information sharing and within group relational synergies could outweigh the negative effects that may arise from concentration of control in the hands of a few directors. This is also consistent with De's (2001) finding that directorial interlocks in India are predominantly 'related industry' interlocks suggesting the existence of positive synergies from directorial experience and specialization.

The evidence on interlocking and performance in India, albeit limited, does seem to suggest that multiple directorships and the incidence of interlocking in its current manifestation do not negatively impact on company performance. What remains to be seen in the case of India is whether the recommendations of the governance committees with regard to structuring more independent boards translate in better governance in future. As Lipton and Lorsch (1992) comment, '...the norms of behavior in most boardrooms are dysfunctional because directors rarely criticize the policies of top managers or hold candid discussions about corporate performance'.[10] Such a possibility remains even with a board with the statutory number of independent directors. Existing evidence on board independence and company performance with regard to developed countries like the US is mixed. For instance, while Hermalin and Weisbach (1991) and Bhagat and Black (2002),[11] for instance in studying US firms, do not find any relation between firm performance and the fraction of outside directors, Baysinger and Butler (1985) find evidence to the contrary.

The Role of Foreign Equity in Governance

Several papers analysing the role of large shareholders in corporate governance in India have, under different empirical specifications, looked into the question of how company value is related to the proportion of equity held by foreign investors (Chhibber and Majumdar, 1999; Khanna and Palepu, 2000; and Sarkar and Sarkar, 2000). This issue becomes important in view of substantial foreign participation in Indian companies (Table 8.8).

All the studies analysing corporate sector data at several points of time in the 1990s unambiguously report that foreign equity ownership has a significantly positive influence on company value in India. This result, put in the context of the evidence presented in Tables 8.1 and 8.2 of increased foreign participation in corporate sector activities through cross-border mergers and acquisitions as well as foreign direct investment, implies increased competitive pressures on domestic firms to perform and to adopt corporate governance practices in line with international best practices that foreign firms are generally considered to adhere to. Among the various positive spillovers that foreign direct investment can have on domestic firms is the diffusion of organizational and managerial skills and practices. In an empirical examination of the effect of foreign investors and foreign directors on self-interested strategizing behaviour of managers in large manufacturing companies in India, Ramaswamy and Li (2001) find that the level of foreign representation on the board of directors dampen the incentives of managers to behave strategically, thereby reducing managerial agency costs.

Finally, cross-listings of domestic Indian firms in international exchanges can have important effects on the quality of corporate governance at home. Essentially, such listings are argued to serve as a commitment device to align better the interests of the controlling shareholder with that of other shareholders, thereby reducing the possibility of expropriation of minority shareholders (Reese Jr. and Weisbach, 2001; Doidge et al., 2001). Evidence to this effect with respect to Indian firms as of now is limited to the fact that firms seeking listing abroad have to adopt international norms of accounting and disclosure. For instance, a non-US firm seeking listing in the US is subjected to a number of provisions of US securities law and the firm is also required to conform to generally accepted accounting principles in the United States US GAAP. Such stipulations, it is argued, increases the expected cost to managers of extracting private benefits, and commits the firm to protecting minority shareholders' interests in the home country (Reese Jr. and Weisbach, 2001). This is borne by empirical evidence with regard to non-US firms cross-listed in the US stock exchanges, which show that firms from countries with weak shareholder protection signal through cross-listings their commitment to protect minority investors in the home country and follows a cross-listing in US with equity issues at home. As of 1997, there is evidence that foreign companies listed in the US have a market valuation that exceeds by 16.5 per cent that of firms from the same country that are not listed in the US and that growth opportunities are valued significantly higher for firms that cross-list than those that do not (Doidge et al., 2001).

Conclusion

This chapter focused on the corporate governance reforms initiated in India since the 1990s and analysed how corporate sector development has co-evolved with such reforms in this period. A summary evaluation of these measures suggests that the emphasis of the reforms is broadly in line with the financial services and the legally based view, where policy makers and industry constituents have attempted to create an *enabling* legal and regulatory framework in which both banks and markets have been provided with incentives to supply efficient financial services to the corporate sector with mechanisms put in place to protect the interests of the outside investors.

This portends well for the Indian economy given the recent cross-country evidence that the overall level of financial development, along with strong investor and creditor rights and contract enforcement mechanisms, fosters the formation of new firms and stimulates the growth of those industries that depend heavily on external finance (Beck and Levine, 2001). Most of the legislations until now have been directed towards the development of the equity market and the market for corporate control. Given that banks in India play a significant role as providers of external finance, reforms at strengthening debt contracts backed adequately by effective and enforceable covenants should take priority now.

Finally, it is important to recognize that the success of corporate governance reforms in improving efficiency and growth of companies will also depend on policies that are geared towards fostering greater competition in the product market. Governance and competition are likely to be complements rather than substitutes, as is borne out by select empirical studies (Grosfeld and Tressel, 2001). High competition in the product market can force managers to focus on corporate performance for fear of takeovers and bankruptcy (Hart, 1983); financial institutions that compete in their own markets would have stronger incentives to demand higher performance on their investments; and lastly, the presence of superior competitors provides a yardstick to measure the performance and remuneration of managers (e.g. Nalebuff and Stiglitz, 1983), thereby strengthening their incentives to perform on behalf of shareholders.

Notes

1. A similar view is expressed in Rajan and Zingales (1998) and Prowse (1998) cited in Claessens et al. (1999).

2. Following Demirguc-Kunt and Levine (1999) we take market capitalization ratio as an indicator of size, value traded to GDP as an indicator of activity, and the turnover ratio as an indicator of liquidity/efficiency of the stock market. Along similar lines, we take assets of scheduled commercial banks and development financial institutions to GDP as an indicator of size, non-food credit to GDP as an indicator of activity, and the net interest margin as an indicator of efficiency of the banking system (defined to include scheduled commercial banks and development financial institutions). Using these measures, we then construct measures of overall financial development and financial structure.

3. Demirguc-Kunt and Levine classify countries into four distinct groups: (i) financially developed and bank-based, (ii) financially developed and market-based, (iii) financially underdeveloped and bank-based, and (iv) financially underdeveloped and market-based, using a *Structure Index*. The index is constructed by combining different measures of stock market and banking sector development.

4. As summarized by Levine (2000) the arguments in favour of a bank-based system are that financial intermediaries can improve the acquisition of information on firms, the intensity with which creditors can exert corporate control, the provision of risk-reducing arrangements, and encouraging managers to commit to longer-term profitable investments. The advantages of systems led by stock market with regard to the quality of corporate governance are stated mainly in terms of the costs of bank-based systems. Thus, 'marketeers' argue that bank-based systems are inimical

to innovation and stymie enterprise by allowing banks to have strong influence on firms, giving them power to extract rents from firms while approving new investments and debt contracts, forcing firms to employ conservative and low-growth strategies, and promoting collusion between bankers and managers.

5. The three major DFIs are the Industrial Development Bank of India (IDBI) with 72 per cent government ownership, the Industrial Credit and Investment Corporation of India (ICICI) promoted by the government-owned mutual fund and insurance companies with a combined share of 32 per cent, and the Industrial Finance Corporation of India (IFCI) promoted by the government-owned financial institutions and insurance companies with a combined share of 42 per cent.

6. The year 1989–90 represents the period from April 1989 to March 1990. Most companies in India adopt the period between April (of one year) and March (of the following year) as the financial year for accounting purpose.

7. As of September 2001, net NPAs (as a percentage of net advances) of the three major DFIs, namely ICICI, IDBI, and IFCI stood at 5.2 per cent, 14.8 per cent, and 21 per cent, respectively.

8. Broadly speaking, an acquisition is defined to be substantial if the acquisition is more than 20 per cent of the equity capital of the target company. Substantial acquisitions of shares are classified into three broad categories by the SEBI, namely, (i) takeovers—where the substantial acquisition leads to a change in management control of the target company, (ii) consolidation of ownership—where the acquirer already has control over the company, but acquires additional shares to further augment his/her ownership, and (iii) others—where the acquisition is substantial but does not lead to a change in management control of the target company in favour of the acquirer.

9. An earlier study by Khanna and Palepu (2000), based on a linear specification of the underlying relation between shareholders and firm value, does not find any statistically significant effect of promoters and corporate bodies on firm value.

10. Quoted in Yermack (1996), p. 186.

11. For instance, Bhagat and Black (2002) undertaking a time-series study examining the relationship between long-term stock performance and the fraction of the corporate board that is composed of independent directors find that the proportion of independent directors has little association with performance. On the contrary, they find that poor performance on the part of firms leads to independent directors being appointed to their boards. The results generate very little empirical support for the current push in the US for a higher proportion of independent directors on large company boards.

References

Au, Kevin, Mike W. Peng, and Denis Wang (2000). 'Interlocking directorates, firm strategies, and performance in Hong Kong: Towards a research agenda', *Asia Pacific Journal of Management*, 17 (1), pp. 28–47.

Baysinger, Robert and Henry N. Butler (1985). 'Corporate governance and the board of directors: Performance effects of changes in board composition', *Journal of Law, Economics and Organization*, 1, pp. 101–24.

Bebchuk, Lucian A., Reinier Kraakman, and George Triantis (1998). 'Stock Pyramids, Cross-Ownership, and Dual Class Equity: The Creation and Agency Costs of Spearating Control from Cash Flow Rights', NBER Working Papers, No. 6951.

Beck, Thorsten and Ross Levine (2001). 'New Firm Formation and Industry Growth: Does Having a Market-or Bank-Based System Matter?', *Journal of Financial Economics*, forthcoming.

Berglof, Erik (2000). 'Reforming corporate governance: redirecting the European agenda', In *Corporate Governance and Globalization*: *Long Range Planning Issues*. (eds) Stephen S. Cohen and Gavin Boyd, Cheltenham, UK: Edward Elgar.

Bertrand, Marianne and Sendhil Mullainathan (2000). 'Ferreting Out Tunneling: An Application to Indian Business Groups', NBER Working Papers, No. 7592.

Bhagat, Sanjai and Bernard Black (2002). 'Board Independence and Long-Term Performance', *Journal of Corporation Law*, forthcoming, Vol. 27, No. 1.

Chhibber, P.K. and S.K. Majumdar (1999). 'Foreign ownership and profitability: Property rights, control, and the performance of firms in Indian industry', *Journal of Law and Finance*, 42(1), 209–39.

CII, 1998, *Desirable Corporate Governance*: *A Code*, Confederation of Indian Industry.

Claessens, Stijn, Simeon Djankov, Joseph P.H. Fan, and Larry H.P. Lang (1999). 'Expropriation of Minority Shareholders: Evidence from East Asia', World Bank Policy Research Working Paper Series, No. 2088, World Bank, Washington DC.

_____ (2001). 'Disentangling the Incentive and Entrenchment Effects of Large Shareholdings', *Journal of Finance*, fourthcoming.

Claessens, Stijn., Simeon Djankov, and Larry H.P. Lang (2000). 'The Separation of Ownership and Control in East Asian Corporations', *Journal of Financial Economics*, 58 (1–2), pp. 81–112

DCA (2000). Report on Corporate Excellence on a Sustained Basis to Sharpen India's Global Competitive Edge and to Further Develop Corporate Culture in the Country, Department of Company Affairs, Government of India, http://www.nic.in/dca/corp-exc.htm#foreword

De, Bikram (2001). *The Incidence and Performance Effects of Interlocking Directorates in Emerging Market Business Groups*: *Evidence from India*. Working Paper, Indira Gandhi Institute of Development Research, Mumbai.

Demirguc Kunt and Ross Levine (1995). 'Stock Market Development and Financial Intermediaries: Stylized Facts', World Bank Policy Research Working Paper Series, No. 1462, World Bank, Washington DC.

Demirguc Kunt and Ross Levine (1999). 'Bank-based and Market-based Financial Systems: Cross-Country Comparisons', World Bank Policy Research Working Paper Series, No. 2143, World Bank, Washington DC.

Doidge, Craig G., Andrew Karolyi, and Rene M. Stulz (2001). 'Why are Foreign Firms Listed in the US Worth More?', NBER Working Papers, No. 8538.

Grosfeld, Irena and Thierry Tressel, (2001). 'Competition and Corporate Governance: Substitutes or Complements? Evidence from the Warsaw Stock Exchange', William Davidson Institute Working Paper No.369, University of Michigan Business School.

Hart, Oliver, D. (1983). 'The Market Mechanism as an Incentive Scheme', *Bell Journal of Economics*, 14, pp. 366–82.

Hermalin, Benjamin E. and Michael S. Weisbach. (1991). 'The Effects of Board Composition and Direct Incentives on Firm Performance', *Financial Management*, 20(4), pp. 101–12.

Johnson, Simon, R. La Porta, F. Lopez-de-Silanes, and A. Shleifer, (2000). 'Tunneling', *American Economic Review*, 90(2), pp. 22–7.

Kannan, Ramaswamy and Mingfang Li (2001). 'Foreign Investors, Foreign Directors and Corporate Diversification: An Empirical Examination of Large Manufacturing Companies in India', *Asia Pacific Journal of Management*, Vol. 18, No. 2.

Keister, Lisa (1998). 'Engineering Growth: Business Group Structure and Firm Performance in China's Transition Economy', *American Journal of Sociology*, 104 (2), pp. 404, 440.

Khanna, Tarun and Krishna Palepu, (1999). 'Policy Shocks, Market Intermediaries, and Corporate Strategy: The Evolution of Business Groups in Chile and India', *Journal of Economic Management and Strategy*, Vol. 8, No. 2, pp. 271–310.

Khanna, Tarun and Krishna Palepu, (2000). 'Emerging Market Business Groups, Foreign Investors and Corporate Governance', In *Concentrated Ownership*, NBER Volume, (ed.) Randell Morck, Chicago: University of Chicago Press.

Kust, M.J. (1964). *Foreign Enterprise in India*, Chapel Hill: North Carolina University Press.

La Porta, R., F. Lopez-de-Silanes, A. Shleifer, and R. Vishny, (1998). 'Law and Finance', *Journal of Political Economy*, 106, pp. 1113–55.

_____ (1999a). 'Corporate Ownership Around the World', *Journal of Finance*, 54, pp. 471–517.

_____ (1999b). 'The Quality of Government'. *Journal of Law, Economics and Organization*, 15, pp. 222–79.

_____ (2000a). 'Investor Protection and Corporate Governance', *Journal of Financial Economics*, 58 (1–2), Oct.–Nov., pp. 3–27.

_____ (2000b). 'Agency Problems and Dividend Policies Around the World,' *Journal of Finance*, 55, pp. 1–33.

Levine, Ross (1997). 'Financial Development and Economic Growth: Views and Agenda', *Journal of Economic Literature*, June, 35(2), pp. 688–726.

Levine, Ross (2000). 'Bank-based or market-based financial systems: Which is better?', Working paper, Carlson School of Management, University of Minnesota.

Lipton, Martin and Jay W. Lorsch (1992). 'A modest proposal for improved corporate governance', *Business Lawyer*, 48, no. 1, pp. 59–77.

Mehta, M.M. (1984). *Structure of Indian Industries*, Bombay: Popular Book Depot.

Morais, Richard. C. (1998). Who Needs P4G?, tubes, 23 March.

Morck, Randall, Andrei Shleifer, and Robert W. Vishny (1988). 'Management ownership and market valuation: An empirical analysis', *Journal of Financial Economics*, 20, 293–315.

Nalebuff, Barry and Joseph Stiglitz (1983). 'Information, Competition, and Markets', *American Economic Review*; 73(2), May, pp. 278–83.

Peng, Mike W. and Kevin Y. Au (2001). 'Interlocking Directorates as Corporate Governance in Third World Multinationals: Theory and Evidence from Thailand', *Asia Pacific Journal of Management*, 18, p. 161–81.

Prowse, Stephen (1998). 'Corporate Governance: Emerging Issues and Lessons from East Asia', World Bank, mimeo.

Rajan, Raghuram. G. and Luigi Zingales (1998). 'Which Capitalism? Lessons from the East Asian Crisis', *Journal of Applied Corporate Finance*, Vol. 11, No. 3, pp. xx-xxx.

Reese, William A. Jr. and Michael S, Weisbach (2001). 'Protection of Minority Shareholder Interests, Cross-listings in the United States, and Subsequent Equity Offerings', NBER Working Papers No.8164.

Sarkar, Jayati and Subrata Sarkar (2000). 'Large Shareholder Activism in Developing Countries: Evidence from India', *International Review of Finance*, vol. 1, no. 3.

Sarkar, Jayati and Subrata Sarkar, (2001). 'Liberalization, Financing Pattern and Corporate Performance', *Revue Tiers Monde*, January–March, pp. 61–82.

SEBI (2000). 'Draft Report of the Kumar Mangalam Committee on Corporate Governance', Securities and Exchange Board of India.

Sen, Kunal and Rajendra Vaidya (1998). 'India', In *Financial Reform in Developing Countries*, (eds) Jose M. Fanelli and Rohinton Medhora, pp. 57–89, Hampshire, UK: Macmillan Press Limited.

Stulz, Rene (1988). 'Managerial Control of Voting Rights: Financing Policies and the Market for Corporate Control', *Journal of Financial Economics*, January–March, pp. 25–54.

——— (2000). 'Financial Structure, Corporate Finance and Economic Growth', *International Review of Finance*, Vol. 1, No. 1, pp. 11–38.

Yermack, D. (1996). 'Higher Valuation of Companies with Small Board of Directors', *Journal of Financial Economics*, 40, pp. 185–212.

Wolfenzon, Daniel (1999). '*A theory of pyramidal structures*', manuscript, Cambridge, Mass: Harvard University Press.

World Bank (2000): 'India's 2000–01 Budget and Recent Policy Developments', Note circulated at the India Development Forum Meeting, Paris.

9

On Economic Reforms, Governance, and Development

Examining the Problematic Role of Corporate Profit Strategies

Ananya Mukherjee Reed

> Almost every bit of empirical data in the government's very own Economic Survey 2002–03 highlights the stark reality of the economic challenges India is facing. Growth has fallen by more than 20 per cent compared to the previous year's modest growth of 5.6 per cent; and to the second lowest figure since the crisis of 1991. Surely all of it cannot be attributed to the drought factor. Employment growth has been dropping during the past decade as compared to the previous one. Yet, over 100 million would enter the age bracket of 15–34 years during the next decade for whom gainful employment would have to be created if they are to be dissuaded from swelling the ranks of the violence-prone.
>
> Editorial in the *Indian Express*, Friday, 28 February 2003

As this piece is being written, significant debates are under way in India about the prospects for its economy and strategies that could help improve these prospects. As indicated by the quote above, aggregate demand is sluggish, growth rates are repeatedly being projected downward, and corporate sector performance is, at best, volatile. In part, of course, this is a reflection of the global trends. However, it is also increasingly being acknowledged that India's domestic reforms are not capable of leading the economy on to a path of steady growth. An issue of particular concern in India's current crisis is the fact that, despite the growth in industrial production and corporate profitability, India's economic dependence on agriculture has not been reduced in any significant way.

In the light of this latter situation, the role of the economic reforms need to be carefully scrutinized in relation to two other critical aspects of the current crisis. The first is a continuing crisis of governance within the leading economic institutions of the country. The second is a continuing inability of the economy to overcome insufficiencies in economic stimulus reflected in both consumer and industrial demand. This issue actually points to a much larger problem, viz., the role that India's industrial sector plays in generating economic growth. Interestingly, the economic reforms were expected to solve precisely these two problems of governance and lack of economic stimulus.

In this chapter, I shall focus on this nexus, the issues of demand and economic stimulus and their interconnections with the issue of governance. A central hypothesis of this chapter is that in developing countries such as India governance reforms alone cannot solve the crisis of economic growth, and even less, problems of employment and income distribution. This is particularly true when the governance reforms are aimed primarily (and even exclusively) at augmenting corporate profitability—and no attention is given to the underlying processes through which corporate profits are generated and distributed.

As we know, the primary argument for the recent reforms lies in their ability to unleash the dynamism of private enterprise, by liberating it from state control on the one hand, and inefficient state protection on the other. These two elements, state control and state protection had allegedly affected corporate profitability in a counterproductive manner. Accordingly, several important changes were put in place that led to the dismantling of the regulatory framework through which the Indian state had historically regulated the activities of the corporate sector. Have these changes affected the Indian economy in ways predicted by the reformers? More specifically, have they been able to unleash a process that stimulates corporate profitability and, in turn, growth of employment, wages, and aggregate demand?

In order to answer these questions, I shall not embark on yet another statistical exercise, as many such exist. Rather, I shall begin by examining the general arguments that theorize the intrinsic ability of corporations to foster economic growth. Next, I shall discuss the general applicability of these theories to the Indian case, especially in the context of the reform efforts. Finally, I shall briefly discuss the historical trends that have characterized corporate profits in India, in particular, to assess the argument that an increase in corporate profitability can engender economic growth.

The paper is organized in three sections. The first section discusses some broad strands in the literature on corporate profitability and economic growth. This section draws extensively on my earlier work (Mukherjee Reed, 2001).

The second section will discuss the applicability of these theories to India, with specific references to the economic reforms. The third section will reflect further on the effect of the reforms and present some concluding observations.

Corporations and Economic Growth: The Arguments

There are several strands of literature I wish to consider, each of which offers explanations as to how modern corporations may contribute to development. In what follows, I shall discuss five approaches to the question: (a) the organizational learning argument, as advanced by Chandler, Amsden, and others; (b) the aggregate demand argument (of Boyer and the regulationists); (c) the transaction cost argument (as developed by Coase and Williamson); (d) the classic finance-theoretic arguments about the centrality of shareholder value maximization (Friedman, Miller, and other Chicago economists); and (e) the corporate strategy-centred argument that critique the finance-theoretic model (Porter and Prahalad). Next, I shall discuss how these arguments hold in the case of India. I shall then conclude by identifying some forces and actors that are likely to affect most the trajectory along which the Indian corporate economy is likely to evolve.

Consider first what might be called the Chandler-Amsden theses, which emphasize the following aspects of the corporate form: (1) its ability to exploit economies of scale; (2) its ability to recruit and develop the kind of human capital necessary for using and commercializing new technologies as soon as they come into existence, and; (3) its ability to become the primary drivers of technological advances and the seat of continuous learning.

As is well known, Chandler emphasizes the superiority of the corporate form with respect to its ability to learn and commercialize technology. He also argues that, despite the fact that the rise of the large corporation led to the early emergence of distorted market structures, such distortion aided—rather than hindered—overall industrial growth rates in the US (Chandler and Daems, 1980; Chandler et al., 1997). Amsden (1989) makes this argument (in my view, even more powerfully) in the context of ('late') development. She demonstrates exactly how the organizational strengths of oligopolistic enterprises were harnessed by the Korean state, which at the same time *proved capable of deterring typical profit strategies associated with oligopolistic behaviour from dampening the speed of growth.* This point is absolutely critical, I think, in understanding the dynamics of growth through big business in east Asia. It provides not only an explanation of east Asian growth, but can also give us important pointers as to why such growth was also conducive to increasing material well-being of east Asian workers, as well as a continuous enhancement of their skills and abilities. This could explain in turn, why east Asia's record of income distribution has been much better than that of the US. However, none of these east Asian successes can take away from the essentially undemocratic political structures to which east Asian workers (and civil societies) were subjected—especially during the miracle years (although assessing them simply by contrasting them to the structures of formal democracy in the West is not likely to be particularly fruitful).

Why, then was it the case in east Asia that growth-dampening oligopolistic behaviour could be contained? Several answers are available in the literature. Amsden, for instance, argues that the answer lies in the particular abilities and visions of the east Asian bureaucracy. Others draw upon the uniqueness of Confucian ethics. Business historians and corporate strategists offer yet a third explanation, namely, that east Asian companies place little value on market profits relative to the expansion of size, assets, and 'corporate honour'. As McCraw points out:

> If there is any one key to the Japanese economic miracle, it lies in the maintenance of a fever pitch of inter-firm competition that by the 1990s had persisted without abatement into its fourth decade. This remarkable aspect of Japanese capitalism is insufficiently understood in the West, and its importance is often underestimated even by Japanese scholars. It is a competition that emphasises market shares as much as profit, if not more. It is a ceaseless, almost obsessive drive to uphold the status of the company—not for the purpose or with the aim of driving domestic competitors out of business, but of maintaining position and corporate honour, and of avoiding shame (McCraw, 1997:543).

Those who espouse this latter view attempt to break with the strong statist interpretation of east Asian success, which portrays business as a passive partner in the process of development (Johnson, 1982; Evans et al., 1985; Amsden, 1989; Haggard, 1990). Not surprisingly, business historians often reject this passive image, as they salvage from the archive of corporate histories the various corporate strategies, decision-making processes and value systems that contributed to the growth process (McCraw, 1997). In any case, the fact remains that the east Asian economies were able to prevent some of the common growth-retarding effects of oligopolistic behaviour, the most important of which was to retain price-based competition, which in turn was predicated on continuous 'learning'. This ability, it may be argued, also accounts for the more egalitarian distribution of income that the Korean model produced, (at least) relative to the US and other parts of the developing world—this, despite the absence of any state-administered redistributive measures.

As has often been argued, this technology-centred argument is necessarily incomplete in that it ignores the other side of the equation, i.e.

the problem of demand. What made this continuous learning, expansion, and commercialization feasible? What guaranteed the requisite increases in the size of the market? The answer to this question is fairly straightforward in the east Asian case; markets were found abroad. A number of scholars have identified this outward orientation of the east Asian regimes as the primary source of their growth, and the inward orientation of countries like India as the primary reason for their stagnation (Krueger, 1974; 1978; Bhagwati, 1988; Bhagwati and Srinivasan,1999).

In the case of the West, however, it is not enough to point to the importance of exports; the dynamics of the domestic market also must be explained. Neither Chandler nor the other growth theorists of his genre address this issue in a fully satisfactory way. Was there anything particular to classic Fordist capitalism that ensured the expansion of aggregate demand? As Boyer (1996) argues, the fact that in the Fordist model productivity gains were directly translated into wage increases lead, in turn, to a synchronization of productivity increases and aggregate demand. In addition to Continental Europe, where this certainly was the case, Boyer argues that this held true even in the US until the 1970s, when US Fordism allegedly entered its process of structural decline. The 'golden phase' in the US was also marked by an unprecedented reduction of wage differentials, which resulted in a similar synergy between growth of productive capacity and aggregate demand (Boyer, 1996:51). Boyer then goes on to make an even stronger argument. Contrary to the neo-liberal assertion that the redistributive elements of Fordism are responsible for its decline, the truth may in fact be the reverse—it is exactly those elements of redistribution, rather than technological learning, that account for the 'golden age', both in the US and in the Continent.

While I accept the general thrust of Boyer's thesis, it is important to add to it the economic relationships between the Third World and the West that also contributed to rising aggregate demand during the golden age. Let us return to the question of aggregate demand at a later point and for now go on to consider several other strands of relevant literature. I wish to consider next the Coase-Williamson type of argument that corporations create wealth by minimizing transaction costs. Despite the growing popularity of this literature, transaction cost economics can have only limited relevance to the problematics of development, however narrowly conceived (Bardhan, 1989). The basis of this limitation is that this approach, because of its normative and epistemological commitment to neo-classical economics, does not provide us with a theory as to why particular transaction costs evolve in particular economies—or more generally why particular institutions emerge in particular contexts. Neither can it explain why 'inefficient' institutions persist over long periods of time. As Bardhan (1989) argues, these 'non-explanations' reflect a fundamental problem with the approach, i.e. its total disregard for the issues of power and inequity. A prime example of this is provided by the managing agency model of governance in colonial India (Mukherjee Reed, 2001). While a transaction cost view could indeed explain its function in the colonial economy, what such an explanation would exclude is the extremely skewed nature of the ownership of capital that made the institution viable. In my view, such exclusion takes away substantially from a full analysis of the impact of the institution in question.

Next, consider the classic argument on value maximization put forward by Friedman, Miller, and their cohorts from the Chicago School. The essence of the argument is, of course, as old as corporate capitalism itself, namely, businesses create value by maximizing wealth for their shareholders. In this model, there is no possibility of a shortage of aggregate demand. According to a tenet that economists call Say's Law, this model believes that an increase in supply automatically creates an increase in demand.

This model has been further developed by finance theorists to argue that, as providers of equity capital, shareholders are the *residual claimants* who bear most of the risk and they accordingly should receive the lion's share of the rewards. Other corporate stakeholders—customers, employees, and local communities—should be *adequately* compensated and no more. Implicit in this view is a clear hierarchy of corporate objectives in which the maximization of shareholder value reigns supreme and 'the ultimate scorecard for managers becomes the current stock price—or more precisely, stockholder returns over a definite time horizon' (Prahalad, 1997: 51).

This orthodox finance-theoretic model has been strongly criticized by corporate strategists like Porter (1997) and Prahalad (1997). Porter's argument is that in order to contribute to economic growth, companies must remain globally competitive. Global or macro-competitiveness, in turn, depends on how well companies invest in *intangibles* like the building of strong networks, process improvements, employee training, etc. In Porter's view, the US system—with its focus of near-term profitability and shareholder value—discourages investment in intangibles and hence undermines the prospects for the long-term growth of the economy. Prahalad (1997) puts forward an even stronger argument; that no significant change in corporate behaviour can be brought about unless we acknowledge that corporations must add value in a way that all its stakeholders' interests are ascribed equal primacy. This would imply eschewing the hierarchy of stakeholders in which shareowners reign supreme and corporate goals are oriented towards maximization of shareholder value.

Both Porter and Prahalad note that the east Asian and European systems of corporate governance are better equipped to discourage short-termism and allocate investment in favour of intangibles. This is so because both these systems are able to control the extent to which the capital market is able to shape corporate, and even some social, objectives. However, they also acknowledge, particularly in the wake of Euro-sclerosis and the Asian crisis, that those systems are also flawed in that there is too little external disciplining (this is the immensely popular thesis advanced by Paul Krueger). What they propose therefore is an amalgamation of the two models.

Their suggested model, however, is quite different from the one that seems to be evolving in Europe, east Asia, and in other parts of the developing world. While they suggest designing governance mechanisms that combine the interests of the various stakeholders—with a clear reduction in the importance of the *stockholder*—what is occurring in reality is quite the opposite. As the Indian case clearly demonstrates, the *maximization of shareholder value* is clearly the shared objective of all the critical actors: the state, business, international donors, foreign institutional investors, as well as a fairly large and influential community of scholars working out of leading institutions in India and abroad. Echoes of a similar commitment to shareholder value can be heard in Mexico, in Brazil, in South Africa, and in much of the developing world, as well as in the transitional economies of Europe. Of crucial importance here is also the global emergence of mechanisms that seek to *legitimate* the concern for shareholder value, especially in the developing world, through the creation of codes, norms of governance, and the various schemes intended to demonstrate corporate social responsibility.

The critical point about shareholder value maximization that is largely ignored in the corporate strategy literature is that profit strategies that maximize shareholder value often inhibit development. Furthermore, this strategy has the potential of pitting the interest of the shareholder against that of the worker. Consider, for instance, the famous Yorkshire businessmen, James Hanson and George White, who during Margaret Thatcher's regime were held as paragons of British business and awarded peerages for their performance as creators of wealth. Hanson became particularly noted for 'commitment to his shareholders' and his ability to acquire companies that continuously maximized shareholder value. The strategy to accomplish this did not, however, come from the growth and expansion of the businesses acquired. Rather it came 'from closing factories, from shedding labour, from pension holidays and appropriating surpluses in pension funds, from avoiding stamp duty on purchases by shuffling assets internationally, by tax evasion through the use of 26 Panamanian companies, etc.' (Hampden-Turner and Tompernas, 1993: 314).

As a contrast to these Anglo-American approaches to wealth creation, consider the Japanese/east Asian strategy:

One key factor in Japanese growth was the willingness to invest heavily in both product development and process development for more than two decades while cash returns were low and growing too slowly .... Over the same period many American firms were actually ceding products and functions to foreign competitors and diversifying into less risky and more profitable areas such as car rentals and financial services, unrelated to their original lines of work.[1]

Applicability to the Indian Case

Let us now consider how exactly the above arguments apply to India. The Chandler-Amsden thesis is an obvious potential explanation for the retarded development trajectories of countries like India. However, it is not clear that technology by itself would have been sufficient to engender the kind of growth that Chandler and Amsden discuss. While it is true that east Asian patterns of 'learning' did not occur in India, a fair amount of technology and capital was accumulated in both the public and private sectors. What remains absent is the diffusion of this technology in a manner that enhances the skills of the average Indian worker. In the light of this observation, it is deeply ironic that Indian corporations enjoy significant tax concessions for investment in research and development. (By way of example, it could be noted that, notwithstanding its record-breaking profit rates, India's most aggressively growing corporation, Reliance Industries, has qualified for *zero* taxes for a number of years on this basis.)[2]

Recent research also points to two disturbing aspects of research and development and its role in corporate profitability. Besant (2000) points out that the growth rates of real private sector R&D expenditure (at 1980–81 prices) has decreased considerably between 1974–75 and 1994–95. The aggregate expenditure ratio across all industries has decreased from 17.1 per cent during 1974–80 to 7.1 per cent during 1991–95. Similarly, R&D to sales ratio declined marginally from 0.76 per cent in 1974–75 to 0.70 percent in 1994–95. In twelve out of twenty-eight industries, real R&D expenditures declined. In six out of twenty-eight industry groups, the rate of growth of real R&D expenditures was positive in the 1990s, but lower than in the late 1980s. More importantly, even in industries where real R&D expenditures have risen, the R&D to sales ratios have either stagnated or declined (see Table 9.1).

TABLE 9.1 *Growth rates of real private sector R&D expenditure by major industry group (1980–81 prices)*

Industry Group	*1974–80*	*1980–86*	*1986–91*	*1991–95*	*1974–95*
Metallurgical industries	21.5	1.5	4.9	3.7	5.1
Fuels	17.9	–6.8	6.5	–16.4	–0.4
Boilers and steam generating plants	–29.5	21.3	53.3	–19.0	10.4
Prime movers	6.5	–6.0	14.9	–24.1	6.6
Electrical and electronics equipment	12.6	5.0	5.8	–1.5	5.5
Telecommunications	23.7	–8.3	–0.7	14.4	8.4
Transportation	27.5	–2.6	28.6	12.0	10.6
Industrial machinery	26.8	12.5	3.9	–4.1	5.3
Machine tools	28.5	9.4	26.3	–16.6	9.3
Agricultural machinery	15.2	–4.3	–0.3	33.9	2.0
Misc mechanical, engineering Industries	–37.3	–4.1	57.6	–6.8	13.3
Commercial offices, household equipment	16.1	12.4	39.6	–15.2	10.8
Industrial equipment	28.8	5.6	–32.6	32.3	9.2
Scientific instruments	44.1	25.8	–4.2	–40.5	6.3
Fertilizers	–12.3	–10.0	42.5	7.4	6.9
Chemicals (other than fertilizers)	20.2	–0.2	–10.2	11.7	5.3
Dye-stuffs	10.4	–10.5	5.5	11.4	2.2
Drugs and pharmaceuticals	7.6	8.2	0.0	14.0	7.2
Textiles (dyed, printed, and processed)	19.9	4.3	–11.9	11.4	4.4
Paper and pulp	17.2	7.6	–30.6	–7.7	–2.4
Sugar	40.9	19.2	16.3	4.4	11.9
Food processing industries	19.5	24.9	29.1	7.2	12.7
Soaps, cosmetics, toilet preparations	9.9	2.3	–7.1	12.3	3.8
Rubber goods	31.9	6.9	32.8	0.4	9.6
Leather and leather goods	NA	1.7	100.0	–11.7	20.8
Glass	13.0	–15.0	9.3	12.4	2.5

(Contd)

Industry Group	*1974–80*	*1980–86*	*1986–91*	*1991–95*	*1974–95*
Ceramics	23.7	2.0	7.2	–2.8	1.7
Cement and gypsum	27.8	0.6	2.0	2.3	1.6
Total	17.1	4.0	7.6	7.4	6.7

Source: Research and Development Statistics, (various volumes), Department of Science and Technology, Government of India, New Delhi, cited in Besant, R. 'Corporate Response to Economic Reforms', *Economic & Political Weekly*, 4 March 2000.

In any event, productivity at all levels remains a major problem in India. Unfortunately, the debate on economic reforms has not focused on productivity—except for the allegations that various forms of state control have stifled productivity—at least until recently. Breaking this trend, a recent study by Accenture, a leading management consulting firm, suggests that 20–50 per cent productivity improvements in Indian manufacturing businesses are possible through internal initiatives. The study refers to the well-known deficiencies of Indian corporates (family-owned businesses and professionally managed companies alike) such as hierarchical management styles, lack of accountability and transparency, indifference to issues of quality and value, inadequacies in organizational and manpower management, etc. These issues, which in some sense are classic problems of governance, can be addressed only by examining the underlying issues of power. Again, in the context of the current debate, the focus has always been disproportionately on state power rather than corporate power.

Let us now turn to the transactions cost approach. As some authors have already pointed out, the transaction cost approach has limited applicability with respect to India, or more generally to the problematic of development. It needs to be acknowledged, however, that this approach enjoys considerable credibility amongst policy makers and academics of a certain disposition. It is strongly believed in these circles that certain elements of the reform programme—particularly those related to the financial sector—have been conducive to significant reductions in transaction costs. While in a strictly technical sense transactions costs may have been reduced due to capital market liberalization efforts, significant new costs have emerged simultaneously. In part these costs have emerged from the paradoxical situation that characterize post-interventionist India, namely, the continuation of some important elements of state intervention *simultaneously* with weakened regulatory powers of the state. The autonomous institutions, which were formed as part of the reform process have, more often than not, failed to ensure that citizens can take advantage of the lowered transactions costs. Much of this failure emanates from, again, the underlying power relations that the reforms have left unchallenged.

Let us turn now to the argument that comprises the basic tenet of the neo-liberal reforms, namely, that corporations contribute most to society when they maximize shareholder value. There are several implications of this in the Indian context. On the one hand, even though there has been considerable growth in the number of share-owning households in India, the proportion of such households remain quite low relative to the Indian population. On the other hand, the growth of this share-owning population and, most importantly, the decision to allow employees' provident funds and pension earnings to be invested in corporate securities ascribes a new salience to the issue. These funds comprise the lifelong savings of millions of working Indians and are currently estimated to amount to Rs 2 trillion (approximately US $40 billion).[3] Historically, these funds could be invested only in government securities and tended to earn low returns. The decision to bring this rather significant amount to the capital market and make it available to the corporate sector raises some very important dilemmas.

First, it is possible that the objective of maximization of shareholder value will yield substantive benefit to the average Indian shareholder, both directly, as well as indirectly by increasing the value of his pension funds. However, as it is being increasingly acknowledged, such value maximization the world over comes about at very serious costs, the most important of which is corporate restructuring (including mergers and acquisitions) along with large-scale retrenchment. In the case of economies like India, value maximization is associated with distorted market structures, the negative impact of which is serious. Further, there is great potential for maximizing shareholder value through insider trading and price manipulation. This is precisely what has been witnessed in the successive capital market scams. Needless to say, the kind of shareholder activism or government regulation that would be required to exclude the possibility of value maximization through these mechanisms is unlikely to emerge in India in the near future. In India, a country that has twenty-three recognized stock exchanges and a 125-year history of organized trading, there exists now only twelve investor associations that are recognized by SEBI.

The extent of shareholder activism cannot be enhanced through simple reforms of the governance structures, as is increasingly revealed through instances like Enron. The problem here is primarily one of power. However much structures of corporate governance are reformed, the broader relationship between state and business continues to place stringent limits on the claims of the small shareholder. In India's case, this is being proved time again in the struggles over the power of SEBI, which become particularly salient at times of severe crisis in the stock market. Despite a number of extremely severe crises, and repeated demands by the SEBI chief for more executive powers, the government has refrained from ascribing to SEBI the autonomy that it required.

Consider for instance a recent complaint filed by an accountant, S. Gurumurthy, against one of India's largest business groups, the Ambanis:

> There has been a "gigantic fraud perpetrated by Ambanis" in allotting themselves 120 million shares of Reliance Industries Ltd in January 2000. The modus operandi was the conversion of a preferential issue of non-convertible debentures with warrants (representing 11.38 per cent of the capital at that time), causing, ...a wrongful loss to the company and its investors a huge Rs 27 billion (approximately $500 million). The crux of the "fraud" according to Gurumurthy is as follows: On December 10, 1992, Reliance Industries passed a single resolution (No. 3) authorising the company to issue Rs 3 billion worth of Non-Convertible Debentures with or without warrants and which prohibited any issue to directors or to entities which the directors were interested or concerned with. However, instead of one issue, the Ambanis allegedly made two issues under this single resolution (Dalal, 2002a).[4]

If this were merely a problem of corruption or misgovernance, perhaps legal solutions could be sufficient. The problem is one of power and of a historical relationship between state and business.[5] This is manifested, for example, in the proposals that come from the government itself and that are obviously intended to work against shareholder activism. As one of India's leading financial columnists reports in her column on 4 December 2001:

> Last week the government attempted to push through an amendment to the Companies Bill 2001 to allow companies to buy back 10 per cent of their capital with a simple board resolution instead of the special resolution. As against this companies could only buy back 5 per cent of their equity in a given year that too after investor approval through a special resolution.
>
> The bill was attempting to convert an ordinance, which was hastily promulgated a few weeks ago, into an Act. And the Ministry of Law, Justice and Company Affairs, justified it as 'a suggestion from the finance ministry' aimed at boosting *market sentiment*... this blatantly anti-investor move was pushed through the Securities and Exchange Board of India with record speed and little discussion, apparently at the finance ministry's insistence. Nobody bothered to notice that it wasn't investors who were demanding increased share buyback but the corporate sector (Dalal, 2001).

What emerges from the above are two primary problems with the value maximization approach. The first is that shareholder value maximization depends primarily on strategies that are inimical to development. The second is the potential that it has to pit the shareholder's interests against the interests of the worker. This assumes greater importance in the current context of widespread retrenchment and voluntary retirement schemes that have been handed out to millions of workers around the globe. These schemes are geared towards turning the worker into the small investor whose material interests thereby get intrinsically tied to shareholder value.

Considerations such as these suggest the importance of perspectives that are critical of the wealth maximization approach. I mentioned two perspectives above, the strategic arguments of business theorists like Porter and Prahalad and the demand-theoretic arguments put forward by left Keynesians. The first set of arguments are important in that they come from within the corporate community and, being cast in terms of corporate strategy, are more likely to find a hearing. However, the strategic orientation of these arguments is also the source of their potential weakness, since they do not address the broader questions as to how strategic interests of capital are contingent upon history and structure.

Let us turn now to the demand-theoretic arguments of left Keynesians. In conjunction with these arguments it may also be useful to consider a wide range of development theorists who have commented on similar issues (Bagchi, 1982; 1994; 1999; Bardhan, 1993; Nayyar, 1994; 1995; Singh, 1994; Stiglitz, 1999). Common to all these authors is the recognition of the importance of aggregate demand, and the analytical assertion that at least in the context of a less-developed economy, supply does not create its own demand. In this sense, they argue that economic reforms—being comprised of policy measures that intend to increase labour market flexibility through wage cuts and retrenchments—are inherently inimical to the expansion of aggregate demand in the long run.

Now, the macro-economic aspects of this problem have already been widely discussed and it is increasingly being admitted by all—even the IMF—that macro-economic management is a necessary precondition for the success of reforms. However, macro-economic analysis often refrains from elaborating how the impact of macro-economic policies are realized through the various profit strategies that corporations employ and how, unless these macro policies are aimed *directly at* altering profit strategies, their intended outcomes are unlikely to be realized. As I have argued elsewhere (2001), such a direct targeting of micro policies (profit strategies) was exactly what was done in east Asia and remains, I would argue, one of the most enduring legacies of the 'miracle'. That said, one has to acknowledge the centrality of two factors in determining the success of these strategies—the authoritarian political framework within which they were implemented and the exploitation of east Asian labour.

The crucial question that emerges from the above is how to alter profit strategies in a manner that is compatible with democratic norms and with processes that stimulate a virtuous cycle of aggregate demand, employment, and redistributive growth. At the very least, the processes through which corporate profits are generated should not be directly conducive to the reduction in employment and demand. In order to answer this question, it may be useful to explore exactly what the profit strategies in India have historically been and how the recent reforms affect them. For limitations of space, I shall simply summarize below some of the major features of Indian profit strategies, and then go on to locate the possible trajectories of change that may emanate from the process of reforms.

CONCLUSIONS

As was argued in Chapter 2, India's corporate history can be sketched in terms of three historical models, namely, the *managing agency* model of the colonial period; the *business house* model of the interventionist period; and the *Anglo-American* model of the post-interventionist period. Throughout this history, profits in India have arisen primarily from non-market forces, as well as from market manoeuvres associated with distorted market structures. As was previously argued in Chapter 2, the interventionist state played a critical role in making these profit strategies viable.

As is well known, advocates of economic reforms have claimed, first and foremost, that their reform measures would be successful in 'uncoupling' the state and business, so that neither could amass gains by using the other. However, as I continue to find in my own research, the reforms have not altered, and are not likely to alter, the sources of corporate profitability of Indian firms in any significant way. Exactly as in the interventionist era, state support—in particular in the form of project finance, infrastructural support, and foregone tax revenues—remains crucial to corporate growth in the post-interventionist era. Obviously, the specific conduits through which such support is administered have changed quite substantially and are increasingly mediated through the market.

In this respect, the intervention of the public financial institutions in the capital market have been critical, with rather serious consequences for the small saver and investor. The UTI crisis and the capital market scams that were briefly discussed in Chapter 2 are important examples in this regard. Most notably, the state is mediating quite systematically (as it did before) the channelling of small savings into investible capital. This is being done in two major ways. First, by using the authority and credibility of large public financial institutions an attempt is made to attract small investments and then administer 'new' market instruments like private placements, book, building, and initial public offerings (IPOs). Second, the state has also aided the supply of capital by allowing workers' pension funds to be invested in equity. The impact of the first strategy has clearly been disastrous, with each of the measures resulting in severe losses for millions of small investors. While the verdict on the second strategy is still awaited, given the 'structural' problems with stock markets globally, as well as in India, it is probably not difficult to guess the outcome we could expect.

Contrary to the claims of neo-liberal economists, the relationship between corporate profitability and development (even when narrowly construed) seems far from positive. The present stage in the economic reforms indicates in fact a simultaneous crisis in development and corporate profitability. If one is ready to eschew the neo-liberal economic framework, it is immediately obvious as to where the problem lies and what the remedies could be. The basic problem, as we have seen, is that profit strategies in India are not related to innovation and productivity gains. As a result, the link between profits and economic growth are broken as increased corporate profits do not necessarily translate into increased aggregate demand.

In addressing this situation, there is first of all a need to systematically address the problem of aggregate demand. A second and closely related problem to be tackled is the issue of governance. As is being increasingly indicated by global developments, the foremost problem of governance is the necessity to establish public control over all major public institutions and corporations. The liberal Anglo-American notions of transparency and accountability fall short of the kind of vigilance that is required in a situation such as India's, where business and government share a historical relationship. Finally, it needs to be stated that (minimal and strategically motivated) attention to issues of corporate social responsibility, while important to those who directly benefit, is unlikely to reverse the deeply unequal and undemocratic nature of the corporate economy or to contribute in any significant way to development.

Notes

1. Excerpted from *Made in America*: *Regaining the Productive Edge*, The Massachusetts Institute of Technology Commission on Industrial Productivity, 1989, cited in Hampden-Turner and Tompernas, 1993: 184.

2. In general, it has been observed that 'investments in research and development (R&D) fell as a proportion of GDP through the decade of the 1980s; the share of the

private sector in industrial R&D fell from 58 per cent in 1980–81 to 54 per cent in 1990–91' (Kaplinsky, 1997: 686).

3. Prime Minister's Council on Trade and Industry, *Reforms in the Financial Sector and Capital Markets*, Chapter 7, para 7.4, accessed online http://www.nic.in/pmcouncils/reports/fin/.

4. Dalal was the first journalist to unveil the Indian stock market scam of 1992. See also Dalal (2002b).

5. For a fuller discussion on this, see Mukherjee Reed (2001).

References

Ahluwahlia, I.J. (1985). *Industrial Growth in India: Stagnation Since the Mid-Sixties*, New Delhi: Oxford University Press.

Amsden, A. (1989). *Asia's Next Giant: South Korea and Late Industrialization*, Oxford, NY: Oxford University Press.

Bagchi, A.K. (1982). *The Political Economy of Underdevelopment*, Cambridge: Cambridge University Press.

_____ (1992). *The Political Economy of Underdevelopment*, Cambridge: Cambridge University Press.

_____ (1994). 'European and Indian Entrpreneurship in India 1900–30', In *Entrepreneurship and Industry in India 1800–1947*, (ed.) R.K. Ray, New Delhi: Oxford University Press.

_____ (1999). 'Globalisation, Liberalisation and Vulnerability: India and Third World', *Economic and Political Weekly*, 6 November.

Bardhan, P. (1989). 'The new institutional economics and development theory: a brief critical assessment', *World Development*, 17, September, pp. 1389–95.

_____ (1993). 'Economics of Development and the Development of Economics', 7 (2), pp.129–42.

Bhagwati, J.N. (1988). 'Export-Promoting Trade Strategy: Issues and Evidence', *World Bank Research Observer*, vol. 3 (1), pp. 27–57.

Bhagwati, J. and P. Desai (1970). *India: Planning & Industrialization*, New Delhi: Oxford University Press.

Bhagwati, J.N. and T.N. Srinivasan (1999). 'Outward Orientation and Development: Are the Revisionists Right?', Centre Discussion Paper, No. 86, New Haven: Yale University, Economic Growth Center 17 September.

Business Standard (2001). 'Home ministry objects to more powers for Sebi', 17 October.

Boyer, R. (1996). 'The Seven Paradoxes of Capitalism. Or is a theory of modern economies still possible?', Centre d'Etudes Prospectives d'Economie Mathematique Appliquees, Paper no. 9620, October.

Chandler, A.D. Jr. and H. Daems (eds) (1980). *Managerial Hierarchies: Comparative Perspectives on the Rise of the Modern Industrial Enterprise*, Cambridge, MA: Harvard University Press.

Chandler, A.D.Jr, F. Amatori and T. Hikino (eds) (1997). *Big Business and the Wealth of Nations*, Cambridge: Cambridge University Press.

Conference Board (1999). Institutional Investment Report—Financial Assets and Equity Holdings, vol. 3, No. 1, New York, August.

Dalal, S. (2001). 'Investor activism: Indian capital markets' missing link', Rediff On the Net (www.rediff.com), 4 December.

_____ (2002a). 'S Gurumurthy on the warpath against Reliance again', Rediff On the Net (www.rediff.com), 8 February.

_____ (2002b). 'Corporate power makes putty of Sebi', *The Statesman*, 1 March.

Evans, Peter B., D. Reuschemeyer, and T. Skocpol (eds) (1985). *Bringing the State Back In*, Cambridge: Cambridge University Press.

Evans, P. (1995). *Embedded Autonomy* Princteon, NJ: Princeton University Press.

Government of India (1985). *The Seventh Plan*, New Delhi: Planning Commission of India.

Haggard, S. (1990). *Pathway from the Periphery: The Politics of Growth in the Newly Industrializing Countries*, Ithaca, NY: Cornell University Press.

Hampden-Turner, C. and A. Trompenaars (1993). *The seven cultures of capitalism: value systems for creating wealth in the United States, Japan, Germany, France, Britain, Sweden, and the Netherlands*, New York: Currency Doubleday.

Jalan, B. (1992). *India's Economic Crisis: The Way Ahead*, Oxford: Oxford University Press.

Johnson, C. (1982). *MITI and the Japanese Miracle: The Growth of Industrial Policy, 1925–1975*, Stanford, CA: Stanford University Press.

Joshi, V. and L.M.D. Little (1995). 'Macroeconomic Stabilization in India, 1991–1993 and Beyond', In *India: The Future of Economic Reforms*, (eds) R. Cassen and V.Joshi, New Delhi: Oxford University Press.

Kambhampati, U. (1996). *US. Industrial Concentration and Performance: A Study of the Structure, Conduct and Performance of Indian Industry (1970–85)*, New Delhi: Oxford University Press.

Kaplinsky, R. (1997). 'India's Industrial Development: An Interpretive Survey', *World Development*, 25 (5), pp.681–94.

Krueger, Anne O. (1974). 'The Political Economy of the Rent-Seeking Society', *American Economic Review*, 64 (3), pp. 291–303.

_____ (1978). *Foreign Trade Regimes and Economic Development: Liberalization Attempts and Consequences*, Cambridge, MA: Ballinger.

Kurien, C.T. (1994). *Global Capitalism and the Indian Economy*, New Delhi: Orient Longman.

McCraw, T. (1997). 'Government, big business, and the wealth of nations', In *Big Business and the Wealth of Nations*, (eds) A.D. Chandler, F. Amatori, and T. Hikino, Cambridge, MA: Harvard University Press.

Mukherjee Reed, A. (2001). *Perspectives on the Indian Corporate Economy: Exploring the paradox of profits*, London: Palgrave.

Nayyar, D. (ed.) (1994). *Industrial Growth and Stagnation: The Debate in India*, Bombay: Oxford University Press.

_____ (ed) (1997). *Trade and Industrialisation*, New Delhi: Oxford University Press.

Porter, M.E. (1997). 'Capital Choices: Changing the Way America Invests in Industry', In *Studies in International Corporate Finance and Governance Systems*, (ed.) Donald H. Chew, New York: Oxford University Press.

Prahalad, C.K. (1997). 'Corporate Governance or Corporate Value Added: Rethinking the Primacy of Shareholder Value', In *Studies in International Corporate Finance and Governance System*, (ed.) D.H. Chew, New York: Oxford University Press, pp. 46–56.

Singh A. (1994). *Corporate Financing Patterns in Industrializing Economies: A Comparative International Study*, Washington, DC: IFC.

Stiglitz, J. (1999). 'Labor Participation and The East Asian Crisis', paper presented at the Seoul Conference on Democracy, Market Economy and Development, 26–27 February.

10

The Role of Business in Society

Business-NGOs Partnerships for Development

Shankar Venkateswaran

INTRODUCTION

An issue that is engaging the attention of businesses, civil society leaders, governments, multilateral organizations, and academics the world over is the role of business in development. And each one is seeing the role differently. Some are focusing on the resources that businesses have and how to harness these for the greater public good. Others are researching business models that facilitate their involvement in development. Still others are looking at what needs to be done to change the behaviour of business so that they are concerned about their impact on society while trying to maximize shareholder wealth.

This article attempts to look at how in a country like India, businesses should and must be a partner in development and suggests that partnerships between companies and NGOs can play a crucial role in making this involvement effective. It takes up this question by looking at the self-understanding and experience of *Partners in Change* (PiC).

PiC is a not-for-profit organization that was set up in 1995 by ActionAid to critically engage businesses as partners in development in India. Its mission is 'to increase the understanding and active participation of business in equitable social development as an integral part of good business practice by promoting partnerships between business, disadvantaged communities, development initiatives and government'. PiC believes that businesses have great potential to do good and harm to disadvantaged people, with actual results being greatly dependent on how people in businesses understand their impact on communities. Thus, PiC focuses on maximizing the good and minimizing the harm that businesses can do to society by increasing this understanding and motivating companies to look not just at maximizing shareholder value but also societal value. It does this by advocating businesses to play a greater role in development and by finding innovative ways for people in companies to work directly with and make a lasting difference to the lives of disadvantaged communities and other stakeholders.

Corporate Social Responsibility

As the debates on corporate social responsibility (CSR) increase, so too do the descriptions and interpretations of what CSR really is. Clearly, this is a journey and not a destination, and the question that clearly needs an answer is 'What does CSR mean'?

There are no universally accepted definitions of CSR. One extreme view is that a company that complies with the laws of the land in which it operates is being socially responsible. Another extreme view is that a socially responsible company is one that is purely philanthropic in the sense that it gives without expecting a return or a benefit. There are still companies and NGOs that subscribe to these extreme views.

Increasingly, there seems to be some convergence around the position that neither of these two extreme positions adequately describes CSR. Why? To quote from UNCTAD's report on The Social Responsibility of Transnational Corporations (UNCTAD, 1999: 4), 'an external programme of good deeds will not protect a firm whose actual operations harm its surrounding society'. Thus, just being purely philanthropic externally is not enough. At the same time, complying with the law is just the minimum behaviour to legally stay in business and it certainly has nothing to do with society's expectations, which is essential for the 'social' in CSR to have any meaning.

Framework for CSR Activities

Even a cursory review of the literature on CSR (which predominantly comes from the West) indicates that there are many ways to categorize and report on CSR activities. In what follows, we examine a few of the more prominent examples of the range of views on CSR.

The Prince of Wales Business Leaders' Forum (PWBLF)

The PWBLF is one of the leading international organizations working on the issue of CSR. In a work published jointly with UNDP and the World Bank, it is argued that companies can serve its stakeholders in many ways, including:

- Its core business activities, which looks at its policies, operations, and production activities (in terms of safety, quality, environmental implications, etc.,) both within the business as well as its backward and forward linkages such as suppliers, distributors, and customer relations.
- Social investments and philanthropy, i.e. moving from ad hoc giving to strategic approaches to building community partnerships, looking for 'win-win' solutions, applying core competencies to such investments and linking community investments to mainstream business strategy.
- Public policy dialogue wherein businesses advocate with the state for changes in public policy that may benefit the business but its core motivation is public interest (Nelson, 1996: 58–75).

London Benchmarking Group (LBG) Model

The LBG seeks to develop and expand the reporting of company activities in the community so that they are more transparent and can be judged by the impact they achieve. The Group, which consists of some of the leading companies working in the UK, has devised a model to classify what companies do in the community by their motivation and this is illustrated below in Figure 10.1 (Diageo plc, June 1999). The model consists of four basic components.

The *Philanthropic* component is typically what all companies, including Indian ones, do. What characterizes this component is that companies rarely expect a return other than the reputation of being a 'caring company'. This is a response to a need and manifests itself not just as donations of money or kind but also employee volunteering.

The *Social Investment* component involves companies becoming more systematic and strategic with their community involvement while looking at business benefits in the medium term. Such activities are typically aimed at communities but employees and their families can be the beneficiaries too.

In *Commercial Initiatives*, the company is focusing more on the short-term commercial benefits of the involvement, while addressing social issues. Cause-related marketing or event sponsorships are typical examples of this type of engagement.

The *Business Basics* part of the model relates to how the company does its business and whether it is sensitive about the impact of its business on society and the planet, i.e. societal and environmental returns apart from financial returns—the so-called 'triple bottom line' reporting.

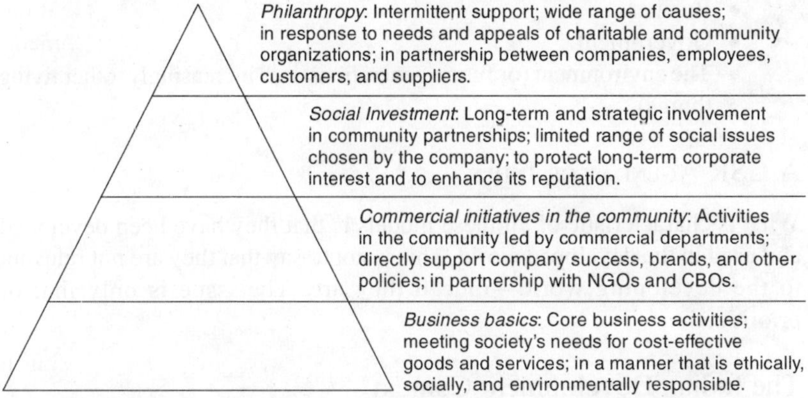

Fig. 10.1 *LBG model of Company Involvement in the Community*

Corporate Citizenship Company (CCC) Framework

The Corporate Citizenship Company is a UK-based organization that advises companies on the issue of social responsibility. Based on its own experience in the field with businesses in the US, Europe, Japan, and in the developing world, its model looks at corporate citizenship (which is the term it prefers to use) as consisting of the following three components (Logan and Tuffrey, undated):

1. The basic values, policies, and practices of a company's owned and operated business, at home and abroad.
2. The management of environmental and social issues within the value chain by business partners, from raw material production to product disposal.
3. The voluntary contributions made by a company to community development around the world.

Of these, the first and the third are an extension of the LBG model. While the first corresponds to the Business Basics section of the LBG, the third looks at the remaining three sections. The CCC model goes on to unpack the Business Basics component of the LBG model by analysing and reporting to and about the following key stakeholders:

- Employees (including contract and part-time).
- Customers.
- Investors.

- Business.
- Government.
- The environment (or future generations and, increasingly, other living things).

A CSR Agenda for India

What is characteristic of all these models is that they have been developed and used in the developed world. This is not to say that they are not relevant to the developing world—indeed they are. The issue is only that of prioritization.

The Indian Development Context

It will perhaps be useful to remember the Indian context. India is a country in which an estimated 350 million people live in absolute poverty. They are poor not *only* because of a shortage of material resources but because social, political, and economic structures have systematically denied them the right to access and control of the resources they need for a life of dignity.

Once this premise is accepted, it is obvious that any attempt to significantly reduce poverty and inequity will require these structures to be reviewed because these very structures ensure that all resource inflows to society go to the rich and powerful. Thus, serious attempts at social and human development in India must recognize these structural imperfections.

Role of Companies in Development

On the continuum referred to earlier (extending from corporate philanthropy to compliance with the law), what is clear is that compliance is *necessary* but far from being *sufficient* for a company to be classified as socially responsible in India. Thus, CSR in India must be closer to what UNCTAD (UNCTAD, 1999: 6) proposes: 'CSR has come to be associated with standards of performance that are applied to both internal and external corporate activities, redressing societal norms that are not (but may become) legally required mandates.'

Thus what constitutes socially responsible behaviour in an Indian context (and indeed in the context of any developing country) is that it would include all activities a company undertakes that benefit people and communities. However, it would exclude activities aimed at:

- those it is contractually obliged to (this excludes employees, suppliers, customers, shareholders, etc.) and

- those who are not socially and/or economically disadvantaged.

This is not to suggest that activities by companies that benefit their employees, shareholders, suppliers, etc., are unacceptable. Rather, it is to argue that companies can make a greater difference if their activities go beyond these stakeholders to benefit those who are disadvantaged.

Public Policy

An important component of the PWBLF model is the issue of influencing public policy. While multinationals are busy lobbying for a liberalized global economic framework enforceable by law (and have made much progress in this direction with the establishment of the WTO), the national business sector increasingly plays a major role in determining national laws, particularly in the developing world. In India for instance, while business is always consulted by the government when formulating key economic policies, civil society is rarely consulted, even in matters that concern them.

Is this rhetoric or is there a basis to say that public policies in India are favouring businesses over the interests of the poor? Here are a few examples:

- The proposed amendments to the Land Acquisition Act will empower the state to acquire land from people even for private investment, which it can declare as 'public purpose'. At the same time, the time frames and the means to protect the rights of the people whose lands have been acquired are proposed to be drastically reduced.
- Under WTO regulations, farmers will be prevented from retaining and exchanging seeds with their neighbours, a practice that has gone on since time immemorial. This will make the already vulnerable small and marginal farmers more and more dependent on seed companies for their own household food security and hence their survival.
- As India moves from a process to a product patenting regime for medicines under WTO, prices of medicines will rise (as many have already risen), making them out of reach of the poor.

These examples point to an important dimension of CSR in the Indian context, one which requires companies not so much to exert influence for their own business benefits, but to actively influence public policy in favour of the poor and the environment. At the very least, a socially responsible company will not argue for policies that it knows will harm the poor and the environment.

Towards an Indian Definition of CSR

Using the framework of CSR that has been discussed above, the Indian definition of CSR would look at the following in descending order of importance:

- Activities aimed at communities (be they philanthropic, social investment, or commercial initiatives) that benefit them in a sustainable manner. (Of course, a company that undertakes such activities but does not comply with business basics cannot be termed as socially responsible.)
- Basic business practices and value chains that go beyond legal compliance to benefiting the disadvantaged amongst the company's stakeholders, e.g. contract/casual labour, marginalized producers (small/marginal farmers or traditional craftpersons, for instance) and so on.
- Advocating change in public policy and laws that benefit disadvantaged people.

Business-NGO Partnerships

Non-government organizations or NGOs are not-for-profit organizations that dedicate themselves to working on issues of social and human development. They range in form from those that work directly with communities at the grass roots to those that support grass-roots activities (like CRY or Oxfam or ActionAid) or advocate for changes in public policy (like Greenpeace).

Potential for Partnerships

While NGOs are not the largest development player in India in terms of resources (the Indian state is), they are often seen as more effective and are increasingly emerging as the most significant sector, both in India and the world over. However, while the NGO sector has some key strengths, it also has its limitations, limitations which make them incapable of effectively promoting sustainable development alone.

The grid below attempts to identify the key success factors for being successful in development, and rates NGOs and companies on these factors:

Success factor	*NGO*	*Company*
Development skills—core competence	Medium to high	Low
Commitment to development	High	Low

(Contd)

Success factor	*NGO*	*Company*
Understanding of issues	Medium to high	Low
Trust of the community	High	Low
Range of resources	Low to medium	High
Influence with governments	Low to medium	Medium to high
Strong systems and procedures	Low to medium	Medium to high
Flexibility and adaptability	High	Low

What seems quite apparent from this grid is that companies and NGOs are natural allies. Their respective strengths and weaknesses are complementary. Thus, the process of development has the potential to be greatly enhanced if businesses and NGOs became partners.

But what happens in practice? A survey on corporate involvement in development (Partners in Change, 2000: 54) indicates that in 87 per cent of the cases, companies involved in development preferred to implement programmes directly rather than in partnership with an NGO. In the few cases where there were partnerships, social clubs like the Lions and the Rotary or the local government were the partners, not development NGOs. However, the same survey is optimistic about the future of such partnerships, as companies that had worked with NGO partners found the experience greatly beneficial and were keen on expanding their cooperation.

Barriers to Partnerships

Experience suggests that there are several reasons why there are so few business-NGO partnerships in practice.

Many companies are extremely uncomfortable about working with NGOs. This is especially true of those who have never worked on a long-term basis with NGOs. They feel that there are many NGOs who are either amateur 'do-gooders' (who will be extremely inefficient and ineffective) or corrupt money-grubbers (based on media reports of incidents which, though infrequent, are generally highly publicized), and see little point in working with them. Given this scenario, companies feel that they do not possess either the skills or the time to evaluate and assess the good NGOs from the bad, and hence prefer to work directly on their own or with an NGO that is familiar or comes with a strong reference.

Another factor that inhibits companies from working with partners is that their CSR activities are rarely strategic. The survey (Partners in Change, 2000: 33) showed that only 11 per cent of the 600 companies surveyed had a written policy on CSR, which clearly indicated the rather ad hoc nature of this activity. What was also interesting to note was that over 41 per cent of those companies with a written CSR policy actually worked with partners, compared to only 10 per cent of companies without a policy (Partners in Change, 2000: 52).

NGOs too are uncomfortable with companies. Some NGOs have ideological problems in working with a sector that is motivated by profit maximization. They often see business firms as exploitative. The past record of some companies in India has helped reinforce this perception. On the other hand, NGOs that are willing to work with companies often either do not know how to approach and deal with them or underestimate the time and effort required to actually build a partnership with companies, especially those who do not understand development and consider it a low priority and largely unimportant.

Then there are many other cultural differences that inhibit partnerships. For instance, companies tend to be focused on 'product' and are looking at short-term quantitative outputs while NGOs see development as a process and hence focus on qualitative outcomes. Companies like to see regular reports, with variance analysis and reasons for variance, while NGOs feel that their time is better spent working with communities than sitting in the office and writing reports. The fact that there are very few fora where NGOs and companies can meet, discuss, and understand each other makes reconciling these differences very difficult.

Role of Intermediaries

It is because of these barriers for partnerships that there is a need for intermediaries like PiC. Intermediaries bring the two partners together by trying to interpret and reconcile each other's understandings, concerns, interests, and perceptions of the benefits that are expected to derive from the partnership. They do this through dialogue, arranging field visits, relating past experiences of successes and failures and so on.

To be effective in this role, intermediaries must:

- be convinced that partnerships between companies and NGOs play a crucial role;
- have a good understanding of sustainable human development processes and corporate priorities;
- be both recognized and trusted by both companies and NGOs as playing a critical role in the process, and this is essential both to promote the concept of corporate involvement in development as well as to meaningfully make this happen; and

- be more than a broker and instead be someone who ensures that the partnership sustains and strengthens the relationship between the partners.

PiC's experience in working with two international consulting firms—one a failure and the other a success—clearly illustrates the role that an intermediary can play. Soon after it was set up, PiC was approached by a well-known firm to put together a volunteer programme for its consultants. PiC met with the volunteers, mapped their skills and interests, and worked with several NGOs to help identify specific problem areas where they could seek help from the volunteers. These were documented and sent to the volunteers who were keen to set up meetings themselves directly with the NGOs. After one visit to some of the NGOs, the programme came to a grinding halt, thereby reducing the effort put in by the NGOs and PiC to nought. On analysing the reasons for this debacle, the following factors came to light:

- While the consultants were interested, one enthusiastic staff member drove the programme. When he was transferred soon after the programme was launched, it came to a halt and there was no one within the system to carry it forward;
- Work schedules made it very difficult for the consultants to keep to time commitments;
- The consultants had never worked closely with an NGO in India and were unprepared for the working conditions there;
- The NGOs were not very clear on how to deal with the consultants and what to expect from them.

A few years later, PiC was contacted by another international firm of consultants. Learning from its previous experience, PiC:

- worked closely with a few staff members and the managing director to understand what the long-term vision of the firm as a good corporate citizen was;
- identified one potential partner and, over several meetings, ensured that the firm and the NGO knew what to expect from the engagement; and
- arranged for a presentation by the NGO to all the staff of the consulting firm so that they all understood the work of the NGO and what to expect in the field. This was preceded by a presentation by PiC to the consultants on what working with an NGO entails in terms of working conditions, quality of staff, facilities available, and so on.

The partnership worked well and delivered results, both to the NGO and to the firm.

THE FUTURE OF BUSINESS-NGO PARTNERSHIPS

International interest in business-NGO partnerships as well as the survey findings quoted earlier clearly indicates that the future lies in partnerships between businesses and NGO, with perhaps the state as the third partner. Two factors will accelerate this process. One is that successful examples of such partnerships will become more widely known (with the Internet playing a huge role in faster and wider dissemination of such examples from around the globe). The second is that the state and development agencies see an increasing role for NGOs in development, which would increase their legitimacy and importance as key development players. As a result:

- Mutual suspicion between businesses and NGOs will be reduced;
- Many more fora where companies and NGOs can interact will be created, which would again lead to an increased understanding of each other's skills and strengths. This is already happening with NGOs being increasingly invited to participate in meetings and committees set up by industry associations like CII, for example;
- The number of intermediaries that promote such partnerships will grow. The last few years has seen the setting up of new intermediaries in India like PiC, the Business and Community Foundation, and the Charities Aid Foundation as well as a diversification of industry bodies like CII and FICCI in playing this role.

Having said that, there will be many factors that will hinder such partnerships. As the globalization and privatization agenda become more firmly entrenched, businesses will become more and more powerful and will play a bigger role in determining public policy. This is likely to bring it in conflict with human development objectives, which can increase suspicion of civil society actors, thereby inhibiting partnerships. Also, increased competition will mean that businesses will put a greater emphasis on survival, which will be at the cost of CSR activities. Better and faster communication too can inhibit partnerships, as instances of irresponsible behaviour of companies in other parts of the globe will become public knowledge much sooner than ever before.

However, the weight of the evidence suggests that business-NGO partnerships are not just the flavour of the month—they are here to stay for a long, long time.

Making it Happen

If the process of business-NGO partnerships is to be accelerated and scaled up, there are a number of actions that must be taken by the various players. More and more companies must commit themselves to being socially responsible in the form of a written policy, one that also specifies working in partnership as a way forward. NGOs need to set aside their inherent suspicions of the business sector and engage them in issues where partnerships help the process of development, without losing their right to be critical when they have to. The state and multilateral organizations must increasingly find innovative ways to encourage such partnerships and create fora for dialogue and better understanding. Setting up of intermediaries would play a huge catalytic role in making this happen.

References

Diageo plc (1999). *Global Brands Local Citizens–Corporate Citizenship Guidelines*, London: Diageo plc.

Logan, D. and M. Tuffrey (Undated). *Companies in Communities: Valuing the contribution*, London Charities Aid Foundation.

Nelson, J. (1996). *Business as Partners in Development*, London: Prince of Wales Business Leaders' Forum.

Partners in Change (2000). *Report on Survey of Corporate Involvement in Development in India*, New Delhi: Partners in Change.

UNCTAD (1999). *The Social Responsibility of Transnational Corporations*, New York and Geneva: United Nations.

11

From Social Responsibility to Development-driven Business

The Ongoing Experience of the TATA Group

Anant G. Nadkarni

The Tata group of companies is the largest of India's business houses. The Tatas have a long history of involvement in social causes, going back to the nineteenth century and the founder of the firm, Jamshedji Tata. Over the years it has earned a reputation as being among the leaders in social responsibility, not only in India, but throughout the world. Changes in the Indian and global economies over the past decade or more, however, have led the Tata group to reflect on what corporate social responsibility means in our changing times.

In this paper, I first examine how the Tata group initially responded to the process of economic reforms in the early 1990s by trying to develop a more systematic approach to unfolding a corporate social responsibility programme. These efforts included the establishment of the Tata Council for Community Initiatives (TCCI). Next, I examine a somewhat subtle, but significant, development in the group's self-understanding of its social responsibilities. This change is best expressed as a shift to a notion of 'development-driven business'. While we are just beginning to understand the implications of this shift ourselves, it is hoped that sharing our initial experiences might stimulate others to reflect, as well as helping us to better understand what it is that we are trying to achieve.

Corporate Social Responsibility at TATA in the 1990s

When the process of economic reform began in earnest in India during the early 1990s, Indian companies were forced to rethink how they did business. The Tata group, like all major Indian business houses, began to contemplate how to restructure its businesses to make them more competitive, both in terms of domestic and international competition. Restructuring in the Tata group involved radical changes across the full range of functional areas, e.g. economic, fiscal, procedural, and administrative. It also involved attention to the question of what social responsibility means in the changing circumstances of the emerging global economy and an increasingly interconnected society, both nationally and internationally.

In an effort to address this issue of the changing nature of social responsibility, three major consultations were held for community development representatives of Tata companies during 1993–1995. Two basic convictions emerged from these consultations. First, the belief was expressed that, any process of managing change—whether at a national level or in the corporate environment—should put people first. Second, the understanding emerged that corporate social responsibility should be seen as a service to the nation. The basic understanding of the specific role of the corporate sector in promoting social responsibility that emerged from these two convictions, then, was that corporations should be involved in a conscious and dedicated effort to assist social reform in building the nation.

With this purpose in mind, at the end of 1994 the board of directors of Tata Sons Limited appointed two senior directors to form the Tata Council for Community Initiatives (TCCI). This network was charged with facilitating the development of a common direction for all Tata companies on social responsibility. Today, the guidelines for community development formulated by TCCI are being implemented by twenty-eight major Tata companies, which form the critical mass of the Tata group. The commitment of the group is reflected in the level of outlays on community initiatives in recent years, which amounted to US $13 million in 1998, US $22 million in 1999, and US $36 million in 2000. This is in addition to donations received from various Tata trusts and contributions rendered in kind by volunteers.

In attempting to renew our self-understanding of social responsibility and implement it in the practices and policies of the group, during the 1990s TCCI focused its efforts around six themes.

Developing Long-term Programmes with Stakeholder Groups

For over a century the TATA group has been known for its contributions to the broader society. In the 1990s, the nature of the contribution of the Tatas to societal betterment was reconceived in terms of a coordinated process of managing multiple stakeholders interests, such as those of government, non-governmental organizations (NGOs), and local communities. We believe that the corporate sector has an important but specific role to play in societal betterment (in addition to its programmes of corporate giving and charity), which primarily involves contributing managerial expertise, skills, and talent, as well as providing some financial assistance in projects that involve the active participation of local communities.

There is an increasing recognition, both by corporate actors like the Tatas as well as NGOs, that the most effective use of resources involves implementing long-term programmes around the concept of self-help and self-reliance. In terms of Tata involvement, the programmes that have been supported are not large-scale operations. Rather, they are initiatives in the form of pilot projects that show new ways to build a 'can-do' confidence. This offers possibilities to the community and the authorities of making attitudinal and procedural changes.

Towards this end of developing a long-term approach to stimulating new initiatives, we formed clusters of Tata company representatives in major cities in India like Bangalore, Kolkata, Jamshedpur, Hyderabad, New Delhi, Mumbai, and Pune. The goal of this two-year experiment was to encourage collaboration among the group's companies in developing new community initiatives. This experiment has resulted in about seventy-six initiatives and mobilized several hundred volunteers who are working in micro-level programmes.

The Triple Bottom Line

The nature of the Tata group's commitment to corporate social responsibility is perhaps best summed up in its brand declaration: *TATA—improving the quality of life*. The Tata group has always been well known for its leadership, not only in adhering to quality-driven business practices and procedural ethical norms, but also for adding a lateral dimension to its overall vision by demonstrating a deep concern for the environment and genuine care for the community. In line with this commitment, in 1999 the Tata group formally adopted the concept of the triple bottom line to reinforce the larger social purpose to our businesses.

In the following years a conscious effort was undertaken to institutionalize this concept of the 'triple bottom line' as an integral part of business strategy and performance. Thus, for example, social expenditure is not considered as an allocation out of surplus (as charity), but is budgeted well in advance as a business cost like any other. Social responsibility is an important part of the leadership process under the Tata Business Excellence Model. Tata companies have declared specific goals and policies on social responsibility to employees. Tata companies draw up annual programmes as part of the business plan based on their core competencies. For instance, Tata Consultancy Services and Tata Infotech are engaged in mainstreaming computer-related education and application to assist programmes for the underprivileged in urban and rural areas. The Taj group of hotels has worked out possibilities with NGOs to make use of their skills in the hospitality business. Chefs volunteer to train a significant number of slum women to make baked goods and other confectioneries as part of an income-generating programme. Volunteers help in managing public kitchens and other events to show a better way to the less privileged. Tata Steel and Tata Engineering impart vocational training of sorts for underprivileged youth. The environmental component of the triple bottom line is discussed later. At present, 20 Tata companies are in the process of completing the triple bottom line reporting.

Community Champions

Traditionally, Tata companies operated through specific departments, societies, or designated officers to conduct community work. Such designation was often based upon the initiative that individual employees had taken. While this provided a steady form of support to the community, it *assumed* that other company employees would participate in community work by default rather than by design. In the 1990s, a more proactive approach has emerged, one which involved the designation of 'community champions' and 'key result areas' to be targeted. The notion here was that when the heads of human resources identified specific employees who were to be actively involved with local communities ('community champions'), their function was no longer just to engage with the communities themselves, but more importantly, to motivate other Tata employees to become involved in community development projects as volunteers. The champions were to encourage the participation of employees through a common process (the Tata Way), which was developed at the group level. This process, along with the designation of 'key result areas' was designed to ensure uniform outcomes that serve to effectively realize the claim of the Tata Brand: *Improving the quality of life*. This experiment, which began with barely nineteen community champions, quickly proved to be quite popular and successful. In 2000–2001, for example, the human resource department assigned 'key result areas' to 191 community champions, a tenfold increase in the number of champions in four years.

Tata Corps of Volunteers

The Tata group firmly believes that active involvement by its employees is the key to effective corporate participation in social activity. The group has a large and highly skilled workforce. Through volunteer activity, individual members of the Tata group of companies are able to make very tangible contributions to local communities and individuals. As a result of this direct contact, the large pool of active volunteers provides not only a reliable and knowledgeable resource base for social activity, but also lays the foundation for building high-trust communities.

In an effort to improve the volunteering process and make it more effective, all major Tata companies are in the process of instituting specific schemes for volunteering and are recording volunteering days on their data banks. Even the relatively smaller and newer companies have demonstrated commendable interest by structuring this process. In 1999, for example, Voltas registered over fifty volunteers. Similarly, Rallis have over forty, Tata Special Steels registered 115, the Taj group of hotels declared forty-eight volunteers—all these in Mumbai alone. These numbers, of course, represent only a fraction of the estimated over 20,000 volunteers in the Tata group. As of today, 10,417 volunteers of the 20,000 estimated are registered.

Improving Quality of Life: The Tata Way

Through TCCI, the Tata group has been trying to systematize its approach to community initiatives. As part of this effort, known as the Tata Way, it created 'thrust areas' for community development. The areas designated were vocational training, primary education, computer education and application, health and family welfare, supply of drinking water, and irrigation. In 1999, a series of guidelines on community development were released. As a result of the eleven-point process advocated by the guidelines, several companies were spurred to reorienting the ways that they organize their programmes. Tata Engineering at Jamshedpur, for instance, has reoriented its effort for the rehabilitation of persons afflicted by leprosy. Its programme now covers 214 villages (with a combined population of half a million) and addresses

3000 cases. It has been successful in lowering the rate of infection from twenty-one cases per thousand in 1989 to five per thousand in 1999. At present there are 700 cases under rehabilitation. The programme is holistic and covers the children of these very isolated parents. In 2000, as a result of the programme, 255 children entered mainstream school education.

Another initiative has involved the Taj Mansingh in New Delhi, which has collaborated with an NGO, Katha Khazana, to train nearly a hundred ladies from the Govindpuri slums to make bakery items and other confectioneries. Taj volunteers imparted 120 man-hours of training in the process. Part of this training involved issues relating to quality control, which helped the women deal with recurring customer complaints and regain lost business from competitors. As a result of such ongoing connections, during 1999 these women were able to improve the efficiency of their operation and double their average monthly income to Rs 6500.

Among other initiatives, a Tata business manager through the Computer Society of India, at Pune, mobilized 100 computers and managed to train 200 municipal teachers in one year during 1998–99. This work resulted in motivating yet another Tata manager to add ten more computers to three municipal schools to intensify introductory computer education. Private schools were surveyed and he assisted the school committee of the Pune Municipal Corporation in reviewing its syllabus. As a result the budgets for this purpose were enhanced from nearly half a million rupees to ten million rupees, thus impacting that system. Similar efforts are under way to enhance the capability and improve the quality of computer education provided in municipal schools in Mumbai.

From 1995 to 1998, a Tata officer coordinated programmes for municipal corporations of Bangalore, Mumbai, and Pune to build networks with more than twenty NGOs in each city on a consorted one-year programme each to improve various public utility services beginning with better solid waste management. Tata volunteers later worked with the municipal corporations of Mumbai and Pune to release the Citizens' Charters linked up with the media and NGOs and commendably redressed day-to-day consumer grievances.

Environmental Management and Social Auditing

The Tata group spends an estimated amount of Rs 70 lakh annually on conserving natural resources and preserving the environment. In 2000, the Tata Group Environment Network was formed with the objective of providing a further impetus to the excellent work already being done, to take it beyond the requirements of regulations through a formal system that encourages companies to be proactive. All major companies have complied with the

Tata plan on the environment that was jointly worked out through a process of consultation. Plans are afoot to integrate community and environmental initiatives under a structured social audit to meet international standards.

Development-driven Business

Over the course of the past decade, the experiences of the Tata group in the field of social responsibility—including countless inputs from community workers, development agencies, the media, NGOs and others—have led us to believe that a major shift in corporate social responsibility is in the offing. We believe that it is time to review the fundamental purpose of business. It is our conviction that contemporary business should become more 'development-oriented'. This non-negotiable affirmation has surfaced from our five years of 'action learning' with the community. Today, as new ideas emerge on building contemporary society, 'enlightened business' needs to align with the accepted tenets of development if improving the quality of life is a serious goal.

Undertaking such a shift in our understanding of business is a challenging endeavour. It calls for a radical change of mindset. The leadership of the corporation is required to develop a new understanding of the balance between the 'top line' (purpose) and 'bottom line' (profit or advantage) of all its actions. This is not an easy task. Indeed, at TCCI we regularly encounter Tata colleagues who believe that (even) community programmes can be run like a traditional shop-floor routine! Thus, in trying to change our understanding of business, TCCI has come to realize that it is most important to first attend to basic conditioning before we set out to implement any change. We need to ask ourselves whether we really know what community development is all about. Have we understood the basic ideas on development? Have we properly recognized our role as corporate facilitators? In attempting to answer these questions and understand what incorporating a development perspective into business means, it may be helpful to look at four key levels where the concept needs to be applied.

Incorporating the Notion of Development at Different Levels

Institutions

Historically, before the emergence of development NGOs, most institutions involved in community development were either charitable organizations or traditional businesses. The form of these institutions promoted and reinforced certain understandings of the nature of problems, the appropriate solutions to address them, and the criteria for measuring success. Charitable organizations generally conceived of their activities in terms of 'givers' and 'receivers' of goods and did little to encourage the active involvement of recipients. Many business organizations also adopted this same conception of what was involved in community initiatives and employed their hierarchical management structures to address social problems. Typically, success was measured in terms of donations (or PR value) rather than the actual impact on human lives. If corporations are to be 'development-driven', they need to develop new institutional frameworks that are more appropriate to their task.

If we can suppose for a minute that institutions should be oriented towards encouraging active involvement by target populations and community development is not about people in organizations doing something for others, our notion of institutions must change. One possible model for new institutions is the notion of community. While the notion of community as an institution might strike us as a bit odd, this is primarily because we have been led to conceive of institutions as hierarchical and bureaucratic in nature. They need not be so, however. Institutions can be viewed more in terms of networks of partners cooperating for a common goal. Communities provide such an example of networks. The advantage of conceiving of institutions as communities are many. The notion (and experience) of community gives the fullest expression to the social and affiliation needs of people—the sense of belonging and togetherness. As such, groups with common interests and goals can come together to form communities. Communities have the power to facilitate networking among a variety of traditional institutions, organizations, interest groups, and 'beneficiaries' for the purpose of achieving one common goal. People can readily decide, 'look, this is the *issue* and this is the *community* for it', ignoring any ethnic, professional, and organizational barriers. Communities provide a flexible and evolving shape, which encourages more democratic participation, solidarity, and taking responsibility for one's own actions and situation. In this way, adopting community as a model for institutions helps to create and reinforce a *development-centric* approach to business in which corporate social responsibility is an integral part and not just an appendage of the firm.

Purpose

Can making cars or assembling computers have a 'purpose' on their own? We believe that it takes a larger 'purpose' for products and services to *actually* improve the total quality of life. Clearly no one would deny that running a school profitably should be balanced *with* the larger 'purpose' of the institution (e.g. instilling self-confidence and a desire for knowledge and self-development in children, etc.). Even though it is often difficult to measure elements of the larger purpose (e.g. self-confidence), we do not think that it is good to be obsessed *only* with the bottom line (e.g. on the number of children passing out through the public examination) as the ultimate focus. The situation is similar with other social institutions as hospitals. To concentrate on the bottom line is to forget and marginalize the ultimate purpose of the institution. In the case of hospitals it results in an emphasis on the revenue and the turnover of patients rather than bringing people back to health.

Business, too, however, is also a social institution. Yet in this institution, there is a strong tendency to focus on the bottom line to the exclusion of the larger social purpose. (Ironically, this exclusive attention to the bottom line often serves to undermine the bottom line. It is common knowledge that an enterprise often turns around through troubled times because it pursues a vision no matter what the bottom line looked like at that time.) Our concern is to highlight how business needs to incorporate the notion of (and costs involved in) development as part of its understanding of its top line (purpose). Again, for the Tatas, this purpose (which has already been incorporated in its brand) is improving the quality of life for all people.

Performance

In all organizations, performance needs to be evaluated. The key questions here, of course, are what is to be evaluated and what are the best indicators. In many organizations there is a tendency for performance indicators to be simple (as opposed to complex), static (as opposed to dynamic), and micro (as opposed to macro) in nature. Using these types of indicators is frequently problematic for organizations, as they do not do justice to what is to be measured. Simple indicators (e.g. GDP/capita), for example, often fail to measure important components (e.g. access to health care and education, security, etc.) of the object to be measure (e.g. development). Similarly, static measures do not allow for the fact that the key variables to be measured may change over time. A hospital, for example, may look at improving *accessibility* at one time and then shift focus to improving *response time* at another moment depending upon circumstances. We frequently find parallel situations of changing priorities in our community development projects. Most important, however, is the fact that micro-level performance indicators often fail to take into account the larger purpose of organizations. It is well known, for example, that in business, indicators of success (which are typically linked to individual rewards) in one branch of the operations (e.g. marketing, production) may well generate inefficiencies and work against the larger business goals of the firm. The case is similar with respect to our present concern of incorporating a development-driven understanding of business. Here, typical (micro-level) business indicators of performance can lead to results that run counter to the broader purpose of the firm. For this reason, it is essential that firms develop (financial, social, and environmental) indicators in line with the 'triple bottom line' approach. Such an approach views *economic value added* (profit) as only one part of the 'wealth' generated by an enterprise. This more holistic approach to measuring performance includes an analysis of different forms of capital accumulation—economic, natural, and social. Whereas traditional approaches tend to measure particular effects in isolation, this more integrated approach provides a much more comprehensive way to measure 'total development performance'.

Shifting from Management to Governance

The practice of management is almost synonymous with business and is commonly understood to be a major factor in business efficiency. The notion of management, however, brings with it certain connotations (e.g. hierarchy, technical expertise) that are not always the most appropriate values for addressing certain types of problems and situations. This is particularly true of corporate relations with stakeholder groups. In this context, a management approach to addressing problems inevitably smacks of a paternalism in which experts provide the answers to those who do not know how to deal with the situation. For businesses driven by developmental values, such involvement with stakeholder groups is less about 'doing something for the other' and more about cooperating in a network with people who are actively engaged in promoting their own development. Increasingly, studies indicate that active involvement by people is the only effective way to ensure long-term results. In large cities, for example, active involvement by motivated citizens proves to be an effective way to ensure keeping streets clean, whereas regulation alone is generally quite ineffective. In the long run, people do only what they believe. For this reason, solutions generated through self-management or co-determination last longer. An enlightened business conditioned by a developmental mindset by its very nature becomes consultative and seeks participation of all stakeholders concerned and the community to build responsible capital—economic, natural, and social.

The same mindset needs to be evolved within the company, especially, though not only, with the encouraging of volunteers. Everyone likes to be consulted and be involved in decision-making processes. Employee volunteers must feel some sense of ownership over the activities that they are involved in. Such involvement also serves as an important impetus to the company being responsible. It helps to check, for example, any tendencies there might be of the firm's business considerations (e.g. marketing, PR concerns) determining the nature of the company's community involvement. This democratizing approach, which encourages stakeholders and employees to be more active and balanced in decision making and take on greater responsibility, is what we call *governance*.

Incorporating Development Concerns into Everyday Practice

Incorporating the notion of development at the level of daily practice is challenging. In order to facilitate this goal, TCCI has developed a series of questions and suggestions based upon its experience over the last five or six years. These suggestions focus on the importance of understanding leadership in a new way, a way that emphasizes leading by example and involvement in a network rather than providing solutions to problems which others implement. The suggestions were primarily developed for (potential) community leaders in the Tata group. They presuppose the Tata understanding of community development, which highlights the importance of the 'top line', gives priority to governance over management, and incorporates a holistic approach to development. In presenting these 'in-house' suggestions, our hope is not that they will be adopted by others, but that our experience can help to stimulate further reflection in the larger business community on how corporate responsibility should be lived out in our contemporary situation.

Leadership

Let us look at leadership in the community (or business) as an effort to best balance the interests of all stakeholders. While there will be other ways to express a general kind of leadership, there are some distinctions we notice in the course of our work. They are as follows:

(i) During the greater part of the last two years, 'leadership' in a programme meant that you minimized the idea of charity and encouraged involvement. You were certainly more satisfied when superiors took part than merely sanctioned the money or support. Yet, even though we strongly stressed volunteering, the Tata group still spends 40 per cent of social expenditure through donations.

[*Measure*: *How did you measure your success—in terms of increasing volunteer participation and de-emphasizing donations or just signing cheques*?]

(ii) As programme leaders I believe you had to constantly generate a larger purpose, since a common 'direction' was always not possible. Do you agree that your best programmes and partnerships happened because you saw beyond the conventional practices of setting goals closer to known patterns and the bottom lines? Secondly, the ultimate test of your leadership was to provide mini-missions and get people into 'right' action. That means your 'action' at all times had a context rooted in the values of development. A blood donation campaign is not the end in itself. But it *is an end* if you felt: 'we came to know each other better through an event like this one'. Here you test 'participation' as a value. Or 'the local blood bank needed a particular blood group and we gave it'. There you test 'improving access'! The mini-mission balanced with an ordinary piece of action makes it 'right'. In this sense we are 'mission managers' and the basic mission is 'improving the quality of life'. [*Measure*: *How does 'improving quality of life' become central to the context and purpose in the stated objectives of even our smallest programmes*?]

(iii) An ability to raise funds and guide their effective deployment is essential. We earned more respect for our ability to source external funds and function more as fund facilitators for NGOs and government.

[*Measure*: *How do we enhance and measure our capacity to mobilize external funds and resources as a percentage of company resources deployed*?]

(iv) As leaders do we believe in enhancing and applying knowledge (especially knowledge gained collectively in the group) to projects? Do we see a transition in our role from event management to 'knowledge' management or real-time development work?

[*Measure*: *How do you use the platform of the regional group to enhance participation? How do you assess the quality and dissemination of knowledge generated? How do you rate the importance of documentation in the form of cases*?]

Understanding and Heightening Community Perception

(i) The TCCI aims at creating regional groups to act as a 'lever' or 'mechanism' to promote corporate social responsibility in major cities and the country as a whole.

[*Measure*: *How do you measure the impact of programmes, fund raising, creating inputs/expertise in terms of people understanding you 'as a group' perceived under the stewardship of the brand? How is a brand identity developed?*]

(ii) One thing that our programme leaders have learned relates to the notion of developing a kind of a 'market process' for 'beneficiaries'. Many good projects under our supervision often die on our withdrawal. Although sustainability is spoken about, developing a 'market process' for generating new ideas and skills was key to your successful projects.
[*Measure*: *How do we ensure that there is a 'market process' built into a withdrawal plan and issues of sustainability are addressed in our projects?*]

(iii) Although we are business people, we know that in development work one does not offer a 'product' or 'service'. This work is also not managed in the same way. (I am often asked: what does TCCI actually do!) We develop and deploy processes, create and influence by ideas that have worked in our projects, build concepts out of everyday routines, and facilitate a 'transformation of minds'. *Transformation* is the end 'product'. Changed people and government processes are our outcomes!
[*Measure*: *How do you create and record attitudinal changes and shifts in the government processes caused by your intervention? How lasting is that benefit?*]

Human Resources

(i) As a leader you have built good working relationships across borders within the company or the TCCI regional group, staff, and volunteers even when you have had to sometimes compromise on your own ideas. It is said that leaders are good followers too, since they empathize with the difficulty of the person assigned to do a job.
[*Measures*: *1. In important meetings, while encouraging new ideas and inputs, how do we ultimately converge to action with integrity? 2. How do you ensure that all Tata companies and institutions participate in the Regional activity? 3. How do you ensure that a strategy is transparent and fair in selection of projects, and the approach and the scale of work are appropriate?*]

(ii) Ultimately a leader is one who is determined to develop oneself—as a person and at work. If a need for self-improvement is not intense and explicit, it almost indicates that a person claims to be perfect (I know all). And, we all agree that there is really no such limit to improvement at a deeply spiritual level. I am sure we also agree that our best performance is always *yet* to come!

[*Measure*: *How do you reflect, conceptualize, and articulate what really opened up for you while serving the community*? *How do you set personal goals for yourself*?]

(iii) Although our work is 'passion' driven, our facilitators are generally focused on the job and less on their 'self'. He or she is *not* a mere rapport or image builder. There is no hurry to appear on the CNN or the BBC. The intent is never PR or needless seeking of approval. Our people are encouraged to be confident, yet modest. They should not be unduly appeasing, but rather capable of contesting. Above all they are encouraged to be authentic.

[*Measure*: *How do you deal with your professional and personal 'identities' in spirit and in words*?]

(iv) Our community workers constantly move on. So we cannot rely only on employees' personal commitment, which such work badly demands. In five years, 95 per cent of the original community champions have moved up or left. Continued performance depends on systems and conventions being in place and their ownership by the successors 'ex-officio'. So we have always tried to create a system-driven base for work to provide more credibility.

[*Measure*: *How do you and the company's management select your champions and manage a transition when it comes*, *to maintain quality and continuity in performance*? *How do you take care of commitments so that reputation and credibility are built*?]

(v) It is often said that leaders develop leaders. A significant number of us come from a background of ground-level work and we tend to stay at that level, comfortable in 'doing'. At another level we grow into a role of facilitating others. And now, we have discovered that to involve a larger number of employees we need to understand what *enrolling* is all about. It means enrolling peers and superiors so that their own participation in *social development* is the essence of our approach.

[*Measure*: *How do you assess your ability to influence CEOs*, *senior managers*, *departmental heads*, *HR heads and volunteers*?]

Conclusion

Economic reforms in the 1990s provided the Tata group and other corporations with the challenge of addressing what corporate responsibility means in an increasingly global economy. While economic reforms bring with them new opportunities for the business community, we must not forget that the ultimate purpose of business is not to pursue such opportunities purely for the sake of profit. This is especially so in the light of the overwhelming developmental challenges that continue to confront us, both here in India and throughout the developing world—challenges that many claim have been exacerbated by the economic reforms that have provided new opportunities for business. In this context, business cannot ignore the fact that it has a larger social purpose, a purpose that we in the Tata group have expressed as 'improving the quality of life'. If this notion is to be effectively implemented, however—and not just remain another marketing slogan—our understanding of corporate responsibility has to change. The challenge to corporations is to integrate corporate social responsibility into the heart of the corporation's activity and not view it merely as an appendage. This challenge involves new ways of doing business and interacting with stakeholder groups. This is the challenge that we are attempting to take up by defining ourselves as a 'development-driven business'.

In June 2003, the TCCI evolved the Tata Index for Sustainable Human Development in partnership with UNDP, India. This document is a detailed process endeavouring the view that the end purpose of all business or social activity must contribute to human development. This pioneering effort uses the Assurance process of the Tata Business Excellence Model and combines the power of UNDP's Human Development Index to enable business enterprises to genuinely strive for human excellence! This document is a tribute to Jamsetji Tata, our founder, on the occasion of his centenary, who said: 'The community is not just another stakeholder in our business, but, in fact, the very purpose of existence of our enterprises!'

12

The Role of Governance in Promoting Development

Evaluating Governance Responsibilities and Models of Governance

Darryl Reed[*]

With the recent processes of economic reforms that have been occurring in India and other developing countries, corporations have come to be perceived increasingly as (the) primary agents of development. For their part, many corporations have been using the language of development and accepting the notion that they have obligations to contribute to development, both through their business practices and corporate responsibility programmes. If corporations do have responsibilities to promote development, clearly the primary onus to act would seem to fall on the highest levels of the corporation, i.e. in terms of governance. The notion of an obligation to promote development, however, remains controversial. Even when the basic principle is accepted—and it is clearly not universally accepted—the implications are subject to contestation.

This chapter examines the role of governance in promoting development from a normative perspective. Such normative analysis of corporate governance can be broken down into two basic categories. On the one hand, there is the analysis of corporate governance responsibilities within the context of a given system or model of corporate governance. On the other hand, there is the comparative evaluation of different models of corporate governance. In this chapter, I take up these two approaches in turn. First, I

* This chapter is based in part on a paper previously published, 'Corporate Governance Reforms in Developing Countries', *Journal of Business Ethics*, 37 (3), May 2002, 223–47. Sections are reproduced with the permission of Kluwer Academic Publishers.

examine the notion that there might be governance responsibilities to promote development from within the context of the Anglo-American model of corporate governance. After indicating the possible bases for such responsibilities and some of their implications, I go on to examine the question of how the responsibilities to promote development might be most effectively taken up. In this context, I then raise the question of whether the Anglo-American model of governance is likely to be an effective vehicle for the promotion of traditional development goals, or whether alternative policies and models should be considered.

This chapter is structured in the following manner. In the first section, governance responsibilities within the Anglo-American model are explored, first through a distinction between shareholder and stakeholder approaches[1] to governance responsibilities and then on the basis of distinction between different formal tasks of governance. The second section then probes (from the Western and Indian perspectives) the issue of whether there is any responsibility on the part of those responsible for the governance of the corporation to promote development. Next, the implications of a responsibility to promote development are elaborated on the basis of the formal tasks of governance and a distinction between narrow and broad understandings of such an obligation to promote development. The fourth section then investigates the prospects for effectively promoting development by: (1) more effectively implementing the Anglo-American model of governance; (2) adapting the Anglo-American model in different ways; and (3) adopting or developing other models of governance.

Governance Responsibilities within the Anglo-American Model

It is commonly accepted that India is moving in the direction of adopting an Anglo-American model of corporate governance. What this means in terms of the roles and responsibilities of those governing the corporations is a highly disputed question. A basic distinction that tends to divide opposing views into two distinct camps is based upon the notion of 'stakeholders' and whether those responsible for governing the corporation have any responsibilities to such groups. While in the Anglo-American world, the notion that the board and management need only to look out for the interests of shareholders has long held sway (at least among corporate leaders and judges), more recently there has been wider acceptance of the notion that corporations have responsibilities to actors other than shareholders, viz., stakeholders. What remains controversial, however, is the extent to which firms have such responsibilities. In what follows, I first examine the shareholder-stakeholder distinction. Next, following Tricker (1994), I distinguish some basic tasks of governance. After this I go on to note how shareholder and stakeholder approaches to governance differ with respect to their substantial understandings of the nature of these basic tasks of governance.

Shareholder vs Stakeholder Approaches

In analysing the responsibilities of corporate governance it is common to distinguish between shareholder and stakeholder approaches. Shareholder approaches argue that corporations have a limited set of responsibilities, which primarily consist of obeying the law and maximizing shareholder interests (generally understood as shareholder wealth). Justification of the shareholder model is usually based upon one of two foundations. Libertarians base their approach on a claim of strong property rights. Historically, the problem with this approach has been that the assertion of strong property rights has not been accompanied by an adequate (or, in some instances, any) argument (see, for example, Nozick, 1974). Alternatively, a shareholder model might be rooted in utilitarian analysis. Here the basic argument is that corporations, by focusing on shareholder interests, maximize societal utility. The logic of this position goes back to Smith, but is elaborated in detail in neo-classical economics. The shareholder approach is logically most compatible with an Anglo-American model of corporate governance.

For libertarians, the shareholder model has inherent value insofar as it is based upon a rights claim. For utilitarians, however, the shareholder approach is purely instrumental; it has value only insofar as it serves to maximize societal utility. The ability of the shareholder model to maximize utility, however, is tenuous in that it is predicted upon the notion of perfect competition. To the extent that the conditions of perfect competition are not in place, the argument falters. More specifically, as deviations from the conditions of perfect competition increase (e.g. imperfect markets, incomplete contracts, information asymmetries), after a certain point corporations will not be maximizing societal utility by merely pursuing shareholder interests. At this point, such utilitarians may be logically forced to reject their shareholder position and adopt some form of stakeholder analysis.

In contrast to shareholder approaches, stakeholder models of corporate governance argue that those responsible for the governance of the corporation have responsibilities to parties other than shareholders and that, any fiduciary obligations owed to shareholders to maximize profits might be subject to the constraint of respecting obligations owed to such stakeholders. I have argued elsewhere (Reed, 1999) that, in order to be compelling, stakeholder models must undertake several basic tasks, including: (1) providing an account of what stakes are and who has them; (2) circumscribing corporate responsibility to stakeholders; and (3) determining how to evaluate the claims of competing stakeholders. The assumption of these tasks, as Cludts (unpublished paper) documents, can be grounded in any variety of Western normative theoretical perspectives including Kantian ethics, a (feminist) ethics of care, the ethics of fiduciary relationships, social contract theory, a theory of property rights, a theory of the stakeholders as investors, communitarian ethics, critical theory, etc. As discussed briefly below, stakeholder theory can also be grounded in Indian traditions. While it is possible to develop stakeholder analysis from a variety of theoretical perspectives, in practice much of stakeholder analysis does not firmly or explicitly root itself in a given theoretical tradition, but rather operates at the level of individual principles and norms for which it provides little formal justification. Insofar as stakeholder approaches uphold responsibilities to non-shareholder groups, they tend to be in some tension with the Anglo-American model of corporate governance, which generally emphasizes the primacy of 'fiduciary obligations' owed to shareholders over any stakeholder claims.

Formal Roles of Corporate Governance

Understanding how different normative theories might flesh out the requirements of corporate governance can be facilitated by drawing upon a formal account of the responsibilities of governance. Tricker (1994) provides such a formal account of governance responsibilities based upon two key distinctions, conformance vs performance roles and outward-looking vs inward-looking roles (see Figure 12.1). Performance roles, as their name suggests, are oriented towards ensuring efficient performance. On the basis of the second distinction (inward vs outward), performance roles can be divided into strategy formation and policy making. Board members fulfil these roles most directly by contributing know-how, expertise, and external information. They may also contribute to the success of these functions in a somewhat more indirect fashion by networking, representing the company in different fora, and adding status to the company. These roles may generally be described as future oriented. For their part, conformance roles are primarily directed towards ensuring that the company conforms to policies and procedures established by the board. Again, based upon the distinction between outward and inward roles, conformance roles can be split into two categories. First, the board has the function of ensuring accountability. This it does by providing relevant information to shareholders and other stakeholders with legitimate claims. Second, the board has the function of monitoring and supervising management. These two roles may be described as past and present oriented (Tricker, 1994: 98–99).

	Conformance Roles (Past and Present Oriented)	Performance Roles (Future Oriented)
(Outward Looking)	*Accountability*—providing feedback to shareholders, other stakeholders.	*Strategy Formation*—developing plans for the firm's interaction with the external environment (e.g. strategic alliances, profit strategies, financing).
(Inward Looking)	*Monitoring*—questioning, judging, and supervising management.	*Policy Making*—establishing rules and norms to guide the company in achieving its strategic goals.

Source: Adopted from Tricker (1994: 149).

Fig. 12.1 *The roles (responsibilities) of boards of directors*

Virtually all accounts of corporate governance can agree to these formal roles of governance. Where they will disagree, based upon their (explicit or implicit) normative theory, is with respect to the nature of these obligations and to whom they are owed. While it is not possible to examine the full range of possibilities, we can indicate how shareholder and stakeholder approaches to governance will tend to disagree with respect to these tasks.

First, with respect to the task of strategy formation, shareholder approaches are guided by a single goal, viz., maximizing shareholder wealth. Not only are no other goals considered, but no normative constraints (i.e. claims by stakeholders) are imposed upon developing strategies, apart from obeying the law. If stakeholder concerns are taken into account, it is purely out of pragmatic concerns (i.e. because the stakeholders have the power to influence corporate performance) and not on the basis of the validity of their normative claims. Stakeholder models, by contrast, may allow additional goals to guide strategy (e.g. contributing to local/national community economic development) and/or may subject strategies (designed to maximize shareholder wealth) to certain normative constraints (e.g. not operating in countries with repressive governments).

A similar situation holds with respect to policy making. Shareholder models do not take normative concerns (again, apart from obeying the law) into account in developing policy. Stakeholder models, by contrast, subject policy choices and design to certain constraints (e.g. producing in an environmentally sustainable fashion), which may be based upon norms espoused by the organization and/or claims made by stakeholder groups (e.g. local communities).

Third, for shareholder models, accountability is directed exclusively towards shareholders. In stakeholder models, however, obligations of accountability may extend much further. Possible stakeholder groups may include consumers, employees, contractors, local communities, citizens and possibly even competitors, while the nature of the obligations to each of these groups may change with economic, political, and socio-culture circumstances (Reed, 2002).

Finally, the task of monitoring in the shareholder model is exclusively focused upon addressing the principal-agent problem, i.e. ensuring that management runs the corporation in the interests of shareholders. Again, those adopting a shareholder approach in practice may undertake activities to ensure stakeholder interests are addressed, but their motivation in doing so is purely pragmatic in nature (e.g. public relations considerations). In stakeholder approaches, however, the role of monitoring can focus on conformance to normative constraints imposed upon maximizing shareholder wealth (e.g. producing in an environmentally sustainable manner) or even the fulfilment of competing goals (e.g. generating employment).

A Responsibility to Promote Development?

While India and other developing countries have been undertaking reforms moving in the direction of an Anglo-American model of governance, they have not been justifying these moves on the basis of libertarian views about shareholder rights. To the contrary, governance reforms (and liberalization generally) are typically discussed in the context of the long-standing goal of promoting development. This is true not only of states like India, but also of multilateral bodies. A basic question that arises, then, is whether corporations have any responsibility to contribute to development, apart from the development effects that may naturally ensue as a result of their responsibilities to generate profits for shareholders. Arguments for such responsibilities can be developed from both Western and Indian perspectives.

Western Perspectives

Although libertarian advocates of shareholder approaches to corporate governance would obviously not accept the notion of a responsibility to development, such a case can be made from other Western normative theoretical traditions. Clearly, for example, a utilitarian case can be made. To the extent that developing countries tend to define development as their top priority (and the notion that markets will naturally harmonize shareholder and stakeholder interests—based on the assumption of perfect competition—is dropped), a utilitarian would hold that corporations have a responsibility (of an instrumental nature) to promote development. Weaker and stronger obligations could be argued for from a utilitarian perspective, depending upon assumptions about the efficacy of markets, etc. Similarly, arguments for stronger and weaker responsibilities to promote development could also potentially be developed from a communitarian perspective, social contract theory, critical theory, (human) rights theory (e.g. stressing the right to development), and various theological perspectives (including different Christian, Judaic, Islamic variants, etc.). The strongest positions would be those that would hold that corporations' entire raison d'être is to promote development. A more moderate view might hold that corporations have a responsibility to promote development as one of several goals. A weak version might argue that promoting development is not a goal for corporations, but merely a condition that they have to fulfil in order to receive a sanction from society to conduct business.

Indian Perspectives

In India, the dominant source of ethical values and principles continues to be the Vedic tradition, which has served as a foundation for the religions of Hinduism, Buddhism, and Jainism. It is of course a complicated and challenging task to understand how the insights from religions that originated centuries and millennia ago can be incorporated into the analysis of the complex world of the modern business corporation. The most prominent way in which this challenge has been meditated, at least at a popular level, has been through Gandhi's notion of trusteeship. In both the pre-independence period and periodically in independent India, various business leaders (and the occasional academic) have professed the notion as an ideal for understanding the governance responsibilities of senior managers and directors (Choksi, 1966; Moorthy, 1966).

In the last couple of decades, more systematic efforts have been made to understand the implications of the Vedic tradition for contemporary governance and management practices. The most prominent efforts, of course, have been those of S.K. Chakraborty. Although trained in finance, Prof. Chakraborty is well versed in the Vedic literature and tradition. This combination has provided him an insightful lens through which he has not only developed sharp critiques of contemporary business practices, but developed a constructive approach to promoting responsible governance and management. Prof. Chakraborty has been investigating governance practices in India from a Vedic perspective since as early as 1983, long before the notion of governance became a buzzword in corporate boards and multilateral organizations (Chakraborty, 1983). Since that time, he has not only continued to write extensively on these issues (Chakraborty, 1991; 1995; 1998), but has stimulated others to reflect as well, both academics through his editorship of the *Journal of Human Values* and business practitioners through the various management training programmes offered by the Management Centre for Human Values. What is fundamental to Prof. Chakraborty's understanding of governance (and management) issues is that individuals and organizations cannot just operate (either individually or collectively) in accord with the egoism of the logic of the market, but must act with a pure heart and a higher purpose (an understanding which is expressed in the ideal conception of the firm as a 'business ashram').

While committed to the importance of the Vedic tradition for Indian business, Prof. Chakraborty is also quick to point out that most of the key concepts or notions that he draws upon are also available in other guises in Western religious traditions, and even among some secular philosophies. Proof of this is available in a very tangible form in the influence of Prof. Chakraborty's work, both in India and abroad. In India, for example, a number of scholars have developed eclectic approaches to business ethics that integrate Western philosophical and Vedic insights, including more contemporary insights coming from Gandhi and the systematic business ethics of Prof. Chakraborty (Sekhar, 1997; Giri, 1998). It should also be noted that there are efforts within India to develop approaches to governance and management responsibilities from the perspective of Western religious traditions (such as the work of Fr K. Cyriac), again efforts which are generally compatible with those of the Vedic tradition as worked out by Prof. Chakraborty.

These Indian perspectives—which are representative of the overwhelming opinion among scholars of business ethics in India—have key characteristics in common with respect to governance responsibilities to promote development. First, they all recognize that those responsible for the governance of the corporation have (potential) obligations to a wide range of stakeholder groups, including vulnerable groups and the nation as a whole, which would imply development responsibilities. Second, insofar as they uphold the larger social purpose of business, this would imply a responsibility to promote development, not merely as a condition for a licence to conduct business, but as, at least, one of several goals of the corporation.

Governance Implications of the Responsibility to Promote Development

What the responsibility to promote development implies for governance can be worked out in terms of the basic tasks elaborated above. The specifics, of course, will vary with the understanding of the nature of the obligation to promote development (and the normative tradition used to justify the obligation). First, with respect to the question of strategy, only the stronger and moderate versions might have implications. Stronger understandings of a responsibility to promote development would imply that all of the firm's (business) strategy should be oriented towards the promotion of development.[2] What this would mean practically is that corporations would have to take into account the development impact (as either the sole criterion or one of several criteria) when they make decisions about such issues as the sectors of the economy in which they compete, product selection, how they finance operations, where they locate their operations, etc. Such an approach would not generally imply neglecting shareholder concerns (as firms would still have to induce shareholders to invest in order to access capital and shareholders also have valid claims), but would imply a more 'satisficing' approach to dealing with shareholder concerns (Simon, [1945] 1976; Drucker, 1980). In addition, to the extent that stronger versions see the promotion of development as a goal in itself, the corporate social responsibility (CSR) programmes themselves become an important object of strategy. The questions of strategy to be addressed here would include such issues as whether to emphasize local economic development (e.g. support for small business development) or social development (e.g. health and education programmes), whether to cooperate with NGOs, etc. For their part, weaker accounts of development responsibilities might not have implications for (business) strategy as development responsibilities might potentially be fulfilled through CSR programmes.

In India, the best example of a company incorporating development responsibilities into its actual business strategy is provided by the Tata group, as discussed in Chapter 11 by Nadkarni.

Second, in terms of policy formation, a responsibility to promote development would have a range of implications. For the strongest understandings of this responsibility, a variety of concerns would have to be taken into account with respect to their business operations, including capital-labour ratios (to generate employment), setting appropriate wage rates (to stimulate consumption and growth, to allow workers to educate their children, etc.), establishing personnel policies (e.g. affirmative action programmes) to better incorporate marginalized groups (e.g. women, indigenous groups, the otherly-abled, etc.), incorporating research and development programmes oriented towards development impact, etc. Similarly, there would be policy implications for CSR programmes, e.g. not linking them to marketing programmes, incorporating local input into projects, etc. Again, the weakest understandings of a responsibility to development might not acknowledge that there are any implications with respect to (business) policy.

In India (and elsewhere) more enlightened corporations do take (some of) the various concerns noted above into account in developing policy. Again, a prime instance of this is provided by the Tata Group (Reed, 1998). The Tatas, for example, have been in the lead in introducing progressive labour measures for nearly a century. They are also renown for their work in the area of CSR, where they have a very well-articulated 'development' approach to CSR and have been in the lead in cooperating with local community groups, NGOs, and international bodies, (e.g. UNDP).

Third, development responsibilities imply that corporations have a wider range of stakeholders to whom they need to be accountable. These would include, among others, citizens (in terms of political development and the responsibility not to employ questionable practices to influence government policy in their favour), local communities (who are the primary object of social and economic development and who not infrequently suffer negative development effects from irresponsible corporate practice), small businesses partners (insofar as they provide an important complementary basis for economic development, especially through employment generation), development project partners (e.g. NGOs), etc. Again, there are different approaches to accountability. Stronger versions of a responsibility to development are more likely to uphold a need for more active participation by stakeholder groups in corporate activities. This could include consultation (on both business and CSR projects) as well as participation in decision making, either at the board level (e.g. directly through community representatives on the board, or more indirectly through representatives from the company's CSR office on the board) or lower levels in the organization. In addition, in terms of reporting, corporations must provide clear, accurate and timely information on their development impact (e.g. social and economic audits) as well as providing channels of communication through which individual stakeholders and stakeholder groups can raise concerns, provide suggestions, etc. Weaker versions of a responsibility to development are more likely to limit accountability to reporting.

Again, in the Indian context, the Tatas also provide an excellent example of accountability. They have long been in the forefront of promoting of governance reforms (e.g. audit committees, remuneration committee, etc.), a fact that was publicly acknowledged recently with one of the group companies, Tata Steel, winning the National Award for Excellence in Corporate Governance for 2000. Tata Steel was, not coincidentally, also the first Indian company to undertake a real social audit (1980). The Tatas have also recently introduced an arm's-length, transparent, and non-partisan policy on contributions to political parties.

Finally, with respect to monitoring, a responsibility to promote development would imply that corporations have to establish evaluation criteria that coincide with their strategies and policies (that are intended to promote a positive development impact). They would also have to ensure that incentive structures are based upon these criteria. For stronger versions of a responsibility to promote development, this would imply employing such criteria (e.g. environmental and social impact, including livelihood impact, employment generation, etc.) to their business practices as well as to their CSR programmes. Weaker understandings of the responsibility might limit monitoring responsibilities to their CSR programmes.

Again, among Indian firms the Tatas have been exemplary with respect to monitoring. They have, for example, established the JRD Tata Quality Value Award, which is modelled on the lines of the Malcolm Baldridge National Quality Award, but also integrates beneficial attributes from other national quality awards. The award recognizes a company within the Tata group which excels in quality management and the achievement of the highest levels of quality. The Tata group have also adopted other international standards, such as the Social Accountability 8000 Standards. Also, through the Tata Council for Community Initiatives, all group companies are encouraged to examine the impact of the activities on local communities.

Promoting Effective Governance for Development

While there are a few good examples of corporations living up to the stronger understandings of a responsibility to promote development as noted above (e.g. the Tata group), expecting most corporations to live up to such standards is likely naïve.[3] In the absence of corporations with high levels of moral commitment to promoting development goals, developing countries like India face three basic questions as they struggle in their efforts to implement corporate governance reforms and promote development. The first is how they can introduce the basic conditions commonly thought necessary for the effective functioning of an Anglo-American model of corporate governance.

The second is whether in their context they will need to supplement the standard features of the Anglo-American model in order for it to effectively contribute to development. Third, developing countries may ultimately find that they must ask themselves whether the Anglo-American model is the best choice for promoting development or whether, in the longer term, they need to consider other alternatives. In what follows we briefly examine these questions.

Enforcing the Anglo-American Model

Developing countries like India are moving in the direction of an Anglo-American model of corporate governance. The basic areas of reform have included changes to company law (e.g. to strengthen shareholder rights), reforms of the judicial system (to allow for more effective enforcement of contracts), and changes to financial markets (to help induce investment and discipline management and majority owners) as well as related macro-level reforms (e.g. trade liberalization, macro-economic stabilization, etc.). Especially challenging may be juridical reform. In the literature on corporate governance, there has been an ongoing debate about whether financial or banking models are more effective. It is currently being argued that the key to effectiveness does not depend upon whether a country adopts one or the other model, but whether it has a well-functioning legal system which allows for the timely enforcement of contracts (Levine, 2000). If this position is correct, the ability of developing countries to enforce a model of corporate governance may be ultimately tied to larger questions of legal reforms and democratic political reform. Some have argued, however, that this prospect, even in developed countries, is being undermined by the very forces of globalization that are promoting an Anglo-American model of governance (Barlow and Clarke, 2001). Clearly in India, the need for the issue of judicial reform has long been noted. Little effective action, however, has been taken. Moreover, there is reason for concern that any action that is likely to be taken will favour the interests of the economically powerful (viz., management of foreign TNCs and domestic business families) rather than small investors, employees, etc., (Halbe, 1997a).

An important question that the experience of developing countries raises is whether individual countries acting alone will be able to effectively enforce an Anglo-American model of governance in a global economy. A number of initiatives have been undertaken to try and establish international standards, e.g. international principles and standards for corporate governance (OECD, 1999; CAGC, 1999), international accounting standards such as the AA 1000 (Institute of Social and Ethical Accountability, 1999), international sustainability standards (Global Reporting Initiative, 2000), etc. What these initiatives have in common is that they represent a self-regulatory approach to corporate governance. The efficacy of such an approach, however, is open to question. What is particularly at issue in a global economy is the fact that the international realm lacks strong regulatory and legal vehicles that are generally deemed necessary at the national level (e.g. antitrust law). To the extent that the success of the Anglo-American model is largely dependent upon the discipline of the market (product, financial, managerial talent), maintaining competitive international markets should arguably be a key priority. Recent trends in mergers and acquisitions, both generally and specifically in terms of TNCs operating in developing countries like India (Khanna, 1999), however, raise serious questions about the prospects for competitive international markets.

Supplementing the Anglo-American Model

It is arguably the case that, if the Anglo-American model is to be compatible with development goals, it will have to be supplemented by policies and mechanisms not typically associated with it and/or not currently in place. There are two possible reasons for adopting such a position. The first reason would hold that there are inherent problems in the model that have to be addressed. Perhaps, the major problem inherent in Anglo-American models is the phenomenon that Blair (1995) characterizes as 'market myopia'. The basic problem is that managers come under strong pressure to provide returns to shareholders and this inhibits long-term planning. One possible way to address this is to try to revive the practice of 'nominee directors' from financial institutions. It is not entirely clear, however, that this is likely to be effective as, in the new economy, portfolio managers themselves are also coming under increasing pressure to produce short-term profits. A more commonly advocated approach is to encourage greater involvement by institutional investors. While the emphasis on institutional investors is often primarily advocated as a means of increasing investments—both through foreign portfolio investment (FPI) and domestic sources such as pension funds—in principle institutional investors can also help to address the problem of market myopia (in that they tend to have a longer-term approach to investment). They may also have important benefits for the members (especially, employees) of the institutions in question.

In the case of domestic institutional investors, the key to success is the nature of the mechanisms through which funds are invested. In India, however, the tapping of pension funds has not contributed to solving the problem of market myopia and has proven to be a disaster for the supposed beneficiaries of these funds (Mukherjee Reed, 2002). The major problem would appear to be that workers and workers' organizations, which basically own the funds and have the most interest in taking a long-term perspective, have not had any control over the process. Unless there is greater involvement by the principles in controlling funds and greater influence by the funds on firms (e.g. through nominee directors), the prospects of institutional investors inducing increased development seem precarious at best. A related option that would seem to offer potential development effects is greater employee ownership. Recent work in the US seems to indicate that significant employee ownership poses no burdens on firms in terms of efficiency, and may help provide greater stability (and important investment funds) (Blair et al., 2000). In India, however, there has been little support for such options and only isolated instances of this strategy have emerged (e.g. Kobani Tubes).

For its part, FPI has an inherent tendency towards a short-term approach (even when the funds come from institutional investors). This tendency, along with speculative activity in currency markets, has been strongly implicated in the recent 'Asian crisis'. The obvious question that arises is whether in a global economy with high capital mobility there is a need for international regulation to address these problems. In the case of currency speculation, strong arguments have been put forth for the need for a Tobin or Tobin-like tax to decrease speculative activity (Michalos, 1997). A similar argument could be made for the need for capital controls over FPI, e.g. minimum time limits for investment (Kaplan and Rodrik, 2001). Without such measures, developing countries are extremely vulnerable to macro-economic shock and their development prospects are much more precarious.

The second reason why the Anglo-American model may have to be supplemented to be compatible with development goals has to do with the specific histories of developing countries and the current problems that flow from them. One such problem has to do with a lack of fair economic opportunities for disadvantaged and/or minority sectors of the population (generally distinguished in terms of race, ethnicity, or, in India, caste). The standard institutional approach to addressing this problem has been the use of affirmative action policies. Among developing countries, India has long been in the lead in adopting such measures (viz., legislation on backwards and scheduled castes). Historically, such affirmative action programmes, both in developed countries and in developing countries like India, have been limited to the public sector. In terms of promoting development impact, however, a strong normative case could be made that the private sector should also be encouraged to adopt (voluntarily or otherwise) affirmative action programmes.

Another problem that affects development is the ability of countries, especially in a global economy, to set and enforce minimum standards in key areas (e.g. health and safety, wages, the environment, etc.). Again a strong case can be made for the need for international standards. If such standards were made mandatory (a difficult task under the current institutional arrangements), they could serve as an effective brake on the 'international race to the bottom', while placing no substantial demands (in terms of moral motivation) on individual companies apart from obeying the law. If such standards are voluntary, they place greater demands on individual companies (in terms of moral motivation) to comply, are less likely to be effective, and shift more of the risk on to vulnerable populations.

A similar situation exists with respect to social spending. To the extent that economic development is more a function than a cause of social development (Dreze and Sen, 1995), the Anglo-American model needs to be supplemented by much higher levels of social spending. There are two approaches to this situation. One is to rely upon corporations, in cooperation with NGOs, to play a larger role in providing social development programmes. The efficacy of this approach is questionable, however, for at least two basic reasons. On the one hand, while corporations have increased their funding in such areas and are cooperating more closely with NGOs, their participation is generally sporadic and frequently reflects marketing and public relations concerns more than development impact (Partners in Change, 1997). For their part, development NGOs, while possibly well motivated, do not have the resources to meet the needs. They are, in effect, being asked to take over the role of the state and, as their track record indicates, they do not have the capacity to do so.[4] The other alternative is state involvement in the provision of social development programmes and projects—an approach that does not sit well with most advocates of Anglo-American corporate governance reforms (Sen, 1998).

Moving Beyond the Anglo-American Model?

As indicated above, there are obvious reasons why developing countries are moving in the direction of an Anglo-American model. Partly, the move is due to structural changes in the global economy. Even if developing countries were inclined to other models, this is clearly the path of least resistance. Second, it could be argued that the Anglo-American models can serve as an effective method for breaking unhealthy state-business relationships and imposing more discipline on domestic corporations. It is not clear, however, that these reasons are sufficient for adopting an Anglo-American model of governance, especially when development impact is the main goal. While it is probably too early to evaluate the Anglo-American model in most developing countries, the concerns raised above, including early empirical evidence (Stallings and Perez, 2000), should at least indicate a need for developing countries to leave open the possibility of alternative models.

One geographic area where a lot of concern has been raised is east Asia, in both the newly industrialized countries (NICs) and the second-tier countries. Here, the experience of development has been different than in India and other parts of the developing world, both in terms of the emergence of globally competitive corporations and the generation of sustained economic growth. Many analysts argue that the success of the NICs (and also the second-tier countries) has been due to a strong role for government in industrial planning and a relationship-based approach to governance. Such analysts are not blind to the fact that there are obvious problems that have been associated with the model (e.g. abuse of minority shareholder rights, unfair practices vis-à-vis small- and medium-sized businesses, abuse of worker rights, etc.). They argue, however, that these abuses can be best resolved within the system, while the adoption of an Anglo-American model could have a potentially devastating impact on development. Indeed, they argue that the recent Asian crisis (which had devastating consequences in terms of growth, employment, etc.) was the result of liberalizing measures associated with the Anglo-American model (Bardhan, 2001; Chang, Park, and Yoo, 1998; Wade, 1998). They also respond that charges of 'cronyism' against east Asian countries not only represent a new version of 'orientalism', but question how different the practices of Western countries and international financial institutions (especially the IMF) have been (Johnson, 1998). Thus, in east Asia, the question may not be so much going beyond the Anglo-American model, but evolving new ways on the basis of their previous model.

If a reformed version of the previous model of governance is preferable for east Asia, it is questionable whether such a model could or should be adopted in other geographic areas. In these other regions (e.g. South Asia, Latin America, Africa) it may be more a question of moving beyond the Anglo-American model. One key area where India and other developing countries might consider moving beyond the Anglo-American model is with respect to governance structures. In particular, it could be argued that the incorporation of more participation into governance structures (e.g. along the lines of a German model which allows employee participation) is required. While this notion has been dismissed out of hand by business groups such as the Confederation of Indian Industry (1998), advocates argue that such changes would place a much greater practical emphasis on the generation and retention of jobs. Similarly, it could be argued that developing countries like India might want to do more to encourage more cooperative models of governance (e.g. along the lines of the Mondragon model). Possible related development benefits of such models might include inducing more investment from workers and local communities, greater provision of information, etc.

Another area where developing countries might consider alternatives is with respect to industrial policy. Around the world, despite pressures to liberalize, there are still calls in developing countries for interventionist policy (Rabelo and Vasconcelos, 2002). Such calls are often understandable, especially given the problems that corporations in developing countries face in competing against TNCs. Given these problems, and the lack of international regulation to address them (e.g. the lack of international antitrust law), strong industrial policy may well be capable of improving development impact. Again, the ability to effectively implement industrial policy is dependent upon, among other things, a strong (democratic) state and a favourable international environment. The former implies a strong civil society and the establishment and enforcement of limits on the ability of corporations to influence state policy. The latter would be facilitated by more democratic control over the international economy.

Conclusion: Evaluating Corporate Governance Reforms

Around the globe, countries are introducing corporate governance reforms in the context of more extensive programmes of economic liberalization. These reforms are, by and large, moving developing countries like India in the direction of an Anglo-American model of corporate governance. The basic reason for this, as I have argued in the opening chapter, is that the Anglo-American model is the logical counterpart of macro-level changes that have occurred in the international economy with processes of economic globalization. These recent changes in corporate governance, and the processes of globalization that have induced them, are obviously of historic proportion, radically altering as they have economic, political, and social structures.

The stakes in these reforms are high—indeed, they may be literally a question of life and death for the most vulnerable populations. How then are we to evaluate recent governance and economic reforms in India, especially with respect to their development impact? Three distinct, but related areas of questions would seem to come into play in making an informed judgment.

The first area of questions involves the promotion of an Anglo-American model of governance. One set of concerns here is whether the state has been able to effectively establish the basic features of an Anglo-American model of governance (and, if not, why not). While some success has been made in this direction, critics would argue that business and bureaucratic concerns have slowed or diverted the process with respect to key issues such as (small) shareholder rights, a truly independent board to regulate capital markets, etc. (Mukherjee Reed, 2001). Another set of questions involves the empirical analysis of whether these reforms have had any significant development impact as measured through standard economic criteria (e.g. unemployment, growth, innovation, etc.). In this collection, while some of the authors seem sanguine about future prospects, Mukherjee Reed and I have argued that the model has clearly not yet operated in accord with textbook logic and has resulted in few unambiguous indicators of development. Rather, what has most clearly characterized the reform experience so far has been increased instability in the system, a result that is likely to have adverse development effects, especially on the most vulnerable populations. A third set of concerns relates to whether the shift to the Anglo-American model has encouraged corporate boards to take up their responsibilities to promote development. In this chapter I have argued that from the perspective of most ethical traditions, especially Indian traditions, a strong case can be made that corporate boards have significant responsibilities to promote development, both through their business practices and through corporate social responsibility programmes. While there has clearly been more noise made around these issues in recent years, critics will argue that this is largely just that, noise designed to ensure that the state continues on with its (selective) policy of liberalization. While this evaluation may seem a bit harsh, there are still few compelling examples of companies committed to living up to development responsibilities in any significant or systematic fashion that would contradict it.

The second set of fundamental questions involves not the effects of and responsibilities within the Anglo-American model, but rather the desirability of the model vis-à-vis other possible models. This is a topic that I have raised in this chapter, but have not fully addressed. Evaluating this issue is a challenging endeavour to the extent that a variety of concerns (e.g. growth, employment, risk) and normative values (e.g. freedom, equity) come into play in choosing one model over another. In a global economy it becomes even more complicated, especially for developing countries. This is because in a global economy, multinational corporations, foreign states and other international actors play a key role in determining economic performance. Insofar as they have a preference for a certain model of governance and an ability to significantly influence the economic performance of a developing country, their preferences (as embedded in international economic and political structures) inevitably influence the desirability of a given governance model. This can lead to choices being made that might not be made under other structural arrangements, as strategic analysis largely dominates normative concerns. I have argued in this chapter that if India is serious about its commitment to development, it probably needs to reconsider its pursuit of an Anglo-American model of governance, either adapting it in some ways (e.g. through more effective use of nominee directors and institutional investors) or even moving to an alternative model of governance.

This leads us to a third set of issues involving governance reforms, viz., the procedural questions of how governance models are chosen. Two realms come into play here, the domestic and the international. At the domestic level, the question is how democratic are the procedures through which reforms have been implemented. More specifically, at issue is the degree to which corporations have been able to promote their ideas and interests over those of other groups. Clearly, with respect to such issues as company law reform, reforms to financial markets, etc., the government has given greater opportunity to business (over labour groups, consumer groups, etc.) to express their opinions and have taken these opinions more seriously in developing legislation and regulations (Halbe, 1997b). From the perspective of normative analysis, at issue is the need for reforms to a range of issues involved in business-government relations (e.g. lobbying practices, conflict of interest regulations, campaign financing, etc.).

At the international level, the basic concern is that developing countries, like India, are forced to choose reform strategies and models in the context of a global economy that they have had little role in shaping. Not only is it the case that the governance of the international economy is not democratic, but it fails even to live up to minimal standards of transparency. The irony, if not hypocrisy, of key international economic institutions calling for developing countries to live up to standards that they themselves do not practice has not been lost on many commentators. Indeed, it is this lack of transparency and democracy that has led to the protests that have greeted all major international economic policy meetings recently (e.g. G-7, Free Trade Area of the Americas [FTAA] etc.). What this points to is the notion that more fundamental than the nature of responsibilities with a model of governance, or even the choice of a governance model, is the manner in and conditions under which choices about governance are made. Ultimately, the legitimacy of corporate governance reforms in developing countries like India can only be predicated upon governance reforms occurring in the larger global economy. The challenge to large developing countries like India is to strive not merely to be included in multilateral financial and political organizations (as representatives of the developing world), but to make multilateral processes and institutions more transparent and democratic, a challenge which they can only credibly take up if they are committed to similar reforms at home. Fortunately, for India, it has a rich, if not pure, tradition of democratic practice and thought to draw upon in taking up these challenges.

Notes

1. Elsewhere I have addressed the issue of applying stakeholder theory in the context of developing countries in more detail (Reed, 2002).

2. It could be argued that it is unrealistic to expect corporations to take other goals into consideration. Certainly, there are few obvious empirical examples of traditional corporations that seriously take other goals into consideration in terms of strategy. Examples of this type of behaviour can be found, however, among cooperative corporations, such as the Mondragon Cooperative Corporation in Spain (MacLeod, 1997).

3. As noted above, some cooperative corporations have demonstrated a commitment to promoting economic development goals, but there are few examples of traditional corporations doing so. Among the more socially responsible corporations, it is often the case that they are anomalous in different ways. In the Tatas, for example, more than 60 per cent of the shares of the apex company are held by private charitable foundations (established by or in the name of family members). This not only enables the Tatas to direct 60–70 per cent of the profits of the apex company to charitable organizations, but also to promote a more enlightened approach to business without any effective opposition by other shareholders (or potential corporate raiders).

4. Historically, as Sinha notes in Chapter 4, the public sector in India has been very active—by government mandate—in terms of social responsibility programmes, including the provision of social services. It seems unlikely, however, that this model could be extended to the private sector without encountering extreme resistance and having adverse effects on FDI.

References

Bardhan, P. (2001). 'Development Thinking Today in an Asian Perspective', Global Finance and Development Symposium sponsored by the World Bank, Tokyo, Japan, 1–2 March, accessed at: http://www.worldbank.org/japan/sympo/bardhan.htm.

Blair, M. (1995). *Ownership and Control: Rethinking Corporate Governance for the Twenty-First Century*, Washington: Brookings Institute.

Blair, M., D. Kruse and J. Blasi (2000). 'Employee Ownership: Unstable or Stabilizing?', In *The New Relationship: Human Capital in the American Corporation*, (eds). M. Blair, D. Kruse, and J. Blasi, Washington: The Brookings Institute, pp. 241–88.

Cadbury Report (1992). *The Financial Aspects of Corporate Governance*, London: Gee and Co. Ltd.

Chakraborty, S.K. (ed.) (1983). *Boards of Directors in India: Their Statics and Dynamics*, New Delhi: All Indian Management Association.

Chakraborty, S.K. (1991). *Management by Values*, New Delhi: Oxford University Press.

____ (1995). *Ethics in Management: Vedantic Perspectives*, New Delhi: Oxford University Press.

____ (1998). *Values and Ethics for Organizations*, New Delhi: Oxford University Press.

Chang H.J., H.J. Park, and C.G. Yoo (1998). 'Interpreting the Korean crisis: Financial liberalisation, industrial policy and corporate governance', *Cambridge Journal of Economics*, 22, 735–46.

Choksi, P. (1966). 'The Gandhian Concept of Trusteeship', In *Social Responsibilities of Business*, The Institution for Gandhian Studies, Bombay: Manaktalas, pp. 85–100.

Commonwealth Association for Corporate Governance (CACG) (1999). *CACG Guidelines: Principles of Corporate Governance in the Commonwealth*, London: CACG.

Confederation of Indian Industry (1998). *Desirable Corporate Governance—A Code*, Delhi: Confederation of Indian Industry.

Dreze, J. and A. Sen (1995). *Economic Development and Social Opportunity*, New Delhi: Oxford University Press.

Drucker, P. (1980). *Managing in Turbulent Times*, New York: Harper & Row.

Giri, A.K. (1998). *Values and Ethics in Business*, Jaipur: Rawat Publications.

Global Reporting Initiative (2000). *GRI Guidelines*, London: GRI, available at http://www.globalreporting.org.

Halbe, S.R. (1997a). 'Much ado about nothing', *Business Standard*, Monday, 8 September.

____ (1997b). 'A law for the corporates and by the corporates', *Business Standard*, Friday, 8 August.

Institute of Social and Ethical Accountability (1999). *AA 1000*, London: ISEA, available at http://www.accountability.org.uk/aa1000/default.asp

Johnson, C. (1998). 'Economic Crisis in East Asia: The Clash of Capitalisms', *Cambridge Journal of Economics*, 22, 653–61.

Kaplan, E. and D. Rodrik (2001). 'Did the Malaysian Capital Controls Work?', National Bureau of Economic Research Working Paper No. W8142.

Khanna, S. (1999). 'Financial Reforms and Industrial Sector in India', *Economic and Political Weekly*, xxxiv (45), 6 November.

Levine, R. (2000). 'Bank-Based or Market-Based Financial Systems: Which is Better?' Institute of Financial Studies, Carlson School of Management, The University of Minnesota, Working Paper *0005.

MacLeod, G. (1997). *Mondragon To America: Experiments in Community Economic Development*, Sydney, NS: University of Cape Breton College Press.

Michalos, A.C. (1997). *Good Taxes: The Case for Taxing Foreign Currency Exchange and Other Financial Transactions*, Toronto: Dundurn Press.

Moorthy, M.V. (1966). 'Gandhiji's Idea of Trusteeship', In *Social Responsibilities of Business*, The Institute of Gandhian Studies, ed., Bombay: Manaktalas, pp. 145–51.

Mukherjee Reed, A. (2001). *Perspectives on the Indian Corporate Economy: Exploring the paradox of profits*, London: Palgrave.

____ (2002). 'Corporate Governance and Economic Reforms in India', *Journal of Business Ethics*, 37 (3), May, pp. 249–68.

Nozick, R. (1974). *Anarchy, State, and Utopia*, New York, Basic Books.

Organization for Economic Cooperation and Development (OECD) (1999). *Principles of Corporate Governance*, Paris: OECD Publications.

Rabelo F.M. and F.C. Vasconcelos (2002). 'An Overview of Corporate Governance in Brazil', *Journal of Business Ethics*, 37 (3), May, pp. 321–35.

Reed, D. (1998). 'Corporate Social Responsibility and Development in India', *Journal of Human Values*, 4 (2), pp. 201–17.

____ (1999). 'Stakeholder Management Theory: A Critical Theory Perspective', *Business Ethics Quarterly*, 9 (2), pp. 453–83.

____ (2002). 'Employing Normative Stakeholder Theory in Developing Countries: A Critical Theory Perspective', *Business and Society*, 41 (2), June, pp. 166–207.

Sekhar, R.C. (1997). *Ethical Choices in Business*, New Delhi: Sage, Response Books.

Simon, H.A. ([1945] 1976). *Administrative Behavior*, New York: Macmillan.

Sen, A. (1998). *Development as Freedom*, New Delhi: Oxford University Press.

Stallings, B. and W. Perez (2000). *Growth, Employment, and Equity: The Impact of the Economic Reforms in Latin America and the Caribbean*, Washington: Brookings Institution Press.

Tricker, R. (1994). *International Corporate Governance: Text, Readings and Cases*, NY: Prentice Hall.

Wade, R. (1998). 'From "Miracle" to "Cronyism": Explaining the Great Asian Slump', *Cambridge Journal of Economics*, 22, pp. 693–706.